ELIZABETH WIDVILLE, LADY GREY

livelifeaberdeenshire.org.uk/libraries

Che in tal maniera ti sia sottoposto
el corpo mio, Signor, non mi par degno,
ch'io pur a sangue assai nobil m'accosto.
Ch'io sia tua moglie, ciò passaria il segno.

Antonio Cornazzano, *De mulieribus admirandis*,
'*La Regina d'ingliterra*', lines 190–3, *c*.1467.

(That in such a way my body should be subordinated
to you, Lord, does not seem right,
even when I'd be close to such noble blood.
That I should be your wife, *that* would be good enough.

Antonio Cornazzano, *The Wonderful Women*,
'The Queen of England', lines 190–3, *c*.1467. Trans. J.A-H)

ELIZABETH WIDVILLE, LADY GREY

EDWARD IV'S CHIEF MISTRESS, AND

THE 'PINK QUEEN'

JOHN ASHDOWN-HILL

PEN & SWORD
HISTORY

AN IMPRINT OF PEN & SWORD BOOKS LTD.
YORKSHIRE - PHILADELPHIA

First published in Great Britain in 2019 by
Pen and Sword History
An imprint of
Pen & Sword Books Ltd
Yorkshire - Philadelphia

Hardback ISBN 978 1 52674 501 9
Paperback ISBN 978 1 52676 583 3

Typeset in Ehrhardt MT Std 11.5/14 by
Aura Technology and Software Services, India

Printed and bound in the UK by TJ International Ltd.

Pen & Sword Books Ltd incorporates the Imprints of Pen & Sword Books
Archaeology, Atlas, Aviation, Battleground, Discovery, Family History, History,
Maritime, Military, Naval, Politics, Railways, Select, Transport, True Crime,
Fiction, Frontline Books, Leo Cooper, Praetorian Press, Seaforth Publishing,
Wharncliffe and White Owl.

For a complete list of Pen & Sword titles please contact

PEN & SWORD BOOKS LIMITED
47 Church Street, Barnsley, South Yorkshire, S70 2AS, England
E-mail: enquiries@pen-and-sword.co.uk
Website: www.pen-and-sword.co.uk

or

PEN AND SWORD BOOKS
1950 Lawrence Rd, Havertown, PA 19083, USA
E-mail: Uspen-and-sword@casematepublishers.com
Website: www.penandswordbooks.com

Contents

Introduction – problems in this story

The subject of this present study seems recently to have become known in historical fiction as 'the White Queen'. But of course, historical fiction is not reality. In reality, as she herself knew very well (and it worried her greatly), it was and is definitely questionable whether Elizabeth Widville should really be accepted as a genuine *queen*. As for her associated colour, on the basis of the flower emblem which she herself chose and adopted (see below, Chapter 10), it seems it would actually be more accurate to call her 'pink' rather than 'white'. An additional advantage of referring to her colour as pink lies in the fact that it also highlights her having been eventually acknowledged as of royal status by both white rose and red rose kings (Edward IV and Henry VII). However, another accurate colour word which might be used to describe her – a colour word which may actually have been applied insultingly to Elizabeth during her lifetime and which also figures in the title of this book – is 'grey'.

In 1938 an earlier account of Elizabeth Widville was produced by David MacGibbon.[1] That account applies no colour word to her. It does include genuine valuable research in respect of her ancestry. But apart from the name spelling problems (see below) MacGibbon's book also contains a number of other worrying issues which arise from the much earlier rewriting of history, by the government of King Henry VII and his immediate successors, after that sovereign's seizure of the English crown. They include, for example, MacGibbon's chapters on the alleged 'usurpation of Richard III', and on the alleged 'murder' of the so-called 'princes in the Tower'. Although the present author has already attempted to present the true stories in respect of both of those issues elsewhere,[2] they will of course be re-examined here as part of this present history (see below, Chapters 10 & 11). However, the first and most major predicament in MacGibbon's study actually presents itself very clearly in his Preface. It relates to Elizabeth Widville's rank and status.

Was she really a queen?

In his Preface MacGibbon states that in his initial publication year (1938) England was 'fortunate enough to have another Queen Elizabeth'. He was referring to Elizabeth Bowes-Lyon, the consort of King George VI – and the mother of that king's heiress, who subsequently succeeded to the throne as Queen Elizabeth II. The fact that Elizabeth Bowes-Lyon was then the queen consort made it, he argued, especially appropriate for him to publish his 'biography of our first Queen Elizabeth'. His reference to 'our first Queen' does focus attention on the interesting fact that, prior to Elizabeth Widville, the name 'Elizabeth' had never actually figured prominently in the English royal context. The name in question had been given to one or two junior royal daughters (Elizabeth of Lancaster, Duchess of Exeter, a younger daughter of John of Gaunt, and Elizabeth of York, Duchess of Suffolk, a younger daughter of Richard, Duke of York), but it had never previously been held by an alleged queen.

However, by referring to Elizabeth Widville as 'our first Queen Elizabeth', MacGibbon ignores – or deliberately conceals – the highly significant fact that, for the greater part of her fifteenth-century adult life, the right of Elizabeth Widville to be named as England's queen consort had actually been a matter of dispute. After her coronation, at two stages in her life she actually lost the title of 'queen' (see below, Chapters 13 and 17), and at the second of those two points she was officially judged by parliament never to have had a right to the queenly title. That explains why the title of 'queen' is not included in the main heading of this present study. As for the issue in question, that will be dealt with in detail later (see Chapter 7).

Name spelling problems

English historians sometimes appear to have strange problems with accurately recording names as they would have been heard in the past. For example in eastern England, where I live, historians refer to an ancient British tribe, the name of which is written using the letters I-C-E-N-I. Nowadays, those letters are generally all pronounced according to their modern English norm, producing the sound 'Ay-seen-ay' or 'Ay-seen-ee'. Yet the British tribal name in question had originally been recorded in Latin texts by Roman writers. Therefore the Roman letters which they chose to register the sound of the British tribal name as it was heard 2000 years ago must have originally had their classical Latin values. That means that in reality the tribesmen presumably called themselves 'ik-ain-ee'. Logically, modern spelling of the word should therefore be altered, in order to reproduce accurately a sound of that name which the tribesmen in question would themselves have recognised and understood.

In respect of the present study, the historical spelling problem occurs in two instances. First, although spelling of the family name is usually modernised to 'Woodville', it was spelled 'Wydeville' in

Carta Baroniæ Roberti Foliot.

DE Baronia Roberti Foliot de veteri fefamento.
    Michaël Befet . IIII. milites.
Thomas de Andeli . IIII. mllites.
Abbas de Weftmonafterio . I. militem.
Ernulfus de Bofco . I. militem.
Johannes de Argentune . I. militem.
Henricus de ¹ Aldwincle dim.
Willelmus de ² Widuill dim.
Willelmus de Franceis dim.
Philippus de Infula tenet quartam partem militis.
Ipfe Robertus Foliot tenet in Dominio unum militem de veteri fefamento.

Et de novo fefamento, poft mortem Henrici Regis, Adam de Bernavilla tenet . IIII. partem militis.
· Rolandus de Dinant tenet feodum . I. militis & dim. in voluntate Domini Regis.

Rogerus de Moubrai militem & dim. unde detinet michi fervitium.

Poft Conquæftum Angliæ tenuerunt Antecefſores ipſius Roberti Foliot per fervitium . XV. militum, & ipfe poft illos.

---

1 *Sive* Oldwincle. 2 *Hinc liquet, Widvillorum familiam admodum effe antiquam. immo longe vetuftiorem quam voluerunt nonnulli. Nec quidem. quid de antiquitate· ejufdem flatvendum fit, fatis compertum habuit* 'Dugdafius. qui nempe de eadem mentionem nullam invenerat ante annum

Hearne, *Liber Niger Scaccarii*, p. 213.

contemporary publications by Caxton, and her tomb at St George's Chapel, Windsor Castle is inscribed thus: 'Edward IV and his Queen Elizabeth Widvile'.[3] In fact the earliest recorded spelling of the fifteenth-century Elizabeth's maiden surname in her male line of ancestry is either *de Widuill* or *de Widvill* (see Family Tree 5). De Widuill was the form in which the surname was written about three hundred years earlier than Elizabeth's own period – in the twelfth century for one of her Northamptonshire male line ancestors. That fact is recorded in Hearne's published version of *Liber Niger Scaccarii*, p. 213 (see above).

Nowadays, of course, the letter 'u' is only employed as a vowel. But in the Middle Ages it could be used to represent the modern English consonant 'v'. In other words the equivalent modern spelling of that version of the name would obviously be *de Widvill*, which is very close to the surname form which is generally employed in the present work.

Moreover, the inclusion at that stage of the word *de* ('of') clearly reveals another significant point. It shows that, in origin, the surname in question was a toponym. Therefore, presumably, it relates to the village of Wyville, near Grantham, in Lincolnshire, which must be where the family came from before it began to establish itself in Kent and Northamptonshire.

Since it was later Elizabeth's maiden surname, the name in question obviously figures as a centrepiece of this present study. Many versions of it were subsequently recorded in the fifteenth century – though not specifically in respect of Elizabeth herself. The recorded fifteenth-century forms include: Wedevill, Wideville, Widevlle, Wodeville, Wodevyle, Wodevyll, Wydevile, Wydevill, Wydeville, Wydevyle, Wydevyll, Wydevylle, Wydewyll, Wyndevyll. In the Yorkist period the spelling which was most commonly used seems to have been Wydeville – which would presumably have been pronounced as *WID-VIL*. There was no difference in terms of pronunciation between 'I' and 'y' in the fifteenth century. For example, Lord Hastings signed his name 'Hastyngs' (see below, Chapter 7).

However, for some curious – and unknown – reason, the most widely used modern sound of Elizabeth's surname has come to be *WOULD-VIL*, and the most widely used modern spelling is 'Woodville'. Yet only three of the 14 fifteenth-century name forms listed above actually include the letter 'o' in the first syllable. According to his eighteenth–century editor, it seems that in the 1490s the chronicler John Rous may have employed the spelling 'Woodvyle'.[4] Certainly, by the second half of the seventeenth century, Francis Sandford (Lancaster Herald) seems to have been one of the first to have utilised the spelling 'Woodvile'. And it is probably from his spelling that the most commonly used modern version appears to have come. Nevertheless, the fact remains that no early sources for that particular spelling seem to exist.

In this present study, therefore, account has been taken of the prevalence of the vowel sound 'i / y' in the first syllable of most of the recorded medieval versions of the name. Account has also been taken of the spelling 'de Widvill' as its earliest recorded version. Thus the spelling WIDVILLE (for which some earlier records do exist – see Plate 11) is the form of the surname which is generally employed here. This spelling has been chosen because in modern English the retention of the letter 'e' at the end of the first syllable, after the 'd' (where it figures in medieval spellings), might appear to suggest the lengthening of the vowel sound of that first syllable (as in the modern English word 'wide'). In the medieval period, however, the inclusion of that letter 'e' in the spelling at that point would probably not have created that effect. In other words, although it was not the most common medieval written version of the name, the modern form 'Widville' appears to reproduce more or less accurately the *sound* of her maiden surname, which Elizabeth herself seems likely to have normally heard.

But of course in actuality she herself was generally referred to in the fifteenth century under a different name entirely – her married surname of Grey. For example, that was how Richard III referred to her.[5] Some later accounts continued to refer to her under her husband's surname. For example, George Buck's account refers to 'Lady Elizabeth Gray'.[6] Therefore the appellation 'Grey' is also applied to Elizabeth in the title of the present study, and is sometimes referred to in the text.

A second historical spelling problem occurs in respect of the first name of Elizabeth Widville's mother. Her native language would have been French, and in that tongue she was called Jacquette de St Pol or Jacquette de Luxembourg. But oddly her first name is generally given in modern English accounts as 'Jacquetta'. In reality there is absolutely *no* evidence that the lady in question ever used that spelling herself, or employed the modern English three-syllabled version of her Christian name.

For example, in her own petition to King Edward IV she very plainly called herself 'your humble and true liegewoman Jaquet duchesse of

Bedford, late the wyf of your true and faithfull knyght and liegeman Richard late erle of Ryvers.'[7] Similarly, there are confirmatory sources from other contemporaries. For example, there is:

> an acknowledgment (in English) by Will. Yelverton, Knt., Just[ice] of [the] K[ing's] B[ench], of the receipt from Bishop Waynflete of £87, in full satisfaction of all claims on Sir J. Fastolf by Jaquet, Duchess of Bedford.[8]

As for William Worcester's dedication of his work to King Edward IV, he there refers to her as 'dame Jaques, duchesse of Bedforde'.[9] Presumably that is a little spelling mistake, and what was really intended was 'dame Jaquet'. Also, in June 1483 (after she herself had died), when the three estates of the realm put their petition to Richard Duke of Gloucester, asking him to accept the crown, they referred to Elizabeth Widville's mother as 'Jaquett, Duchess of Bedford'.[10] Thus, based on her own clear evidence, the Oxford acknowledgment, the petition of the three estates, and also William Worcester's probable evidence, the modern French two-syllabled form of her first name – Jacquette – will be employed for her here, accurately reproducing the name sound which she herself obviously utilised throughout her life.

Nevertheless, it is actually true that the three-syllabled form 'Jacquetta' is used in relation to Elizabeth's mother in some surviving fifteenth-century English government records. However, that was not at all because the lady in question used that form of her name *in everyday English*. Rather the explanation is the simple fact that the original documents in question were actually written, not in *English*, but in *Latin*. In other words, they were actually recording her name form in *that* language – and not in English.

It is therefore simply the prevalence of *Latin* as the language employed in official documents and records for the greater part of the fifteenth century which explains how the three-syllabled Latin form of Jacquette's name was subsequently picked up by historians. Initially it was picked up – and erroneously applied to her for the first time in an *English* context – by the editors of the *Calendars of Patent Rolls* and similar government records. Unfortunately their mistaken version of her name was then assigned to Jacquette by other historians who employed the published English *Calendars of Patent Rolls* as source material in their writing of her history – even though *their* accounts were obviously being written not in Latin but in English.

Maiden names or married names?

Another point which it will be relevant to consider in respect of this present study is the fact that in the context of English history there is a complete lack of logic in the matter of how to refer to prominent widows (and divorcees). Widows (and divorcees) who have been associated with royalty are shown in Table 1.

FIRST NAME	MAIDEN NAME	PREVIOUS HUSBAND	CHILDREN?
Catherine	de Roët	Swynford	yes
Joana	of Navarre	of Brittany	yes
Elizabeth	Widville	Grey	yes
Eleanor	Talbot	Butler	no
Catherine	of Aragon	Tudor(?)	no
Catherine	Parr	Borough / Neville	no
Bessie Wallis	Warfield	Spencer / Simpson	no
Camilla	Shand	Parker-Bowles	yes

Royal consorts who had earlier husbands, and the surnames by which they are usually known.

In each of these eight cases as listed in Table 1, the surnames which are most commonly applied to them today are underlined. Fifty percent of them tend to be known by their maiden names, but the other fifty percent tend to be referred to under the surname of a previous husband. That is totally illogical. Certainly it does not depend on whether or not they produced children for their previous spouse. Moreover, what is done today in respect of the surname does not always correspond with what was done in the past. For example, those surviving fifteenth-century sources which refer to Elizabeth Widville in terms of a surname employ, not her maiden name, but the surname of her first husband (Grey). However, the present text will simply seek to be consistent, and will primarily refer to all such women by using their maiden surnames.

Dating

Finally, it is important to explain that in medieval England the New Year began not on 1 January, but on 'Lady Day' (25 March). Therefore events which took place in January, February or most of March occurred in medieval England in the last three months of the preceding calendar year in terms of numbering. For example, the Croyland Abbey Chronicle continuations record the birth of Elizabeth of York junior (later wife of Henry VII) as follows:

> This took place in the month of February, it being the year of our Lord according to the computation of the English church, 1465, but according to that of the church of Rome 1466.[11]

Thus, for example, Edward IV's accession to the throne took place on 4 March 1461 in terms of the wider European medieval calendar and also of the modern English calendar – but on 4 March 1460 in terms of the English calendar of his day. For that reason, all events which occurred between 1 January and 24 March will here be dated using both the medieval and the modern year numbers, linked with a forward slash. In other words, it would be stated here that Edward IV became king on 4 March 1460/1, and that his daughter, Elizabeth, was born in February 1465/6.

Chapter 1

Imperial Ancestry

Through her mother, Jacquette de St Pol (or Jacquette de Luxembourg), Elizabeth Widville had a highly significant channel of ancestry. Jacquette was descended – in several lines – from the Emperor Charles I ('Charlemagne') and his immediate imperial heirs. Family Tree 1 shows one of her lines of imperial descent.

'Charlemagne' himself was not actually of royal descent from a long line. His grandfather, Charles Martel, had been the power *behind* the Frankish throne while the land was still theoretically ruled by the Merovingian dynasty. But by taking over the royal title, Charles Martel's son (and Charlemagne's father), Pepin the Short, created a new Frankish royal line – the Carolingians. Subsequently, Charlemagne recreated for himself the title of Western Roman Emperor. That imperial title was later held by his son, Louis the Pious, and by his grandson, Charles the Bald, both of whom were also ancestors of Jacquette de St Pol and her daughter, Elizabeth Widville.

As can be seen from Family Tree 2, by the eleventh century the descendants of the Emperor Charlemagne in the cadet line in which Jacquette de St Pol was ultimately to be born had acquired the county

The Emperor Charles I ('Charlemagne').

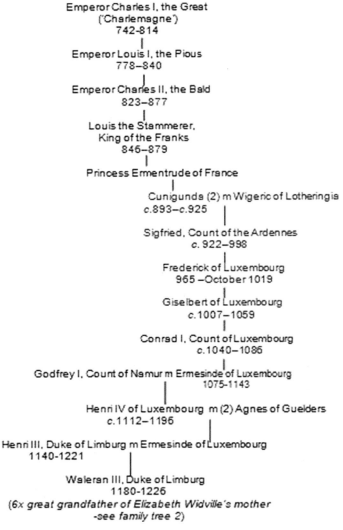

Emperor Charles I, the Great
('Charlemagne')
742-814

Emperor Louis I, the Pious
778-840

Emperor Charles II, the Bald
823-877

Louis the Stammerer,
King of the Franks
846-879

Princess Ermentrude of France

Cunigunda (2) m Wigeric of Lotheringia
c.893-c.925

Sigfried, Count of the Ardennes
c. 922-998

Frederick of Luxembourg
965 -October 1019

Giselbert of Luxembourg
c.1007-1059

Conrad I, Count of Luxembourg
c.1040-1086

Godfrey I, Count of Namur m Ermesinde of Luxembourg
1075-1143

Henri IV of Luxembourg m (2) Agnes of Guelders
c.1112-1196

Henri III, Duke of Limburg m Ermesinde of Luxembourg
1140-1221

Waleran III, Duke of Limburg
1180-1226
*(6x great grandfather of Elizabeth Widville's mother
-see family tree 2)*

Family Tree 1: Elizabeth Widville's descent from the Emperor Charlemagne.

of Luxembourg. Subsequently, however, her ancestors in the direct line acquired the title Count of St Pol (see below).

As a result she can be referred to either as Jacquette of Luxembourg or as Jacquette of St Pol. In the present study the second of those forms will normally be employed.

As for one of Jacquette's ancestral cousins – the Emperor Henry VII (Henry of Luxembourg) – he put forward a very intriguing claim in

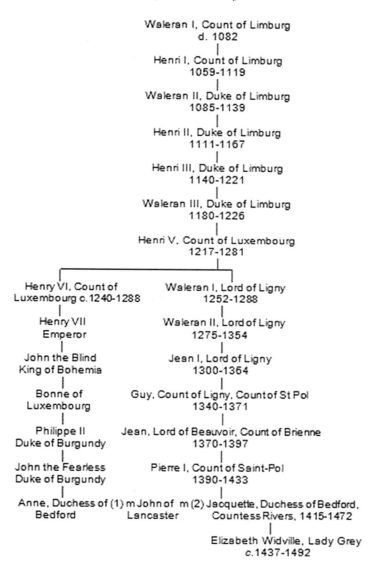

Waleran I, Count of Limburg
d. 1082

Henri I, Count of Limburg
1059-1119

Waleran II, Duke of Limburg
1085-1139

Henri II, Duke of Limburg
1111-1167

Henri III, Duke of Limburg
1140-1221

Waleran III, Duke of Limburg
1180-1226

Henri V, Count of Luxembourg
1217-1281

Henry VI, Count of Luxembourg c. 1240-1288	Waleran I, Lord of Ligny 1252-1288
Henry VII Emperor	Waleran II, Lord of Ligny 1275-1354
John the Blind King of Bohemia	Jean I, Lord of Ligny 1300-1364
Bonne of Luxembourg	Guy, Count of Ligny, Count of St Pol 1340-1371
Philippe II Duke of Burgundy	Jean, Lord of Beauvoir, Count of Brienne 1370-1397
John the Fearless Duke of Burgundy	Pierre I, Count of Saint-Pol 1390-1433

Anne, Duchess of (1) m John of m (2) Jacquette, Duchess of Bedford,
Bedford   Lancaster   Countess Rivers, 1415-1472

Elizabeth Widville, Lady Grey
c. 1437-1492

Family Tree 2: The male line of ancestry of Elizabeth Widville's mother.

respect of another aspect of their family ancestry. That claim will be explored in the next chapter.

Significantly it was, of course, from her mother that Elizabeth Widville inherited her mitochondrial DNA. Mitochondrial DNA (mtDNA) is inherited by all offspring from their mother only, because sperm do not carry mtDNA. Thus the mtDNA haplogroup subgroup of Elizabeth

Imperatrice d'Arco, *c*.1237-*c*.1309
|
Isabella d'Acquaviva, Countess of Celano, *c*.1262-?
|
Francesca di Celano, Countess of Anglone, 1310- *c*.1378
|
Jeanne Gorizia de Sabran, Countess of Nola, 1322-1379
|
Justine Sueva Orsini, Duchess of Andria, *c*.1365-*c*.1422
|
Margherita del Balzo, Countess of St Pol, 1394-1469
|
Jacquette de St Pol, Duchess of Bedford, Countess Rivers, *c*.1415-1472
|
Elizabeth Widville, Lady Grey

Family Tree 3: The female line ancestry of Elizabeth Widville – source for her mtDNA.

Widville, which, with the help of Glen Moran, the present author recently discovered and published, came to her from Jacquette de St Pol, who in turn had inherited it from *her* mother. The lines of descent from Jacquette (and of collateral descent from Elizabeth) in that respect will be explored in Chapter 21. Meanwhile, Family Tree 3 shows what is known of Elizabeth's maternal line female ancestry – the line of descent from which she inherited her mtDNA.

Interestingly, it is traceable two or three generations further back than the female line ancestry of Joy Ibsen and Cecily Neville, Duchess of York, which the present author traced and revealed some years ago. That was the line which I discovered in 2004, thereby revealing the mtDNA of all Cecily's children, including Edward IV and Richard III.[1] Of course that information was subsequently used to help to establish the identity of Richard III's bones, which were found by the LOOKING FOR RICHARD PROJECT (of which I was one of the founder members) in a Leicester car park in 2012.

The mtDNA haplogroup of that earlier and very significant discovery appeared to have descended to English royalty via a fourteenth-century lady from Hainault. In the case of Elizabeth Widville, Jacquette de St Pol, and the origin of their possibly equally important mtDNA haplogroup, however, Family Tree 4 reveals that the female line ancestry in question can be traced back to the thirteenth century. As for its geographical source, at that period it appears to have been Franco-Italian.

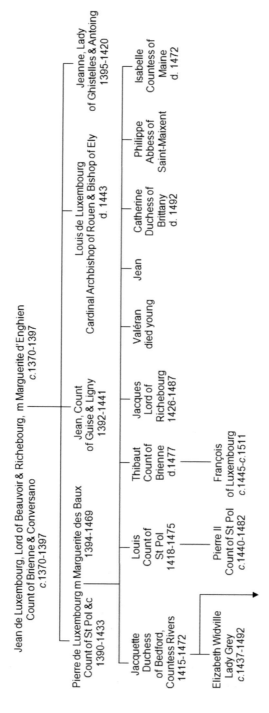

Family Tree 4: The House of Luxembourg.

Chapter 2

Descended from a Water-Fay?

The story about his family ancestry which, as we have seen, was accepted and promoted by the Emperor Henry VII – ancestral cousin of Jacquette de St Pol – was extremely curious. It claimed that the house of Luxembourg was descended from a fairy who had aquatic links! The water-fay story in question appears to have originated in France, though later it spread more widely.

Initially it was claimed that in western France, in a great forest around the knoll on which stood the town and castle of Poitiers, the young Raymond of Poitou discovered near a fountain 'three maidens in glimmering white dresses with long waving golden hair, and faces of inexpressible beauty'.[1] One of the three was Melusine (or Melusina). According to her self-description 'she was a water-fay of great power and wealth'.[2]

Melusine and her sisters, Melior, and Palatyne, were said to be the daughters of a fairy called Pressyne. However, their father had been a mere human. What is more, reportedly the three girls had later attacked their human father. As a result they had then all been punished by their mother. In the case of Melusine the punishment in question condemned her to take every Saturday either the form of a serpent from the waist down, or the form of a mermaid.[3]

In spite of (or perhaps because of) her sorcerous connections, Melusine reportedly became Raymond's wife, and bore him children. She is also said to have enlarged her husband's castle, and strengthened its fortifications. Reportedly she then re-named it 'Lusinia' after herself! According to the story it was that name which subsequently evolved into the modern form of Lusignan.[4]

> Stephan, a Dominican, of the house of Lusignan, ... made the story so famous, that the families of Luxembourg, Rohan,

and Sassenaye altered their pedigrees so as to be able to claim descent from the illustrious Melusina*[2]; and the Emperor Henry VII[5] felt no little pride in being able to number the beautiful and mysterious lady among his ancestors. "It does not escape me," writes the chronicler Conrad Vecerius, in his life of that emperor, "to report what is related in a little work in the vernacular, concerning the acts of a woman, Melyssina, on one day of the week becoming a serpent from her middle downwards, whom they reckon among the ancestors of Henry VII. ... But, as authors relate, that in a certain island of the ocean, there are nine Sirens endowed with various arts, such, or instance, as changing themselves into any shape they like, it is no absurd conjecture to suppose that Melyssina came thence*[3]."[6]

*2. Bullet, *Dissertat. sur la Mythologie Française*. Paris, 1771, pp. 1–32.
*3. Urstisius, *Scriptores Germanias*. Frankfort 1670.

The members of the house of Luxembourg claimed descent from their own version of Melusine. Their claim was made on the basis of a very similar story to the one we have already explored. However, the Luxembourg version contained a different human character who was named as the husband of the water nymph. In their case the connection was reputed to be via Count Siegfried of the Ardennes, who founded the city of Luxembourg towards the end of the tenth century. Melusine was said to have magically created for him the Castle of Luxembourg on the morning after Count Siegfried married her. And in the case of the Luxembourg Melusine it was definitely alleged that on one day every week she became a mermaid.[7]

Of course, this story appears simply to have been a myth. Nevertheless, it may have been considered significant in England. There an attempt had also been made to adopt it earlier on the part of King Richard I. 'The chronicler Gerald of Wales reported that Richard I of England was fond of telling a tale according to which he was a descendant of a countess of Anjou who was in fact the fairy Melusine, concluding that his whole family "came from the devil and would return to the devil"'.[8]

A fifteenth-century imagination of how Melusine might have looked.

The diabolic link via Melusine explains why subsequently, in fifteenth-century England, the story may have come to be regarded as a possible explanation which could account for certain evil activities of which Jacquette de St Pol and her daughter Elizabeth found themselves accused. Those activities included the allegation behind the 1469–70 prosecution of Jacquette. That was based upon evidence that she had committed assassinatory sorcery. The evidence in question – in the form of a statuette – was brought against her by Thomas Wake, a retainer of the Earl of Warwick (see below, Chapter 10). They also include the claim that the casting of love spells which had allegedly been carried out on the part of Jacquette and her daughter was the cause which had led firstly to Edward IV's attachment to Elizabeth, and subsequently to his bigamous secret marriage with her (see below, Chapters 7 & 11).

Chapter 3

Anglo-Norman Ancestry?

As for Elizabeth Widville's paternal ancestry, as was shown in the Introduction, based upon the surname which that family employed it seems probable that Elizabeth may have been descended in that line from a family which had at some stage been located at the hamlet of Wyville, near Grantham in Lincolnshire. According to the *Domesday Book* survey of 1086, at that time Wyville was quite tiny (containing only half a dozen households). It formed part of the manor of Denton, and was then under the lordship of Robert of Tosny, who had been one of King William I's Norman conquerors of England.[1] Thus the family which adopted the name of the hamlet might perhaps have been partly Anglo-Saxon in origin. Probably, however, it was also partly descended from a Norman soldier in the service of Robert of Tosny. In other words it may have comprised a mixture of the two races in terms of its origin.

Eighty years later, in the reign of Henry II, Willelmus de Widuill (William de Wivill) was renting land at Grafton in Northamptonshire from the Benedictine Abbot of Grestein (Grestain) in Normandy.[2] Nevertheless, it seems clear that, at that time, and also a little later, in the reign of Henry II's youngest son, King John – and also in the reign of *his* son, King Henry III, the family surname was most often spelt as *de Wivill* or *de Wyvill*. Normally the letter d was missing. Obviously that supports the theory that they may previously have been living at Wyville in Lincolnshire.[3] From the same twelfth- and thirteenth-century evidence it also seems clear that the family was sometimes already involved in disputes! In addition, some members of the family – though possibly not in Elizabeth Widville's direct line of ancestry – appear to have become established in Sussex by the reign of Henry III.[4]

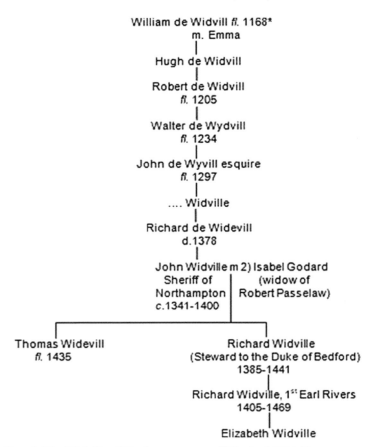

Family Tree 5: The Widville of Grafton ancestry of Elizabeth Widville.

Apart from the all male line of descent, some information is also available in respect of other lines of Elizabeth Widville's paternal English ancestry. For example, her father's mother, Joan Bittlesgate, belonged to family lines all of which seem to have been based in the West Country (Devon, Dorset and Somerset).

The West Country ancestors included Somerset Beauchamps. It is therefore possible that Elizabeth Widville may have been distantly related to Eleanor Talbot and to Margaret Beaufort, both of whom were also of Beauchamp descent in their maternal lines. Eleanor's mother was a Warwick Beauchamp, and Margaret Beaufort's mother was a Bletsoe Beauchamp. Those two families definitely had shared ancestry, though the two fifteenth-century ladies were only distant cousins.

Family Tree 6: Widville Ancestry

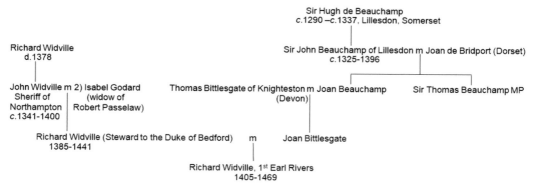

Family Tree 6: Other aspects of the ancestry of Elizabeth Widville's father.

Probably the Somerset Beauchamp ancestry of Elizabeth Widville means that she was also a distant relative. But in her case the precise connection cannot be determined.

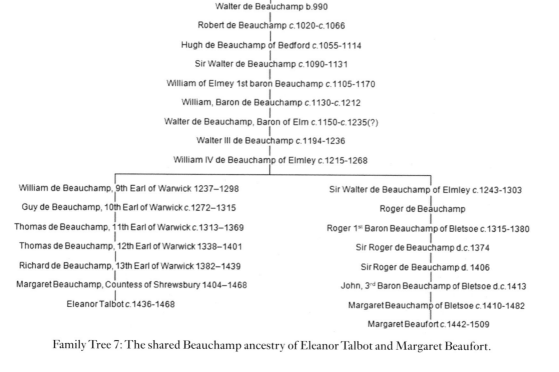

Family Tree 7: The shared Beauchamp ancestry of Eleanor Talbot and Margaret Beaufort.

Chapter 4

Born in France?

Elizabeth's father, Richard Widville, is thought to have been born in 1405 at Maidstone in Kent, where his father held the Mote estate.[1] He was named after his own father (Elizabeth's grandfather), who was later the chamberlain of John of Lancaster, Duke of Bedford, regent of France. As for his paternal grandfather (Elizabeth's great grandfather), John Widville (see Plate 7), he had been three times sheriff of Northampton, in 1380, in 1385 and in 1390.

Possibly Richard's sharing of his father's names creates a little confusion in respect of the surviving fifteenth-century records relating to a 'Richard Widville'. Reportedly Elizabeth's father was a captain in 1429, and was serving in France in 1433. Certainly on Thursday 3 June 1434, a Richard Wideville esquire was one of the six people who were commissioned to take, at Dover, on the following Monday week (14 June), the next muster of men for service in France.[2] Possibly, however, on that occasion 'Richard … *esquire*' refers to the elder of the two Richard Widvilles. That might perhaps be the case because two weeks later, on Friday 18 June, three people in France were commissioned to take muster of men arriving in Calais, and they were told that the men in question would include Richard Widville, *knight*, and his retinue (20 men at arms and 60 archers).[3] That same year a Richard Widville was also named as a knight of the shire for Kent.[4]

Hicks claims that 'the knighting of the younger Richard [was carried out] by Henry VI in 1426.'[5] However, he cites no source for that statement. Obviously Henry VI would have been rather young for carrying out knighting ceremonies *himself* at that time. He was only five years old. For example, the knighting of Henry's young cousin, Richard, Duke of York – which was definitely carried out in 1426 – was performed, not by the child king himself, but by his uncle, the Duke of Bedford.

Certainly Richard Widville is said to have been a knight of the English regent in France, John of Lancaster, Duke of Bedford, by 1435. However, on Saturday 8 October 1435 Richard Widville was cited as the Lieutenant of Calais, but on that occasion the person in question was again referred to as an esquire. At that point the Richard Widville in question was one of the people being requested to conduct a survey of the soldiers whom the Duke of Bedford had stationed in Calais on the day of his death.[6] The duke had then died just over three weeks earlier, at Rouen, on Wednesday 14 September 1435. He was interred in Rouen Cathedral.

John of Lancaster, Duke of Bedford, had been born in England in 1389. He was the third son of Henry, Earl of Derby. The Earl of Derby later succeeded *his* father, John of Gaunt (third adult son of King Edward III), to the Dukedom of Lancaster, and he subsequently usurped the English throne as King Henry IV.

John of Lancaster's two elder brothers were King Henry V and Thomas of Lancaster, Duke of Clarence. Humphrey of Lancaster, Duke of Gloucester, was John's younger brother. Thomas, Duke of Clarence, died in 1421. That was followed by the death of Henry V in 1422. Thus it was John who then became regent for his baby nephew, King Henry VI. However, John was focussed principally on the ongoing war in France – of which country the baby Henry was also meant to be king. Thus control of affairs in England found itself chiefly in the hands of John's younger brother, Humphrey.

In his mid thirties – on 13 May 1423 – the Duke of Bedford married the nineteen-year-old Anne of Burgundy, daughter of the Burgundian Duke John the Fearless. Anne was a distant cousin of her husband. They shared common descent from King Philip III of France. Anne was the great granddaughter of King John of France and his consort, Bonne (or Jutta) of Luxembourg (also known as Bonne – or Jutta – of Bohemia), and King John had been the second cousin of his captor – and the Duke of Bedford's great grandfather – King Edward III of England.

Anne's marriage to the Duke of Bedford was celebrated in Troyes, and it seems that the couple were happy together for the next nine years. Curiously, however, they produced no children. On Wednesday 30 May 1431, as part of the preparations for the forthcoming coronation of his nephew, King Henry VI, in Paris, Bedford had Joan of Arc martyred in Rouen. Sadly, the following year (in the autumn of 1432) his wife, Anne, caught the plague in Paris. She then died there.

Anne of Burgundy,
Duchess of Bedford,
predecessor and distant
cousin of Jacquette
de St Pol.

The following year (1433) the forty-four-year-old John, Duke of Bedford took a second wife. This time he wedded a distant cousin of his previous spouse (see Family Tree 2). The girl in question was Jacquette of St Pol. Like her predecessor and distant relative, Anne of Burgundy, Jacquette was probably about nineteen years old when Bedford married her. Indeed, it is even possible that she may hitherto have been in the service of her cousin, the earlier duchess. John's marriage to Jacquette was celebrated 'at the cathedral of Thérouanne in France, in a ceremony presided over by her uncle Louis, then bishop'.[7] However, John's second marriage also proved childless. Indeed it only lasted for just over two years.

In June 1433, shortly after their marriage had been celebrated, Jacquette accompanied her husband to England, visiting London and the duke's estate at Fulbrook in Warwickshire. But just over a year later the couple returned to France. Jacquette was presumably with the Duke of Bedford 'when he died in Rouen Castle on 14 September 1435, two years and five months after their marriage'.[8] Thus, in September 1435, the twenty-year-old Jacquette suddenly found herself a widow.

On 6 February 1435/6 she was formally granted by Henry VI's government 'that she may sue out livery of her dower of the lands of her late husband by parcels ... provided always that the bishop of Térouane [Thérouanne], king's chancellor of France [Jacquette's uncle, Louis], and the lord of Talbot [later the Earl of Shrewsbury, the father of Eleanor Talbot], be empowered to receive her fealty and that she do not marry without the king's consent'.[9] However, Jacquette seems to have quite quickly found herself attracted to one of her late husband's former officials – Sir Richard Widville. He was about ten years older than she was. At the time of her first husband's death Richard was about thirty. He figures in the 'List of the retinue of the duke of Bedford in the French wars.'[10] There he is listed as 'Richard Wideville, knight bachelor in the regentes court, and after erle Rivers.'[11]

It is just possible that Elizabeth Widville, who is thought to have been born in 1437, might have been conceived before her parents were married. Her mother should, in theory, have avoided a second marriage while she was in mourning for her first husband. Jacquette's official status in that respect would have ended in September 1436. However, if she had wedded her second husband in that month, and conceived her first child as a result of the consummation of their marriage, Elizabeth would probably have been born in June 1437. Birth in June 1437 could also account for the name which the baby was given (see below). It is therefore equally possible that the affair between Jacquette and Richard Widville was conducted morally, and that Elizabeth, their first child, was born in June 1437.

However, Jacquette's relationship with Richard Widville was definitely not conducted legally. The widowed Duchess of Bedford was not supposed to remarry without receiving official authorisation from her nephew by marriage – and her sovereign, both in England and in France – King Henry VI. In September 1436 that young king would have been approaching his fifteenth birthday. When the truth was revealed of Jacquette's conduct regarding matrimony it was therefore probably the young king's surviving uncle (and Jacquette's surviving brother-in-law), Humphrey of Lancaster, Duke of Gloucester, who was chiefly responsible for the action taken. Humphrey had previously been restrictive nine years earlier in the context of the wished-for remarriage plans of another sister-in-law, Catherine of France, widow of Henry V.[12]

Probably it was Jacquette's first pregnancy – when she apparently found herself bearing the foetus who was to become the future Elizabeth Widville – which made it necessary for her to acknowledge her second marriage in public and admit that she had done wrong. The consequence was that on Saturday 23 March 1436/7, the Duchess of Bedford and her second husband, Richard Widville, knight, found themselves fined the sum of £1,000 in order to obtain a pardon for having married without the consent of the young king.[13]

Certainly it seems that Elizabeth must have been the first child of Jacquette's initially secret second marriage. Curiously, MacGibbon's earlier account of Elizabeth Widville proposed that the little girl 'was born, in all probability, at Grafton, sometime in 1437'.[14] A more recent account proposes, on the basis of absolutely no presented evidence, that:

> It was around this time [24 October 1437] that Jacquetta [*sic*] gave birth to her first child, a daughter named Elizabeth, who is likely to have arrived at the Woodville's [*sic*] home of Grafton Manor in Northamptonshire.[15]

As we have seen, the year that MacGibbon proposes is probably correct. However, there is no reason to suppose that the birth probably took place in about October. Also the birth place which MacGibbon and the more recent account both propose for Elizabeth is almost certainly incorrect. After all, it seems that Jacquette 'probably spent a considerable amount of

1 (♀1) Elizabeth Widville, Lady Grey (*c.*1437-1492)
2 (♂1) Louis Widville (*c.*1438-?)
3 (♀2) Anne Widville, Viscountess Bourchier (*c.*1439–1489) — all probably born in France
4 (♂2) Anthony Widville, 2nd Earl Rivers (*c.*1440-1483)
5 (♀3) Jacquette Widville, Lady Strange (*c.*1442-1509)

6 (♂3) John Widville (*c.*1445-1469)
7 (♀4) Martha Widville (*c.*1447-?)
8 (♀5) Eleanor Widville (*c.*1449-?)
9 (♂4) Lionel Widville, Bishop of Salisbury (*c.*1452-1484)
10 (♂5) Richard Widville, 3rd Earl Rivers (1453–1491)
11 (♀6) Margaret Widville, Countess of Arundel (1454-1490)
12 (♀7) Mary Widville, Countess of Pembroke (*c.*1456-1481)
13 (♀8) Catherine Widville, Duchess of Buckingham; Duchess of Bedford; Mrs Wingfield (1457/8-1497)
14 (♂6) Sir Edward Widville ('Lord Scales') (*c.*1459-1488)
15 (♀9) Agnes Widville (*c.*1460-?)

Elizabeth Widville and her siblings.

time in France during the first years of her second marriage, litigating to secure her dower lands there, while Sir Richard served intermittently in France until at least 1442'.[16] Therefore her first five children, Elizabeth, Louis, Anne, Anthony and Jacquette, who were born between 1437 and 1442, were probably all born in France.

In any case, it appears highly unlikely that Elizabeth could have been born at Grafton in 1437, because the manor of Grafton in Northamptonshire was actually only acquired by Sir Richard Widville and his wife, Jacquette, on 10 June 1440. On that day King Henry VI issued a 'licence, pursuant to letters patent dated 20 March, 14 Henry VI [1435/6], for William [de la Pole], earl of Suffolk, and Alice [*née* Chaucer] his wife, to grant the manor of Grafton, co. Northampton ... to Richard Wydevyll, knight, and Jacquetta [*sic – the orginal text of this document is in Latin – hence this 3-syllabled Latin form of Jacquette's Christian name in the CPR*] his wife'.[17]

As we have seen, although she was probably born somewhere in France, and at some time in 1437, it is not certain *precisely* where Elizabeth Widville was born, nor precisely on what date. Nor do we know for certain why she was baptised as 'Elizabeth'. Of course, a slightly different version of that name was held by one of her mother's younger sisters – Isabelle, Countess of Maine. After all, *Isabel, Isabelle, Isabella* and *Elizabeth* are all variant European versions of the same originally Hebrew name *Elisheva*.[18] On the other hand, the possibility was explored earlier that the baby girl might possibly have been born in June 1437. At that period babies would always have been baptised as soon as possible after their birth, for the sake of their soul's safety from a religious point of view. Therefore it is conceivable that Elizabeth Widville might have been baptised on 24 June 1437. That date is the feast of the Nativity of St John the Baptist, and the name of John's mother is traditionally said to have been Elizabeth. In other words, the baby may have been given that name because of the date on which she was baptised. But of course there is no solid evidence in that respect, and it is simply a hypothesis.

From the list of Elizabeth's siblings (see above), it is obvious that Jacquette's marriage to Richard Widville was an active affair in terms of love-making. Soon after the birth of her first baby, and her own subsequent churching, Jacquette seems to have found herself pregnant once again. In 1438 she probably gave birth to a second child – this time a son. He was given the popular French name, Louis. But in those days not all children survived to adult life. And in Louis' case he seems to have died young. The next few years then saw the births of Anne, Anthony and Jacquette. Probably all those children were born in France.

In the 1430s one of the prominent Englishmen who had served in France had been Henry VI's cousin, Richard, Duke of York. After the death of the Duke of Bedford, York was appointed lieutenant and governor of France, and in 1441 he and his wife, Cecily Neville, settled at Rouen. It was at Rouen Castle that, on an unknown date, probably in 1442, Cecily gave birth to York's eventual son and heir, Edward – who later became King Edward IV. Of course, many published sources readily cite an alleged birthdate for Edward. Unfortunately, however, they do so without bothering to research the sources for the date which they attribute to him. The huge problem which, in reality, concerns the future King Edward IV's authentic birth date has been fully explored in the present author's earlier works.[19]

York subsequently remained in command of the English situation in France until 1445. Indeed, he organised the ceremony at Rouen which formed part of Margaret of Anjou's procession to England as that country's new queen consort. Accompanied by Lady Talbot, the Countess of Salisbury, and many others, the Duke of York received Margaret at Rouen where she was given a banquet at the town hall.[20] Since Jacquette appears to have accompanied the new English queen on her subsequent storm-ridden sea journey to England, presumably she was one of the many people present at the ceremonies in Rouen. In other words, both Jacquette and her second husband must have been acquainted with the Duke and Duchess of York in France. However, it seems unlikely that at that time and place their own young children – including Elizabeth Widville – would have actually met Richard and Cecily's slightly younger children, including the future Edward IV.

Chapter 5

Brought up in England

In November 1444 Jacquette was one of the members of the retinue which accompanied Henry VI's bride, Margaret of Anjou, from France to England.[1] Her sixth child – and third son – John Widville, might therefore have been born in England. It is even possible that he was born at Grafton in Northamptonshire (the manor which his parents had acquired in 1440), probably in 1445. Also, presumably all the children of Jacquette and Richard Widville – including young Elizabeth – were then basically brought up in England.

'For the rest of Henry VI's reign', it is said that Jacquette 'was one of the pre-eminent noblewomen at court.'[2] Nevertheless, the fifteen remaining years of Henry VI's first reign were also to be filled for Jacquette with a series of at least ten further pregnancies, so of course she can hardly have been at court all the time. Also, in spite of the fact that she had briefly

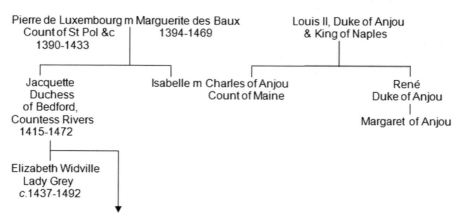

Family Tree 8: Jacquette's connections with Margaret of Anjou.

19

been Henry VI's aunt by marriage, the precise nature of her relationship with Margaret of Anjou is somewhat questionable. Jacquette's younger sister, Isabelle de St Pol, had become Margaret's aunt by marriage in 1443 (see Family Tree 8). However, a possible problem lies in the fact that in 1431 Jacquette's paternal uncle, Jean de Luxembourg (see Family Tree 4) had seized the county of Guisne from Margaret's father, René of Anjou, at a time when René had found himself captured by the Duke of Burgundy.[3] Their contest over the county of Guisne hardly seems likely to have made the two men in question close friends.

On 9 May 1448 Jacquette gained a new title. Theoretically she then became Lady Rivers, because her second husband was created Baron Rivers by King Henry VI.[4] In reality, however, as the Paston letters (and other contemporary documents) still show clearly, she was actually always referred to by the general public in England as 'my Lady of Bedford'.[5]

In 1450 'Rivers took part in the suppression of Cade's rebellion and was apparently considered as a possible constable of England.'[6] But at that point he still had a role in Calais, which he visited in the winter of 1451/2 for its defence against the French.[7]

The pattern of her frequent pregnancies suggests that Jacquette must have been with her husband a good deal. Therefore, since he remained Lieutenant of Calais at least until 1455, more of the couple's children might possibly have been born in what we would now call France. Also, existing children might possibly have accompanied their parents there sometimes. However, Elizabeth is not very likely to have gone back to France in the 1450s, because by then there were marriage plans for her (see below, Chapter 6). Also, subsequently, 'Rivers was not retained as lieutenant of Calais by Richard Neville, earl of Warwick, after 1456 and from 1457 occurs frequently on commissions in Northamptonshire and Kent. In 1457 he became constable of Rochester.'[8] Thus the family may then have been based mainly in the south east of England.

In 1458, in response to news brought to England from France by the Earl of Warwick's supporter, John Wenlock, 'with a great number of soldiers, the archbishop of Canterbury, the lord of Rieveres, and Sir Girvais Clifton'[9] were commissioned to defend the country from a possible invasion. Two years later, after the Yorkist Earls of Salisbury, Warwick and March had fled to Calais, Lord Rivers was involved in the preparation of forces against them at Sandwich. However, when the three

Yorkist earls sent men to invade Kent, Rivers found himself captured by them. As curiously reported at the time, 'the Lord Rivers, Sir Anthony his son, and others *have won Calais*.'[10] Presumably this simply refers to the fact that the men in question had arrived at Calais as prisoners.

> The victors did not fail to turn the incident to their account by exhibiting as much contempt as possible for their unfortunate prisoners. 'My Lord Rivers', writes William Paston, 'was brought to Calais, and before the lords with eight score torches, and there my lord of Salisbury rated him, calling him knave's son, that he should be so rude to call him and those other lords traitors; for they should be found the king's true liegemen when he should be found a traitor. And my lord of Warwick rated him and said that his father was but a squire, and brought up with King Henry V, and since made himself by marriage, and also made a lord; and that it was not his part to have such language of lords, being of the king's blood. And my lord of March [later Edward IV] rated him in like wise. And Sir Anthony was rated for his language of all the three lords in like wise.'[11]

It is interesting to see that both the Earl of Warwick and his cousin, the future King Edward IV, clearly looked down on the Widvilles at that time and felt extremely critical of them.

In February 1460/1 Lord Rivers' wife, Jacquette, found herself requested by the mayor and aldermen of London to protect the city by negotiating with Margaret of Anjou, because the queen's forces were then just outside the capital.[12] On 29 March her husband and her eldest surviving son, Anthony, were captured by the Yorkists at the battle of Towton. As a result Lord Rivers acceded to the Yorkist take-over. Probably he was not strongly 'Lancastrian'. Hitherto he had simply been supporting what had appeared to be the existing regime. Now he gave his support to the new government.

Subsequently he therefore found himself employed by the young Edward IV on royal commissions. On Sunday 12 July 1461 he was pardoned for all his offences, and eleven days later his eldest surviving son, Anthony, was also pardoned.[13] On Saturday 12 December 1461 Lord Rivers was granted the office of chief rider of the king's forest of Saucy [Salcey] in Northamptonshire.[14] His wife's connections with the Burgundian ducal family might possibly have been in his favour. Thus by 1463 it appears that Rivers himself might theoretically have been able to offer a link to the new Yorkist king for his widowed eldest daughter, Elizabeth. However, as we shall see shortly, in reality it appears to have been another relative of the young widow that introduced her to the king.

Chapter 6

Married to Sir John Grey

By the early 1450s a marriage had been arranged for Elizabeth by her parents. The husband they chose for her belonged to a family which was then based at Groby in Leicestershire. However, the fact that Groby had become the family home was thanks to the mother of Elizabeth Widville's chosen husband – not thanks to his paternal ancestry.

The husband who was chosen for Elizabeth was John Grey, son of Sir Edward Grey, and a grandson of Reginald, Baron Grey. At the time when Elizabeth Widville's marriage to John Grey was arranged, John's father also had baronial status. He held the title of Baron Ferrers of Groby. However, like his tenure of the Groby family home, his tenure of the Groby title was by right of his marriage to John's mother, Elizabeth Ferrers, because she was the Ferrers heiress.

The marriage between John Grey and Elizabeth Widville appears to have been celebrated at some point between 1452 and 1454. Assuming that it took place around 1453, Elizabeth would then have been about sixteen years old. As for John Grey, in 1453 he would have been about twenty-one years old. Therefore the marriage could almost certainly have been consummated more or less immediately.

The young couple are said to have resided at Astley Castle in Warwickshire (see Plate 9), and at Elizabeth Widville's parental manor of Grafton in Northamptonshire.[1] They produced two children – both sons. Thomas Grey, who later became the Marquess of Dorset, was the first child of the marriage. He is said to have been born in 1455, in the vicinity of Westminster. Subsequently a younger son, Richard Grey was also born. Apparently he was named after his maternal grandfather.

In 1457 John Grey's father died. His mother remarried several years later. Her second husband, John Bourchier – the fourth son of Henry Bourchier, Earl of Essex – then adopted the Ferrers baronial title and he used it until

Elizabeth Ferrers died herself, in 1483. On his mother's side Sir John Grey had a family connection which was subsequently to help his widow arrange a meeting with King Edward IV. One of his mother's cousins was married to Anne Hastings. She was one of the sisters of William, the future Lord Hastings and the chamberlain to King Edward IV. It was reportedly Lord Hastings who later assisted Elizabeth Widville to meet the young king. Unfortunately, though, in the longer term, as we shall see later, Lord Hastings was to prove to be an enemy of Elizabeth Widville and her family.

As for Sir John Grey's younger brother, Edward (see Plate 10), he was to make a very intriguing marriage a little later. The young girl whom he wedded in the 1470s was Elizabeth Talbot junior, eldest daughter (and eventual heiress) of John Talbot, Viscount Lisle. So that girl was the niece of Eleanor Talbot. In July 1464, when their widowed mother had died (leaving her three children as orphans) Elizabeth Talbot junior and her brother and sister had become the wards of their grandmother, Margaret Beauchamp, dowager Countess of Shrewsbury. But about three years later, on 14 June 1467, Margaret Beauchamp also died. Thus, at that point, the three Lisle children found themselves the wards of Eleanor Talbot and her younger sister, Elizabeth Talbot, senior Duchess of Norfolk.

As for the subsequent descendants of Edward Grey and Elizabeth Talbot junior, interestingly they were to include a girl who shared Elizabeth Widville's (and Eleanor Talbot's) fate of being a disputed Queen of England. The descendant in question was Lady Jane Grey – popularly known as the 'nine-days queen'.

Sir John Grey was knighted in 1458. However, he was subsequently killed fighting on the Lancastrian side on 17 February 1460/1, at the second battle of St Albans. It is not known where he was buried. Possibly it was on the battlefield, or maybe it was at St Alban's Abbey.

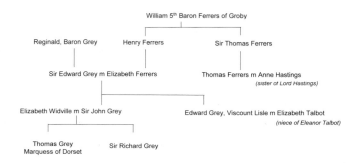

Family Tree 9: The family connections of Sir John Grey.

Chapter 7

Relationship with Edward IV

It seems to have been at some point between his accession to the English throne (March 1460/1), and 25 March 1464 (i.e. the beginning of the medieval English year 1464), that the young Yorkist king, Edward IV, met Elizabeth Widville. Then he gradually became actively involved with her. The impetus in that respect must have come from Edward's side. After all, his taking of the English crown more or less coincided, for Elizabeth, with the loss of her husband, Sir John Grey. And, although she may never have been deeply in love with her first husband (whom she herself had not chosen), his death also robbed her of financial security.

Previously, both her husband and her parents had been supporting the Lancastrian side – or at least, supporting the existing government of Henry VI. Therefore Elizabeth had presumably not hitherto been feeling 'Yorkist'. That being the case, she might never have sought to meet the young king if she had not found herself in need of his assistance, for material reasons which will be presented shortly.

Nevertheless, as we saw in Chapter 5, in the summer of 1461 Edward IV had formally pardoned both her father and her brother, Anthony, for their earlier 'Lancastrian' (existing government) support, and Lord Rivers began to work for the new regime. It therefore seems that the Widville family may not have been strongly partisan in either direction. Rather they simply accepted working for the existing officially-recognised government.

Shortly afterwards Elizabeth's younger brother, John, also met the new Yorkist king. It seems that John may have needed a little money as well. On 20 October 1463, at the age of about eighteen, he was with Edward IV at Pontefract in Yorkshire.[1] And there he was lent a gold noble (six shillings and eight pence) by his older namesake, Sir John Howard, a cousin of the Mowbray Dukes of Norfolk (and their eventual successor).[2]

A gold noble of Henry VI.

Since King Edward IV had certainly been born in France, and given that Elizabeth Widville was probably also born there, some historians have claimed that the young man who became the new king of England in March 1460/1 'had known [Elizabeth] literally ever since he was born, as her father was attached to the Duke of York's staff in Normandy'.[3] However, there is absolutely no real evidence to that effect. Indeed earlier (see above, Chapter 4) it was suggested that most probably no such meeting had taken place between the children in France.

Also, although Edward's precise date of birth is uncertain, he appears to have been born some time in 1441–1442. Thus Elizabeth would probably have then been about five years old when he was born. When her family left France two years later with England's new queen consort, Margaret of Anjou, Elizabeth would have been about seven and Edward would then have been about two. So if they had met in France it must have been when she was six and he was one. It is not common for socialising to take place between girls and boys of those ages. Additional evidence comes from my memory of my own family. My younger sister was three years old when our maternal grandfather died, and she does not really remember him. Thus, logically, it seems that if little Edward ever had seen Elizabeth Widville in France, he would probably not subsequently have remembered her.

Certainly Thomas More – the most commonly cited source for the story of how Edward and Elizabeth met – offers no suggestion for such an earlier meeting (see below). Of course, as we shall see presently, More's account in respect of the Yorkist period is by no means accurate overall. He was born towards the end of that era, in February 1477/8. Subsequently, in 1490, at the age of twelve to thirteen, the young Thomas was placed by his father in the Lambeth household of Archbishop (later Cardinal) John Morton.[4] As a result, the young Thomas More found himself being educated under the guidance of the manipulative politician who led the political rewriting of history in the late fifteenth and early sixteenth century. Morton was working on behalf of King Henry VII, who had usurped the English throne in 1485. However, it is also the case that no solid evidence exists in any contemporary sources indicating that Edward and Elizabeth had been acquainted in any way with one another prior to their meeting as adults in the early 1460s. Therefore Thomas More's account may well be correct in that regard.

As for the new evidence of Edward IV's movements which was produced recently by the present writer,[5] it shows that, if, in the period 1461–64, Edward IV met Elizabeth at or near her parents' manor of Grafton, in the vicinity of Northampton, the young king would have been in the right area in July 1462, in July, August and/or September 1463, and/or in January 1463/4.

It seems that, when they did meet, Edward IV's conduct with Elizabeth Widville closely reproduced his earlier conduct with another attractive Lancastrian widow – Lady Eleanor Talbot, daughter of the late John Talbot, Earl of Shrewsbury, and widow of Sir Thomas Boteler, son and heir of Lord Sudeley. Edward appears to have met Eleanor in about 1460, when she too was a young widow, and he appears to have secretly married her on Monday 8 June 1461.[6] Subsequently, however, that relationship remained secret. Full details in respect of Eleanor can be found in the publication of earlier research by the present writer.[7]

Phillippe de Commynes was a contemporary who had met Edward IV on various occasions – though he only wrote down his account in about 1490, after Edward had died. He states that when he met Eleanor, Edward 'promised to marry her, provided that he could sleep with her first, and she consented'.[8] Initially that seems to make Eleanor sound more potentially susceptible than Elizabeth Widville. However, Commynes also reports that Edward 'had made this promise in the Bishop [of Bath]'s presence. And having done so, he slept with her.'[9] Indeed, in another part of his account Commynes reports explicitly that actually the bishop in question 'had married them',[10] and as we shall see later, there is other clear contemporary evidence that Edward had secretly married Eleanor.

In 1461 the 'Bishop of Bath' to whom Commynes refers (Robert Stillington) was a priest of course, but he had not yet been promoted to the rank of bishop. It is also worth noting that actually in those days priests were not considered necessary for the celebration of a valid marriage. All that

An early nineteenth-century imaginary image depicting the meeting of Edward IV and Lady Grey (Elizabeth Widville). Interestingly, Edward IV appears to have already been with a *Talbot hound* when Lady Grey arrived.

was required was the exchange of oaths between a valid bride and groom, followed by consummation. Indeed, 'priests were forbidden to participate in any clandestine marriages.'[11] Nevertheless a priest is certainly reported to have officiated at Edward IV's clandestine marriage to Elizabeth Widville in 1464. And it seems certain that the future Bishop Stillington similarly officiated at Edward's earlier secret marriage with Eleanor Talbot.

In many respects Edward IV's two secret marriage stories – with Eleanor and with Elizabeth – seem to be very similar. The two women were both widows whose backgrounds had been Lancastrian. Just like Lady Eleanor Talbot, Lady Boteler, Elizabeth Widville, Lady Grey, was apparently older than Edward IV. In fact she was probably of more or less the same age as Eleanor (who may possibly have been about a year older than Elizabeth). Lady Grey is also generally said by historians to have been a beauty – as Eleanor probably was. In neither Lady Grey's case nor Lady Boteler's case are there any surviving contemporary sources which specifically make the claim of beauty in respect of the lady in question. However, Eleanor Talbot's younger sister, the Duchess of Norfolk, definitely was so described in a surviving contemporary source.[12]

The claim has often been made that Lady Grey had fair hair. If that claim was true, in that respect she would probably have contrasted with Eleanor Talbot, who appears most likely (based on close family evidence) to have been a brunette. However, while it is true that two surviving manuscript illustrations do depict Elizabeth Widville with golden hair,[13] what is believed to be a life portrait of her, at Queens' College, Cambridge (a reproduction of which figures in Plate 12), depicts her with quite dark auburn hair, and definitely shows her to have had brown eyes.[14]

Moreover, in the case of Elizabeth – as in the case of Eleanor – the available family evidence seems to suggest that she would probably have been rather unlikely to have been fair-haired. Definitely her brother, Anthony Widville (2nd Earl Rivers), together with both her maternal grandfather Pierre, and her first cousin, Pierre II – two of the Counts of St Pol – are all depicted in contemporary portraits as having dark hair (see Plate 4).

Interestingly, other fifteenth-century evidence suggests that in actual fact manuscript illustrations of English queens are by no means always to be trusted in terms of the hair colour which they depict. For example Margaret of Anjou is also represented in a manuscript with fair hair.[15] Yet she is known to have actually been described as dark.[16] Apparently, therefore, such manuscript-depicted fair-haired queens 'were represented as fulfilling an ideal which may not always have been the case'.[17] As a result it is extremely difficult to assess Elizabeth

Widville's colouring for certain. Thus, although she is generally said, rather naïvely, by modern writers to have been blonde, that may merely be yet another example of historical mythology. As we have now seen, the real evidence in that respect is far from clear, and actually Elizabeth may well have been a brunette.

As we have also seen, whether or not she resembled Eleanor Talbot in her colouring, when she met the king, Elizabeth did resemble Eleanor in another way. Just like Eleanor she was a young widow. Significantly, however, unlike Eleanor, Elizabeth had already become a mother. Thus, although initially Edward IV appears to have conducted himself in a similar way in both cases – making a secret marriage, following which initially nothing was announced in public – in respect of the ultimate formal recognition by Edward of his relationship with Elizabeth, that produced for her a situation which differed fundamentally from that of Eleanor.

Sir Thomas More offers the most complete surviving account of the story of what he presents as having been Edward IV's first meeting with Elizabeth Widville.

> After that King Edward the Fourth had deposed King Henry the Sixth and was in peaceable possession of the realm, determining himself to marry (as it was requisite both for himself and for the realm), he sent over in embassiate the Earl of Warwick with other noble men in his company unto Spain, to entreat and conclude a marriage between King Edward and the king's daughter of Spain. In which thing the Earl of Warwick found the parties so toward and willing that he speedily, according to his instructions, without any difficulty brought the matter to a very good conclusion.
>
> Now happed it that in the mean season there came, to make a suit by petition to the king, Dame Elizabeth Grey – which was after his queen, at that time a widow – born of noble blood, specially by her mother, which was Duchess of Bedford ere she married the Lord Woodville [*sic* Lord Rivers], her father. Howbeit, this Dame Elizabeth, herself being in service with Queen Margaret wife unto King Henry the Sixth, was married unto one John Grey a squire, whom King Henry made knight upon the field that he had on Shrove Tuesday at Saint Albans against King Edward. And

little while enjoyed he that knighthood, for he was at the same field slain. After which done, and the Earl of Warwick being in his embassiate about the afore remembered marriage, this poor lady made humble suit unto the king that she might be restored unto such small lands as her late husband had given her in jointure.

Whom, when the king beheld and heard her speak – as she was both fair, of a good favor, moderate of stature, well made, and very wise – he not only pitied her, but also waxed enamored on her. And taking her afterward secretly aside, began to enter in talking more familiarly. Whose appetite when she perceived, she virtuously denied him. But that did she so wisely, and with so good manner, and words so well set, that she rather kindled his desire than quenched it. And finally, after many a meeting, much wooing, and many great promises, she well espied the king's affection toward her so greatly increased that she durst somewhat the more boldly say her mind, as to him whose heart she perceived more firmly set than to fall off for a word. And in conclusion she showed him plain that as she wist herself too simple to be his wife, so thought she herself too good to be his concubine. The king, much marvelling of her constaunce, as he that had not been wont elsewhere to be so stiffly said nay, so much esteemed her continence and chastity that he set her virtue in the stead of possession and riches. And thus taking counsel of his desire, determined in all possible haste to marry her.[18]

However, More's account contains at least one obvious error. He claims that Edward IV had requested the Earl of Warwick to negotiate a possible marriage for him with 'the king's daughter of Spain'.[19] But in the 1460s Spain did not exist as a single state. The king to whom More is referring must be the Castilian monarch, Henry IV (reigned 1454–1474). And Henry was reputed to be impotent. At all events, he had no recognised royal daughter.[20]

It therefore appears that Thomas More must have been mislead by the fact that subsequent diplomatic negotiations had sought to arrange a Spanish marriage not for King Edward IV, but for his younger brother, Richard, Duke of Gloucester (later King Richard III). *That* possible marriage had been negotiated with Henry IV's *sister* (and eventual heiress), Isabel the Catholic.[21] Yet the negotiations in question only took place five years later, in 1468–69.

In 1463–64 the marriage plans for Edward IV proposed by the Earl of Warwick definitely involved no negotiations with the kingdom of Castile. Warwick had proposed the queen mother of Scotland, or Bona of Savoy as possible consorts for Edward IV.[22] And, intriguingly, it is of course quite obvious from his conduct in this respect that the king's cousin, Warwick, had absolutely no knowledge of Edward's relationship, either with Eleanor Talbot (who was the niece of Warwick's own wife, Anne Beauchamp), or with Elizabeth Widville.

Incidentally, other mistakes on Thomas More's part in the above account include the fact that Elizabeth's mother did not marry a *lord* as her second husband. In reality Sir Richard Widville only received a peerage about eleven years *after* their secret marriage – in 1458, when he was given the title Baron Rivers. Also Elizabeth's own first husband, John Grey was not made a knight just before the (second) battle of St Albans (at which he was killed), as More claims. He was actually knighted three years earlier, in 1458. Thus Sir John Grey enjoyed the status of knight for a much longer period than More suggests. In other words, as is sadly so often the case, it is quite clear that Thomas More's historical account is actually repeatedly unreliable and erroneous in this instance. Yet unfortunately, for almost five hundred years, in respect of his account of the meeting of Edward IV and Elizabeth Widville More's report has simply been accepted as completely accurate by most historians.

As we have seen, More states that 'when the king beheld and heard her speak – as she was both fair, of a good favor, moderate of stature, well made, and very wise – he not only pitied her, but also waxed enamored on her. And taking her afterward secretly aside, began to enter in talking more familiarly.'[23] More thus implies that, captivated by Elizabeth's beauty, Edward IV initially thought simply of sleeping with her. Incidently, More's account does suggest clearly that the two of them met frequently. He says that they had 'many a meeting, [and] much wooing'.[24] But Elizabeth rejected the king's initial idea because she 'thought ... herself too good to be his *concubine*'.[25] Partly because of that, and partly because of his growing attraction in her direction, 'taking counsel of his desire, [Edward] determined in all possible haste to marry her.'[26] But of course the marriage which he contracted with her was secret.

If More's account is correct in these respects (and genuine contemporary supporting evidence, in the form of an Italian poem, written on the subject in about 1467 will be presented shortly) the story of the secret marriage between Edward and Elizabeth appears to have been very similar to what had probably happened earlier between the young king and the virtuous Eleanor Talbot. But, of course, because it post-dated his earlier secret marriage with Eleanor Talbot, Edward IV's secret union with Elizabeth Widville was not actually a genuine marriage. Elizabeth herself was not aware of that at the time, but she discovered the truth later.

It has often been assumed that the initial meeting between the widowed Lady Grey and England's new young king took place because Elizabeth was seeking to appeal to him for the restitution of her husband's property, which has frequently been said to have been confiscated by the king himself because Sir John Grey had been one of Edward IV's Lancastrian enemies. However, that story is not accurate. The property had not been confiscated by the crown. In reality, the tenure of it was being denied to Elizabeth Widville by her mother-in-law, Elizabeth Ferrers, Lady Grey, the heiress to the Ferrers barony of Groby. The situation in which she found herself in respect of her mother-in-law is what made Elizabeth Widville appeal to the king, and she made her approach to him with the assistance of Edward IV's chamberlain, Lord Hastings.

As we have seen earlier, he was related to Elizabeth by marriage, because his sister, Anne Hastings, was the wife of Sir John Grey's maternal

The signature of Lord Hastings.

cousin, Thomas Ferrers (see Family Tree 9). Hastings agreed to present Elizabeth and her case to the king. In return she promised him a share of the property if and when she secured it.[27]

As for the final outcome of their meeting,

> In moste secrete maner, vpon the firste daye of May,[28] kynge Edwarde spousyd Elizabeth, late the wyfe of Sir John Graye, knyght, whiche before tyme was slayne at Toweton or Yorke felde [*sic*], whiche spowsayles were solempnyzed erely in ye mornynge at a towne named Graston [Grafton], nere vnto Stonyngstratforde; at whiche mariage was no [moo] persones present but the spowse, the spowsesse, the duches of Bedforde her moder, y preest, two gentylwomen, and a yong man to helpe the preest synge. After which spowsayles endyd, he went to bedde, and so taried there vpon. iii. or. iiii. houres, and after departed & rode agayne to Stonyngstratforde, and came i^n maner as though he had ben on huntinge, and there went to bedde agayne. And within a daye or. ii. after, he sent to Graston [Grafton], to the lorde Ryuers, fader vnto his wyfe, shewynge to hym y^t he wolde come & lodge with hym a certeyne season, where he was receyued with all honoure, and so taryed there by the space of. iiii. dayes. In whiche season, she nyghtly to his bedde was brought, in so secrete maner, that almooste none but her moder was of counsayll. And so this maryage was a season kept secret after, tyll nedely it muste be discoueryd & disclosed, by meane of other [proposed brides] whiche were offeryd vnto the kynge, as the quene of Scottes and other.[29]

Edward's secret marriage with Elizabeth is said to have taken place at her family manor house of Grafton Regis, on 1 May 1464, and the recent evidence of the king's movements published by the present writer shows clearly that the alleged date certainly is possible.[30] As for the secret ceremony which appeared to unite Edward IV to Elizabeth Widville, that is reported to have been carried out for them by a Dominican priest, Master Thomas Eborall.[31]

Since, presumably, at that time Elizabeth knew nothing of the young king's earlier secret relationship with Eleanor Talbot, in her eyes her own marriage with Edward IV, though secret, she would at that stage have considered valid. Thus, following their secret exchange of vows, Elizabeth would have assumed that Edward was then entitled to have sex with her. And apparently they spent three or four hours in bed together that same day. But of course consummating their union did not make their relationship a recognised marriage. As he had done earlier, with Eleanor Talbot, it appears that initially Edward saw Elizabeth, and slept with her, without offering any public announcement of his attachment. Significantly, however, in the case of Elizabeth Widville, her own family was apparently aware of the secret marriage. Possibly the same may also have been true in the earlier case of Eleanor Talbot. If so, that makes the subsequent marriage of Elizabeth Widville's brother-in-law, Edward Grey, with Eleanor's niece, Elizabeth Talbot of Lisle, potentially rather intriguing (see Family Tree 9).

In the case of Elizabeth Widville the secrecy continued for just over four months. In September 1464, however, Edward IV publicly acknowledged Elizabeth as his consort at a meeting of his council at Reading. This was at a time when his cousin the Earl of Warwick was attempting to promote a proposed royal marriage with Bona of Savoy. It has often been assumed that Warwick's pressure on the king to agree to the diplomatic union which he was proposing was what caused Edward IV to publicly acknowledge his marriage to Elizabeth Widville. However, on other occasions, when he disagreed with his cousin Warwick, Edward IV seems to have found it easy enough to simply reject the earl's suggestions. It is therefore probable that on this occasion the young king's revelation of his Widville union was motivated by some other cause.

The most obvious reason for such an action on the part of the king would have been that Elizabeth Widville had then told him that she was pregnant.[32] And indeed, that is definitely reported to have been the situation in the relevant section of a more or less contemporary Italian surviving source – the poem *De mulieribus admirandis*, which was discovered in the 1960s by Conor Fahy. Fahy shows very clearly that the poem must have been written by Antonio Cornazzano between 1466 and 1468 – at the most, about three years after Edward IV had publicly recognised his union with Elizabeth Widville. Also, as Cornazzano himself states very clearly in his introduction to the relevant section of the poem – a section which is entitled *La Regina d'ingliterra* ('The Queen of England') – the account that he presents in respect of Edward IV and Elizabeth Widville is not a story which has been made up.

> questa hystoria non è scripta
> per penna di poeti, ond'altri possa
> improperarla di fiction picta;
>
> (this story is not written
> by the pen of poets, in order that others can
> use it as a fictional depiction;)[33]

In *La Regina d'ingliterra* ('The Queen of England') Cornazzano first introduces the man in the story – Edward IV. He describes

> signioreggia uno eduardo chiamato,
> giovane bello e di sanghue regale,
> ingegnio humano prompt a reger stato
> con militar peritia e disciplina,
> cesare propio in campo et in senato.
> Imperando costui senza Regina,
> da credere è che spesso occultamente
> Si trastullasse in qualche concubina.
>
> (a lord king named Edward,
> young, handsome, and of royal blood,
> an ingenius human ready to rule the state
> with military expertise and discipline,
> a real Caesar in the field and in the senate.
> That man was reigning without a queen,
> there is make-believe that he secretly
> would play around with some concubine.)[34]

And it is very interesting that Cornazzano tells us so clearly that stories about Edward IV being involved with 'concubines' are merely fabrications.[35]

He then goes on to present Elizabeth, her family, and her story. Elizabeth is 'described as pregnant when the [royal] marriage was divulged'.[36] Cornazzano says:

> Dea di castità, cosi raccolse
> el fructo del justissimo semente.

> (Goddess of chastity, thus she gathered
> The fruit of the lawful seed.)[37]

In other words, in Cornazzano's account, the marriage which had hitherto been kept a secret, was publicly acknowledged by Edward IV when Elizabeth became pregnant.

> Questo acto occulto per ogni rispecto
> tene 'l re un tempo; el matrimonio infine,
> gravida facta lei, mandò ad effecto.
> Tutte le Signorie allui vicine
> all 'alte feste convocate furo:

> (This contract the king kept in every respect
> concealed for a time; finally, the marriage
> made her pregnant, and was acknowledged.
> All his supporting Lords
> were summoned to the high feast:)[38]

Oddly, Fahy felt inclined to see Cornazzano's pregnancy reference as an error on the poet's part. Presumably that was because Fahy was focussing his thoughts on the undisputed fact that Elizabeth of York (Elizabeth Widville's first *known* child fathered by Edward) was actually born more than a year after her mother's royal marriage had received public recognition. But of course, actually there are two very simple possible explanations, either one of which would make Cornazzano's contemporary account of an earlier pregnancy entirely authentic.

Obviously for Edward, if a potential heir appeared to be on the way, his secret union with the mother would urgently have needed to be recognised and made official. And since their union had been secretly consummated in May 1464 Elizabeth might very easily have known that she was pregnant four months later, in September of that year. However, if that was her experience then clearly something must subsequently have gone wrong for her, given that her first royal baby was not actually born until 11 February 1465/6. In other words, if she found herself bearing a foetus by the late summer of 1464, presumably Elizabeth subsequently miscarried the baby at some stage, after Edward had formally recognised their union.

A pregnancy which resulted in a premature miscarriage is one of the two possible explanations for what is said in the Italian poem. The other possibility would be that Elizabeth Widville merely *claimed* to be pregnant in September 1484, as a political manoeuvre on her part, aimed at pressurising Edward IV into publicly acknowledging their marriage. However, pregnancies certainly did (and do) sometimes go wrong, so there is no reason to simply assume that Elizabeth must have been telling a lie.

Overall, the start of Edward's Widville marriage story appears to have been remarkably similar in many ways to his earlier relationship with Eleanor Talbot. Significantly, however, there were two major differences in the relationships. First, as we shall see later, Elizabeth Widville proved very demanding in terms of her parents and siblings and their status. On the other hand Eleanor appears never to have been so demanding, although it seems that she did persuade the king to be kind to her former father-in-law, Lord Sudeley. About six months after his secret marriage with Eleanor, on 26 February 1461/2 Edward IV granted 'exemption for life of Ralph Botiller, knight, lord of Sudeley, on account of his debility and age, from personal attendance in council or Parliament, and from being made collector, assessor or taxer of tenths, fifteenths or other subsidies, commissioner, justice of the peace, constable, bailiff or other minister of the king, or trier, arrayer or leader of men-at-arms, archers or hobelers. And he shall not be compelled to leave his dwelling for war.'[39] And three months later, on 30 May 1462, Edward granted Lord Sudeley 'four bucks in summer and six does in winter within the king's park of Woodstock'.[40] Also, approximately one month after the probable date of his marriage with Eleanor, on 6 July 1461, Edward IV granted to her mother, Margaret Beauchamp, dowager Countess of Shrewsbury, the custody of her grandson, Thomas Talbot, Viscount Lisle during his minority, together with his income.[41] The following year, on 20 October 1462, Edward IV granted to Eleanor's sister, Elizabeth Talbot, Duchess of Norfolk, who was then approaching her twentieth birthday, manors and lordships in Suffolk, Leicestershire, Shropshire, Huntingdonshire, Cambridgeshire and Hertfordshire producing an annual income of £130 plus 80 marks.[42] On 14 June 1463 the king restored to Eleanor's mother her dower income of 10 marks a year (which she had apparently lost two years earlier).[43] And on 23 March 1464/5 Edward IV generously granted to Eleanor's brother-in-law, John Mowbray, Duke of Norfolk (who had attained six months earlier the age of 20) 'licence ... to enter freely without proof of age into all the possessions of his father.'[44] The king also appears to have secretly granted royal land in Wiltshire to Eleanor herself.[45] But the gifts made to Eleanor and her family did not at all correspond to the huge change in respect of family status which was later put into effect for the Widvilles. Partly, of course, that was because Eleanor's relatives already had high status.

Secondly, unlike Eleanor, Elizabeth subsequently gave the king a family of numerous children (see below). If that had not been the case, the Widville secret marriage might very well have remained a secret, like the earlier Talbot union. And probably, if that had happened, later historians would have been as doubtful of the true existence of a secret Widville marriage as many of them have claimed to be in respect of the Talbot marriage.

Writing later, after Henry VII had seized the throne, Polydore Vergil suggests that in 1464 Edward IV had himself originally been seeking a political union. He implies that Edward was responsible for his cousin Warwick's embassy to France, seeking a marriage for the young king with Bona of Savoy. Actually there is no proof in that respect, and Warwick certainly acted on his own initiative on other occasions.

Subsequently, Vergil claims that 'King Edwardes mynde alteryd uppon the soddayn, and he tooke to wyfe Elyzabeth, dowghter to Richerd earle Ryvers, ... which mariage because the woman was of meane caulyng he kept secret.' But when the Widville union was publicly acknowledged, Vergil says that the nobility 'found muche fault with [the king] ... and imputyd the same to his dishonor, as the thing wherunto he was led by blynde affection, and not by reule of reason.'[46]

Public opinion in respect of the Widville alliance was certainly to prove very significant. For example, in some quarters the king was thought to be besotted with Elizabeth Widville on account of witchcraft which had been undertaken on the part of his fairy-descended girlfriend and her mother. About five years later, Jacquette was to find herself prosecuted for sorcery by the Earl of Warwick (see below, Chapter 10). 'The sorcery suit ... apparently presumed that necromancy had been necessary to secure such a marriage!'[47]

1 X(?)   conceived Grafton Regis 1 May 1464?   miscarried Oct 1464?
gap 7 months?
2 Elizabeth   conceived Greenwich 11 May 1465   born 11 Feb 1465/6
gap 9 months
3 Mary   conceived Westminster 11 Nov 1466   born 11 Aug 1467
gap 10 months
4 Cecily   conceived Westminster late June 1468   born 20 March 1468/9
gap 11 months
5 Edward   conceived Westminster 4 Feb 1469/70   born 4 Nov 1470
gap 8 months
6 Margaret   conceived Westminster* 10 July 1471   born 10 April 1472
gap 7 months
7 Richard   conceived Westminster 17 Nov 1472   born 17 Aug 1473
gap 18 months
8 Anne   conceived Westminster 2 Feb 1474/5   born 2 Nov 1475
gap 7 months
9 George   conceived Greenwich● June 1476   born March 1476/7
gap 20 months
10 Catherine   conceived Eltham(?) 14 Nov 1478   born 14 Aug 1479
gap 5 months
11 Bridget   conceived Greenwich(?)10 Feb 1479/80   born 10 Nov 1480

* or possibly a few days later at Windsor Castle
● or possibly Westminster

The conceptions of Elizabeth Widville's children fathered by Edward IV.

Chapter 8

Married to the King?

The young widowed Lady Grey had not figured in any way at the Yorkist court of Edward IV in 1461, and she had not had any known meeting with the young king at that stage. It is therefore highly unlikely that she would have known anything about Edward's attachment to Eleanor Talbot. Yet more than half a century later, when Sir Thomas More was playing the game of penning and re-penning his so-called *History of King Richard III* (based, presumably, on information he had received from the late Cardinal Archbishop John Morton), he claimed that in 1464 'the king's mother [Cecily Neville, dowager Duchess of York] objected openly against his [Edward IV's] marriage [to Elizabeth Widville], as it were in discharge of her conscience, that the king was sure [committed] to Dame Elizabeth Lucy [*sic*] and her husband before God.'[1] In other words, More stated that in the autumn of 1464, when Edward IV announced publicly his marriage to the widowed Lady Grey, his mother had told her son that the marriage was illegal because he already had a different wife.

The only thing which is clearly erroneous in respect of the statement penned by Thomas More in this instance is the *name* of the woman who was reputedly said by Edward's mother to be the young king's legal wife. As the present writer has indicated previously, there is actually no evidence whatsoever for the existence of a woman bearing the name and title 'Lady Elizabeth Lucy' at that period.[2] No-one has been able to identify such an individual, though many people have tried.

Additional, highly significant, evidence in respect of that name which is employed by More in his allegation of what Cecily Neville said to her son in 1464 lies in the fact that he also states, later in his 'history', that nineteen years after 1464 – in 1483 – 'Elizabeth Lucy' was the woman behind the subsequent bastardisation of all the children of Edward IV and

41

Elizabeth Widville, and the consequent offering of the English throne to Edward's brother, Richard, Duke of Gloucester.

> It was by the protector and his council concluded that … Doctor Shaa should in a sermon at Paul's Cross signify to the people that … Dame Elizabeth Lucy was verily the wife of King Edward, and so … all his children bastards that were gotten upon the queen. According to this device, Doctor Shaa … declared … that King Edward was never lawfully married unto the queen, but was, before God, husband unto Dame Elizabeth Lucy.[3]

Later (sixteenth-century) preaching at Paul's Cross.

As usual, however, More makes obvious false and erroneous claims at this point in his story. For example, he asserts that in the summer of 1483 the protector (Richard, Duke of Gloucester, later Richard III) also had the claim advanced that Edward IV had *himself* been illegitimate, so that Edward had never been the lawful king of England. A similar claim had been put forward earlier by Domenico Mancini.[4] But of course he had been working on behalf of the government of France, which seems to have invented – or at least propagated – the suggestion that Edward IV had not been of genuine royal birth.[5] The same claim had also been put forward by Polydore Vergil,[6] who found himself writing English history for Henry VII, who had significant links with France. Nevertheless, all the authentic English governmental documentary evidence that survives from the reign of Richard III – and which consistently refers to his deceased brother, Edward IV as a legitimate king of England – clearly disproves More's (Mancini's and Vergil's) claim in that respect. The truth is that, in reality, Richard III consistently referred to Edward as 'oure derrest Brothere late king',[7] and never suggested that Edward IV had not been legitimate.

Moreover, significantly, More's claim that in 1483 Richard III's accession was based on the assertion that the legal wife of Edward IV had been a woman called 'Elizabeth Lucy' can absolutely be proved incorrect. This is because clear parliamentary evidence exists which shows that the woman who, in the summer of 1483, was officially adjudged by the three estates of the realm to have been Edward IV's legitimate consort was not the mythical 'Lady Elizabeth Lucy', but a real person – Lady Eleanor Talbot, Lady Boteler, daughter of the first Earl of Shrewsbury. It was based upon the fact that *Eleanor* was adjudged to have been Edward's legal consort that the throne of England was then offered to Richard, Duke of Gloucester.

The surviving official documentary evidence, in the form of the petition offered by the three estates of the realm to Richard, Duke of Gloucester, in June 1483 (as subsequently quoted in the Act of Parliament of January 1483/4) reads as follows:

> Over this, amonges other thinges, more specially we consider howe that the tyme of the raigne of Kyng Edward IV, late-decessed, — after the ungracious, pretensed marriage (as all England hath cause so say) made betwixt the said King Edward and Elizabeth (sometyme wife to Sir John Grey, Knight),

late nameing herself (and many years heretofore) 'Queene of England', — the ordre of all politeque rule was perverted, the laws of God and of Gode's church, and also the lawes of nature, and of Englond, and also the laudable customes and liberties of the same (wherein every Englishman is inheritor) broken, subverted and contempned, against all reason and justice, so that this land was ruled by self-will and pleasure, feare and drede (all manner of equitie and lawes layd apart and despised), whereof ensued many inconvenients and mischiefs (as murders, estortions and oppressions: namely of poor and impotent people) soo that no man was sure of his lif, land ne lyvelode, ne of his wif, doughter ne servaunt; every good maiden and woman standing in drede to be ravished and defouled. And besides this, what discords, inward battailes, effusion of Christian men's blode (and namely, by the destruction of the noble blode of this londe) was had and comitted within the same, it is evident and notarie through all this reaume (unto the grete sorrowe and heavynesse of all true Englishmen).

And here also we considre howe the said pretensed marriage betwixt the above-named King Edward and Elizabeth Grey[8] was made of grete presumption, without the knowyng or assent of the lordes of this lond, and alsoe by sorcerie and wichecrafte committed by the said Elizabeth and her moder, Jaquett, Duchess of Bedford (as the common opinion of the people and the publique voice and fame is through all this land; and hereafter — if, and as, the case shall require — shall bee proved suffyciently, in tyme and place convenient).

And here also we considre how that the said pretensed marriage was made privatly and secretly, without edition of banns, in a private chamber, a profane place, and not openly, in the face of church,[9] aftre the lawe of Godds churche, but contrarie thereunto, and the laudable custome of the churche of England. And howe also that at the tyme of contract of the same pretensed marriage (and bifore, and longe tyme after) the said King Edward was, and stoode, marryed, and trouth-plyght, to oone Dame Elianore Butteler (doughter of the old

Earl of Shrewesbury)[10] with whom the saide King Edward had made a precontracte [earlier contract][11] of matrimonie longe tyme bifore he made the said pretensed mariage with the said Elizabeth Grey in manner and fourme aforesaide.

Which premises being true (as in veray trouth they been true), it appeareth and followeth evidently that the said King Edward (duryng his lyfe) and the said Elizabeth lived together sinfully and dampnably in adultery, against the lawe of God and his church. And therefore noe marvaile that (the souverain lord and head of this londe being of such ungodly disposicion and provokyng the ire and indignation of oure Lorde God) such haynous mischiefs and inconvenients as is above remembered were used and committed in the reame amongst the subjects.

Also it appeareth evidently, and followeth, that all th'issue and children of the said king beene bastards,[12] and unable to inherite or to clayme anything by inheritance, by the lawe and custome of England.[13]

Since we now know for certain that Thomas More was wrong when he claimed that 'Elizabeth Lucy' was named in 1483 as the legal wife of Edward IV, that means that his earlier citing of the fictional name 'Elizabeth Lucy' in the context of the autumn of 1464 must also be a false claim. Thus, if More was telling the truth when he said that Cecily Neville objected, in the autumn of 1464, to her eldest surviving son's recognition of Elizabeth Widville as his consort, that must mean that, actually, at that time, the king's mother was already well aware of the fact that Edward IV had secretly married Eleanor Talbot, the widowed Lady Boteler, several years earlier. And it must have been Lady Eleanor Talbot (not the mythical 'Lady Elizabeth Lucy') that Cecily named to her son, Edward, as his legal wife.

Interestingly, some further authentic contemporary evidence does seem to exist which supports More's overall claim that some sort of disagreement emerged between Edward and his mother towards the end of 1464. From his accession to the throne in 1461 until 1464 Edward IV had consistently required prayers to be offered for his mother. However, from 1465 onwards, although royal prayers began to be offered for Elizabeth Widville, Cecily Neville's name came to be omitted.[14] That fact strongly suggests that something important had gone wrong between the king and his mother in the autumn of 1464, and that appears to confirm that Cecily may well have questioned the validity of Edward's marriage to Elizabeth Widville. The available evidence also indicates that Elizabeth Widville herself 'appears to have had few personal connections with her mother-in-law'.[15]

Of course, if Cecily did make such a statement to Edward IV in 1464, presumably she herself must have possessed some kind of knowledge in the matter. In other words, even though it had officially remained secret, Cecily must have been aware in some way of the fact that Edward had married Eleanor Talbot. So how might she have acquired that information?

In the previous chapter the point was raised that apparently Elizabeth Widville's immediate family knew about *her* secret 'marriage' with the king. The possibility was also raised that, in a similar way, Eleanor Talbot's immediate family may likewise have been aware of Eleanor's secret royal marriage. In Eleanor's case, the most obvious relatives who might possibly have known were her mother, Margaret Beauchamp, dowager Countess of Shrewsbury, and her sister, Elizabeth Talbot, Duchess of Norfolk. Significantly, Cecily Neville must have known Margaret Beauchamp because their respective husbands had served together in France. Also, Cecily was related by marriage to Elizabeth Talbot, Duchess of Norfolk (Eleanor's younger sister), because her own sister, Catherine Neville, was the dowager Duchess of Norfolk.

In addition, however, the further possibility has now emerged that maybe Edward's own immediate family also knew something about the king's secret marriage with Eleanor. Certainly Edward's brother, George, Duke of Clarence, the heir presumptive to the English throne, also appears to have been aware of something in that respect, because he too appears to have questioned the validity of the alleged Widville marriage.

Writing nineteen years after Edward IV's formal recognition of his Widville union, Friar Domenico Mancini (who had been exploring the situation in England for the government of France) reported, in respect of the action taken by Edward in September 1464,

> Though Edward's brothers, two of whom were then living, were both seriously concerned at the deed – nevertheless, the Duke of Clarence, the one born second after Edward, clearly showed his ill humour, openly denouncing the obscurity of

Elizabeth's family, while proclaiming that the king's marriage to a widow (when he should have married a virgin) was contrary to ancestral practice. But the other brother, Richard (who was then Duke of Gloucester, and who reigns now), both because he was more capable of disguising his feelings, and also because he had less influence (being the younger), neither did anything nor said anything which could be held against him.[16]

It is interesting to note that Mancini says that Richard, Duke of Gloucester never took any action against Elizabeth Widville. His relationship with her will be explored a little further later.

However, while the Duke of Clarence definitely had a personal issue with her, neither he nor Cecily Neville tried to raise the marriage issue in any formal way, via Church courts. That must mean that, even though they themselves may have heard something about what had taken place, neither George nor Cecily was in contact with any witness who had actually been present at Edward's secret marriage with Eleanor. In the 1460s and 1470s it seems that Robert Stillington – who later (in 1483) revealed his own official presence at the secret marriage with Eleanor – must have been keeping quiet. The probable reason for his conduct in that respect will be explored presently.

As for Elizabeth Widville, it is virtually certain that, when she secretly married the king, she herself must have been completely unaware of his earlier commitment to Eleanor Talbot. The reason for that claim is simply that Elizabeth was obviously an intelligent woman. Therefore, if she had possessed any information in respect of the fact that the king had already contracted another seret marriage, she would never have accepted Edward's proposed secret marriage to her. In those days it was well-known that, at a formal marriage ceremony, all the people present were asked whether they were aware of any reason why the union should not proceed. At a public ceremony that was the time when a pre–existing partner (or the representative of one) should have stated, if appropriate, that either the bride or the groom was already married. Therefore if Edward had married Elizabeth *in public*, and if Eleanor Talbot had failed to raise the issue of the validity of that process when the priest asked to know of any impediment, Eleanor's own right to ever be recognised as Edward IV's wife would then have been destroyed in the eyes of the church and its canon law. In other words, whatever Edward may have done previously, Elizabeth Widville could then have become his legal wife. However, in the context of a *secret* marriage no such security was obtainable for Elizabeth.

We have already seen that earlier (in 1460, and in Calais), Edward IV's first cousin, Richard Neville, Earl of Warwick, had displayed strong dislike of the Widville family. Interestingly, at that stage the future Edward IV had shown a similar feeling. Obviously, in Edward's case, that feeling subsequently changed. But in Warwick's case that hostility definitely continued. Thus, in the autumn of 1464, when Edward IV publicly revealed his alleged Widville marriage, Warwick was furious. 'Much heart burning was ever after between the earl [of Warwick] and the queen's blood so long as he lived.'[17]

Indeed, as we shall see later, in 1469 Warwick accused Elizabeth's mother, Jacquette, of using witchcraft for various purposes – possibly including her daughter's alleged seduction of Edward IV. Richard III is also later said to have accused Elizabeth Widville of sorcery. Certainly that issue was raised in the petition put *to* Richard in 1483 by the three estates of the realm (see above). Of course, it is now very hard to be certain that Elizabeth and her mother really had used the black arts in an attempt to bring about Elizabeth's royal marriage. Nevertheless, it seems that there definitely was contemporary gossip in that respect. After all, as the new royal consort, most of the nobility of England viewed Elizabeth Widville as a bad choice.

Thomas Fitzgerald, seventh Earl of Desmond,[18] was an Irish friend and ally of King Edward IV. On 2 August 1462 Edward had granted Thomas stewardship in respect of the king's own hereditary earldom of March in Ireland as a reward 'for his good service to the king and the king's father'.[19] Subsequently, on 15 April 1463, Edward had formally confirmed the appointment (made by his own brother, the Duke of Clarence – who was then the king's Irish lieutenant) of the Earl of Desmond as his lord deputy in succession to William Sherwood, Bishop of Meath.[20]

Shortly after Desmond's appointment as lord deputy lieutenant of Ireland, some complaints were made in Ireland about his governorship. It seems that opposition to the earl was actually being led there by the previous holder of the deputy's post – the English-born bishop of Meath, William Sherwood.[21] As a result of the complaints which had been voiced, both the earl and the bishop then came to England to put their respective cases to the king. However, other people in Ireland also despatched to the king a number of 'letters in commendation of Desmond'.[22] As a result Edward IV judged in Desmond's favour. He also rewarded the earl again on 24 August 1464 with a grant of manors.[23] Subsequently, after the issue had been resolved, 'the earl returned to Ireland as Deputy Governor with many tokens of royal favour.'[24]

Significantly, however, Desmond had found himself in England at precisely the time when the king publicly acknowledged Elizabeth Widville as his consort. It is reported that the king, who trusted Desmond, and who must have known that his marriage was being widely discussed, therefore asked the earl what his people were saying about him. The outcome was later recorded in writing by one of Thomas Fitzgerald's grandsons and successors, James Fitzgerald, 13th Earl of Desmond.

> This Earl's grandfather was brought up in the King's house, and being well learned in all manner of sciences and an eloquent poet, as the author affirmeth, was in singular favour with his Highness, so far forth that his Grace took much pleasure and delight in his talk. And upon a day being in chase a hunting, his Majesty questioned him, and amongst other things said: 'Sir cousin O'Desmound, for as much as I have you in secret trust, above others, and that ye are a man who doth both see and hear many things, as well in my court as elsewhere abroad, which shall not perchance be brought to mine ears, I pray you tell me what do you hear spoken by [about] me?' To the which he answered his Highness and said, 'If it like your Grace nothing but honor and much nobility.' The King, nevertheless, not satisfied with that answer, demanded of him again, three or four several times, what he had heard; and willed him frankly to declare the truth, not hiding one jot thereof from his knowledge; whereunto the Earl made answer as he did before. At last his Majesty, wading still in that communication as most desirous to grope the full, required him, for that he took him to be not only a man of a singular wit, but of a long experience and judgement withal, and none within this realm in whom he had more affiance, to declare his own opinion, and what he himself thought of him. To the which the said Earl lowly made answer and said, 'If it shall please your Grace to pardon

me and not to be offended with that I shall say, I assure you I find no fault in any manner of thing, saving only that your Grace hath too much abased your princely estate in marrying a lady of so mean a house and parentile; which though it be perchance agreeable to your lusts, yet not so much to the security of your realm and subjects.' Whereunto his Majesty immediately condescended, and said that he had spoken most true and discreetly.[25]

Because the surviving written source quoted above is not literally contemporary, it has been dismissed in many quarters as later fabrication.[26] However, it is a family line source, in respect of a family story. In other words, the contents may well have been current orally amongst Desmond's children and grandchildren ever since the earl's conversation with Edward IV had taken place – and long before the account was recorded in writing. Moreover, those who deny the validity of this source (and its alleged consequences – which will emerge later) apparently also ignore King Richard III's obvious awareness of what had occurred in respect of the Earl of Desmond (see below, Chapter 11).

As we have seen, both in the case of Edward IV's secret marriage with Eleanor Talbot, and in the case of his later secret union with Elizabeth Widville, although in theory the activity remained secret, in reality there were obviously a few people in the world who knew what had happened. In the case of Elizabeth Widville key members of her family and a priest were reportedly witnesses of what had been done. In the earlier case of Eleanor Talbot at least a priest had been present at the exchange of vows. The witness in question on that occasion had been Canon Robert Stillington.

Previously a servant of the government of King Henry VI, Stillington subsequently moved into the service of Edward IV. In 1461 the canon became the Keeper of the Privy SeaI. He also held a number of church appointments.[27] At the time when he carried out Edward IV's Talbot marriage Stillington possessed no high office within the church. However, after he had carried out his priestly function at the secret Talbot marriage, Edward IV sought to promote him. First, towards the end of 1461, the king awarded Canon Stillington an annual secular salary amounting to a pound a day (£365).[28] Later, after the king's secret union with Elizabeth Widville had been publicly announced, Edward IV began pushing hard for Stillington's elevation to episcopal rank. The first English bishopric to fall vacant after the Widville union had been publicly announced happened to be the see of Bath and Wells. On 14 January 1464/5, Bishop Thomas Bekyngton of that diocese passed away. On 19 January, a royal licence was issued for the election of a new bishop.[29] And on 20 January the king granted custody of the see's temporalities to Canon Stillington.[30]

Unfortunately, in spite of his clear intention to have Canon Stillington made the new Bishop of Bath and Wells, Edward IV then found himself confronting a problem. Pope Paul II wished to appoint to the office in question a learned English priest who was living in Rome – named John Free. Moreover, earlier the pope had officially reserved to himself the right to nominate the next bishop of Bath and Wells.[31] Thus, when it became apparent that there were two conflicting aims in respect of the appointment of the new bishop a potential diplomatic crisis was born.

Nevertheless, Canon Robert Stillington was already behaving in England as though he were the new bishop. For example, he was already making appointments within the diocese.[32] Then, fortunately for him and for Edward IV, the conflict suddenly found itself resolved by the death of John Free (the pope's proposed candidate). As a result, Pope Paul II then acknowledged King Edward's wish in the matter. Thus, on 30 October 1465, Robert Stillington found himself formally appointed as the new bishop by the pope.[33] Presumably Edward IV hoped that by thus promoting Stillington he had persuaded that priest to remain loyal to him, and to maintain his silence in respect of the matrimonial question.

Incidentally, it is conceivable that another witness may have been present at Edward IV's marriage with Eleanor in Warwickshire. The most likely person for that role is not one of Eleanor's blood relatives, but her father-in-law, Ralph Botiller, Lord Sudeley. The evidence which suggests his involvement comprises Edward IV's initial generosity to Lord Sudeley in the early 1460s (see above, Chapter 7), followed by the king's subsequent hostility from 1468 onwards. The king's hostility – which began following Eleanor's death – led to him forcing Sudeley to surrender all his property to relatives of Elizabeth Widville,[34] followed subsequently by sending Sudeley to prison, where he died in 1473.

Chapter 9

Crowned as Queen

In spite of all the points we have seen, namely that his cousin, the Earl of Warwick, was angry about the king's marriage announcement; that the validity of his marriage may have been questioned by the king's own mother, leading to conflict between them; that the Earl of Desmond may have told the king in a friendly way that his announced consort was not suitable for him; and that other nobles and members of the royal family may have been opposed to her, Elizabeth Widville was subsequently crowned as King Edward IV's queen consort.

Possibly because she experienced a pregnancy which lasted a few months (but which ultimately failed to produce a living child because it ended in a miscarriage), she was actually only crowned eight months after her acknowledgement as Edward's consort. The ceremony was eventually conducted at Westminster Abbey on the Sunday following the Feast of the Ascension – 26 May 1465.

A procession preceded the service at the abbey and in the course of it Elizabeth was greeted on London Bridge by actors playing the roles

Medieval Westminster Palace and Abbey.

of St Elizabeth and St Paul. The identity of those two chosen saints was intended to honour firstly Elizabeth's own Christian name and secondly her mother's maiden surname (de St Pol).

Elizabeth then made her way to the Hall of the Palace of Westminster, where she was prepared for the church service. She was accompanied by

> The Duq Of Clarance Stywarde of Englond ryding in the hall on horseback his coursoʳ rychely trapped hede & body to the grounde wᵗ Crapsiur rychely embroiderd & garnyst wᵗ spangyls of golde.

> The erle of Arundell Constable & Boteler for the feste in like wise on horsebake his coursoʳ rychely trappyd in clothe of goulde to þe grounde.

> The Duq of Norff[olk] m[ar]shall of Englonde in like wyse on horsebak and his coursoʳ rychely in cloth of goulde trapped to the grounde And evryche of thez astates bare in

Three riders from a slightly later (early sixteenth-century) royal procession.

53

his hande according to his office and rode aboute the hall to avoyde þe peple agenste the comyng yn of the Queene into the hall.[1]

[Note: þ is the Old English 'Thorn' character, used rather like 'th'.]

William Fitzallan, 16th Earl of Arundel (1417–1487), was the senior of those three riders in terms of age. He was forty-seven years old. His wife, Joan Neville, was a sister of the Earl of Warwick, and a first cousin of the king, of the Duke of Clarence, and of the Duke of Norfolk.

John Mowbray, 4th Duke of Norfolk (1444–1475/6), was about twenty-one at the time of the coronation. He was a first cousin of the king and the Duke of Clarence, and his wife, Elizabeth Talbot, was a niece of the Countess of Warwick, and the younger sister of Lady Eleanor Talbot.

The youngest of the three riders in terms of age was George, Duke of Clarence (1449–1477/8). However, he was the highest of the three in terms of rank, since he was the king's senior living brother. Thus he was the heir presumptive to the throne of England in 1465. At that time he was not yet married, though his eventual wife would be the elder daughter of the Earl and Countess of Warwick, and a first cousin of the Duchess of Norfolk, and of Lady Eleanor Talbot.

In other words it would be very interesting to know how these three men felt about their participation in the coronation of Elizabeth Widville. None of them left a record in that respect. However, it appears very unlikely that they would have enjoyed taking part. Nevertheless, they had to obey the command of the king and carry out the official function which went with their respective roles.

And at thentring of the Queene into the hail she was under the canapye clothed in a mantyil of purpull & a coronall vpon hir hede brought yn betwix the Bisshop of Derhrn on hir right hande & the Bysshop of SaIybury on hir lyfte hande. And nexte followyng Th Abbot of West m under þe same and the sayde Canapy was borne up over the Queene w^t iiii Barons of þe v portys.[2]

It was slightly unusual that Elizabeth found herself escorted by the Bishop of Durham and the Bishop of Salisbury. Normally the Bishop of Bath and Wells ought to have been one of her escorts. Traditionally it is the Bishop of Durham and the Bishop of Bath and Wells who escort English sovereigns to their coronations. However, as we saw earlier, at this particular moment in time the see of Bath and Wells was vacant. Edward IV was trying to secure the post for canon Robert Stillington – as he later succeeded in doing.

At the time of the coronation the Bishop of Durham was Lawrence Booth (c.1420–1480), and the Abbot of Westminster was George Norwich. As for the Bishop of Salisbury – who found himself required to fulfil at this event a role which would normally have been carried out by the Bishop of Bath and Wells – he was Richard Beauchamp. He was a distant cousin of Margaret Beauchamp, dowager Countess of Shrewsbury and of her half-sister, Anne Beauchamp, Countess of Warwick. His father, Sir Walter Beauchamp, a lawyer and Speaker of the House of Commons (1416) had been 'employed as counsel by his relative, Richard Beauchamp, earl of Warwick',[3] the father of Margaret and Anne. Thus, oddly enough, this bishop who found himself unusually selected to fulfil a special role at the coronation of Elizabeth Widville was yet another relative of Eleanor Talbot.

> And the Duches of Buk[ingham] thelder bare up the Quenys trayne.
>
> Then followed nexte the Queene of ladys the Duches of Suff[olk] & my lady M[ar]grete hir sister and þe Duches of Bedford [4]

The elder Duchess of Buckingham, who bore Elizabeth Widville's train, was Anne Neville. She was a slightly older sister of Cecily Neville and an aunt of Edward IV, of the Duke of Clarence, and of the Earl of Warwick. As for the Duchess of Suffolk, she was Edward IV's middle sister, Elizabeth of York. Her younger sister, Margaret of York, who accompanied her, was the future Duchess of Burgundy. Of course the Duchess of Bedford was Elizabeth Widville's own mother.

> And the Queene standing in hir place of astate betwix the saide ii Bisshoppys helde in the right hande þe Septo[r] of Saint Edward & in the lefte hande the septor of þe Reaume and was so led thrugh thrugh [*sic*] the hall vnto þe monastary of Westm[inster]. And the saide Abbot allway under the Canapye

w^t the saide ii Bisshoppys And fro the nether step of of the
Dore allway goyng barefote vpon ray clothe into the monastry
w^t p[ro]cession And at the p[ro]cession being the Archebisshop
of Caunterbury prymatte of Englonde and Divers Bisshoppys
and abbottys myterde vnto the noumbre of

And goyng before hir vnto the monastry on fote the Duq
of Clarance Therle of Arundell as Constable the Duq of
Norff[olk] m[ar]shall of England the Duq of Buk[ingham]
borne a pon a squyer shouldr and other Diuers Erlys and
Barons and the newe made knyghts nexte before theym
    And of Ladys followyng the Queene in the saide p[ro]
cession The Duches of Buk[ingham] thelder bering up the
trayne the Duches of Suff[olk] my Lady M[ar]grete her
sister & the Duches of Bedford nexte vnto thastate the yong
Duches of Buk[ingham] borne on shoulder And of Surcotys
yn Rede velevet & ermyne in all xiii Duchesses & Countesses,
In scarlet & menyvere xiiii Baronesses And in Scarlet xii
ladys Banarettes ^5

The younger Duchess of Buckingham, and her young husband, the Duke
of Buckingham – both of whom had to be carried on the shoulders of older
people – were Elizabeth Widville's much younger sister, Catherine (who was
then aged about eight) and the young husband to whom she had been married
just a few months earlier, Edward IV's ten-year old cousin, Henry Stafford.

Although the surviving account of Elizabeth's coronation lists all the
principal members of the royal family and nobles who took part in the
ceremony, the name of King Edward IV himself is nowhere mentioned.
Thus there is no evidence to indicate that the king attended the ceremony
in person. Subsequently, however, Henry VII attended the coronation of
his consort, Elizabeth of York, in a private way – watching her coronation
service hidden in a space in the abbey which was curtained for him with
tapestry. It is therefore possible that Edward IV did likewise.

The Resceyving of the Queene into þe Monastry

And so with the saide solempne pcession she was resceyued
into þe monastery & the Northe Dorre [that being the abbey

entrance which was closest to the Palace of Westminster] & conveyhed throgh þe Queere [choir] & so p[ro]ceded vnto the high auter [high altar] there kneling while þe solempnyte apteyneng was red [read] over hir bi the Archebisshop of Caunterbury metropolytane. And þat done she lay before the auter [altar] while certayne supplications was saide over hir bi the saide metropolitane and þᵗ done she was reivently thatyre of vrgins taken of hir hede the attire of virgins reverently taken off her head — i.e. unveiled] anoynted firste þe hede and so forthe as apteyned [i.e. she was anointed on head and body with holy oil]. And þan crownyd bi the seyde metropolytane. The Archebisshop of Yorke holding the holy vnction [holy oil]. And all the Archebisshoppys & Bisshoppys at þe solempne coronaĉon And so conveyhed her vnto the place of astate wᵗ grete reuerence & solempnyte The Abbot of Westm[inster] wayting vpon þe Septors Sp[irit]uall [the ivory rod topped by the dove of the Holy Spirit] And therle of Essex vpon þe Septors temp[or]all [royal gold sceptre]. And at þe begynnyng of the gospell she sitting in hir astate [i.e. enthroned] the sayde Abbot and Erle delyuered vnto hir þe saide septours which she helde unto the fynysshyng of þe gospell. And than [the sceptres] were resceyued [back] by the saide Abbot and Erle giving attendance as apteyned And at thoffering. The saide Abbot & Erle bare þe ceptoʳ before hir to the Auter & so thens to þe place of astate And also the Duches of Suff[olk] þe yong þe Duches of Bedford in þe mas tyme [mass time] attending vpon þe Croune revrently at certayne time of reponse helde ye croune on hir hede And also aft[er] fynysshing of mas[s] al this while barefote going to þe high auter ageyn & þan was comande of the sayde Metropolitane which sang mass, And þan was conveyhed in þe dignite of þe chivalry vnto þe place of astate. And þᵗ done þe Queene sang solempnely *Te Deum* ⁶

The Archbishop of Canterbury, Thomas Bourchier (1404–1486), was a second cousin of the king. His mother had been a granddaughter of Edward III. He himself had previously crowned Edward IV. The Archbishop of York was the king's first cousin, George Neville (*c.*1432–1476), younger brother of the Earl of Warwick. In May 1465 he had only just been appointed Archbishop of York, and had not yet been enthroned at York Minster when he took part in Elizabeth Widville's coronation. It seems that, like his brother, Warwick, he was not well disposed towards the Widville family.

> And fro the Monastry she was led crownyd betwjx the saide ii Bisshoppys [Durham and Salisbury] vnder the Canapye and the sayde Abbot w^t theym vnder þe same.
>
> And the Duq of Suff[olk] beyng nexte on hir right hande bering in his hand the Septo^r of Seint Edwarde. And therle of Essex on the lyfte hande bering the septo^r of Englonde. And all thastates of lordys & of ladys in semblable wise before and behynde at the retournyng as at the goyng oute And so was led from the monastry through the grete hall vnto hir Chambre and than was newe revestyd in a surcote of purpull [7]

The Duke of Suffolk was Edward IV's brother-in-law, John de la Pole, the husband of the king's middle sister, Elizabeth of York.

As we have now seen, at her coronation, in the normal way for an English queen consort, Elizabeth was given her crown and two sceptres. The gold sceptre of St Edward was placed in her right hand, and an ivory rod surmounted by a gilded dove was placed in her left hand. Yet in spite of the misleading fifteenth-century illustration of her which is shown below, Elizabeth definitely did not receive an orb. England's queen consorts never receive orbs. That item is reserved for reigning sovereigns. And of course, no orb is mentioned in the report of her coronation.

Also it is not certain what kind of crown she would have worn. The misleading depiction which shows her with fair hair and which has her holding an orb also shows her wearing a closed (arched) crown. Prior to the fifteenth century, medieval English crowns seem to have been open. But in the fifteenth century, Henry V, Henry VI and Edward IV are all sometimes depicted wearing closed crowns. It therefore appears to be the case that closed crowns were then being introduced for the reigning monarch of England. However, other portrayals of Elizabeth Widville do not depict a closed crown. For example, she is portrayed in the Royal Window at Canterbury Cathedral wearing a large open crown (Plate 14), and a similar large open crown is depicted on her seal (see Plates 1 and 13).

A mythical fifteenth-century image of Elizabeth as queen. It depicts her holding an orb, which a queen consort would never have, and it depicts her with blonde hair, which probably she never had. Redrawn from her Skinner's Book 'portrait'.

It therefore seems most likely that at her coronation she would have worn an open crown.

After the church ceremony, having donned a royal robe, Elizabeth Widville made her way back to the Palace of Westminster, escorted by her entourage. There the coronation banquet was held at Westminster Hall. Three courses were served, comprising seventeen, nineteen and fifteen dishes respectively. For full details, see below. The celebration concluded on the following day when a tournament was held.

And fro the Chambre [Elizabeth Widville] was brought betwixte the sayde ii Bysshoppys into the hail vnto hir place of astate.

And wh[e]n the Queene did wassh the Duq of Suff[olk] stode on hir right hande And therle of Essex or the lefte hande holding the saide septours as before

Therle of Oxon s[er]ued of water the Duq of Clarance helde þe Basyne and gave th assay.

And the Queene than was set in hir astate to mete crownyd the saide lordys knelirig on ayther syde of hir at the Table holding the sayde septours in their handes And the Countess of Shrewesbury the yonger the Countess of

Kent on the lefte hande knelyng helde the vayle before the
Queene at all tymes when she toke any repace & knelyd
nexte vnto thastate. And at any tyme when she so dyd She
hirselfe toke of the croune and when she had done she put
y^t on agayn.[8]

The Earl of Essex was Henry Bourchier, brother of the Archbishop of
Canterbury. Like his brother he was a second cousin of the king. He was
also Edward IV's uncle by marriage. The Earl of Oxford was John de Vere.
He was officiating 'as both Lord Great Chamberlain, in the absence of
the then office-holder, the Earl of Warwick, and as Chamberlain to the
queen'.[9] The younger Countess of Shrewsbury (wife of the third Earl of
Shrewsbury) was Catherine Stafford, the king's first cousin. She was also
the aunt of the young Duke of Buckingham. As for the Countess of Kent,
she was Catherine Percy, a first cousin of the king – and also of the young
Countess of Shrewsbury.

And on the right hande of the Queene sat the Archebisshop
of Caunterbury prymate of Englonde and at all tymes his
s[er]uice couerd as the Queenys.

And on the lyfte hande sat the Duches of Suff[olk] & my
Lady M[a]rgrete hir sister

Officers
(Sir John Hawarde sewer
(The Lorde Cromwell kerver.
(The Lorde Scallys, Coupeberer
(Alyngton of Cantebriggs.

(The Duq of Clarens Stywarde of Englonde
(Therle of Arundell as Constable on his right hande the Duq
of Norff[olk] as (M[ar]shall of Englond on the lyfte hande
And thez astates rode befor the (s[er]uice on courser richely
trappyd to þe grounde as before and þe (Constable & mshall
som dele before my lorde Stywarde And beforne theym (on
fote Erlys Baroas & other noble knyghts

And s[er]uyng the sayde course of any dysshe the knyghts of
the Batthe newe made and at þ^t Cource xvii Disshes.

Knights	(Sir Roberte Constable
Mshalles	(Sir Willyam Brereton
for the	(Sir Robert Chambleyn
Hall	(Sir Roberte Ffynys

And at þe mydjll Table in the hall on the right hande sat xiii Bysshoppys & Abbotts wᵗ the Ane of Excettyr [Edward IV's eldest sister, Anne of York, Duchess of Exeter] not sarved And beneth theym at þe seide Table the chefe Jugges of the kings Benche and of the commone pleas the the Chefe Barone and theire fellowes juges and Barons Sargeants & Diuers others

(At the mydill Table on the lyfte hande sat the Duches of
   Bedford the Countess of
(Essex the Duchess of Norff[olk] thelder [*Catherine Neville,
   sister of Cecily and*
(aunt of Edward IV] the Duches of Buk[ingham] þe yonger
   and of Countesses &
(Baronesses many others
(And beneth theym the knyghts of the Batthe newe made at
   the same Table
(And at þe Table nexte the walle on the right hande sat þe
   Barons of þe V portys
(and theyr felyship bi theire livree of aunctyan time due and
   accustumed for the
(Day.
(And beneth theym at þe saide Table the Clerk of the Rollys
   and maisters of the
(Chauncery.

And at the Table nexte þe Wall on the lyfte hande sat the Maire of London and his brethren Aldermen Diuers officers & Cytezeyns of the same

Ad benethe theym

The ii Course

And at the Seconde Course the sayde astates ryding before the s[er]uyce as they did before and before theym on fote Erlys Barons & Diuers knyghts.

And the sayde course was s[er]uyd yn with the forseyde newe knyghts and the firste of theym in s[er]uyce was was therle son of Arundell And nexte ensuing Therle son of Kent. And at þe course xix Disshes

The iii Course.

At the iiide Course the seyde iii Astates on horsebak before the s[er]uice on coursours rychely trappyd as beforne And before theym on fote Therle of Oxon iiii Barons and other noble knyghtys

And the sayde Course was s[er]uyd yn with the saide newe knyghts as before

And at þ[at] Course xv Dysshes

Also the Wavers were s[er]uyd yn w[t] the seyde knyghts newe made

And ypocras was s[er]uyd yn w[t] my Lorde Scalys coupe berer

And the Quenys Aumoner & a Chapeleyne foldyd up the Table Clothe vnto þe myddell of the Table & before hir reverently toke yt up & bare frome the Table.

And at wasshyng after Dyner Sir John Hawarde layde þe Surnape before þe Quene The Duq of Norff[olk] m[ar]shall of Englonde went before and comandyde And Sir Gilberte Debenhm draweth þe Surnape after

And at s[er]uyng yn of water þe Duq of Clarance Stywarde of Englonde stode yn the myddys And on his right hande the Duq of Norff M'shall and on the lyfte hande Th Erle of Arundell Constable for the feste.

The Erle of Oxo as Chambleyn brought yn the Basyn the Duq of Clarence helde þe Basyn and gave thassay

Ad the knyghts of the Batthe newe made brought the spice
plates vnto the Coupeberde Sir John Say brought the spice
plate vnto Sr Willyrn Bourchier son and hayre to therle of
Essex and he [there]of s[er]uyd the Queene

The Duq of Clarance Delyuerd thassay of the spice plate
The Maire of London bore the coupe w[t] wyne of voyde and
the Coupe of assay.

And at the Comyng yn of ev[er]y course and During the s[er]
uice th[er] of the Trompettys blowyng up solempnely.

And betwix certeyn coursys þe kings mynstrallys & the
mynstrallys of other Lordys playing & pyping in theyre instry
mentys grete & small before the Queene full melodyously &
in þe moste solempne wise

And þe feste done & the Table voyded the Queene was
brought yn to hir Chambre betwix the sayde Bisshoppys of
Durehm and Salesbury

And the septors were borne before hir w[t] the sayde astates in
semblable wise as they were brought yn.

And at the Dep[ar]ting of the Quene from the hail the Coupe
of Wyne of Voyde was s[er]uyd yn to the Queene was borne
thrugh þe hall before þe Maire of London.[10]

One is left wondering how the experience of her coronation had seemed
to Elizabeth Widville. After all, she appears to have been attended by a
number of probable enemies. These included George, Duke of Clarence,
and various relatives of Eleanor Talbot including the Duke of Clarence's
cousin (and Eleanor's brother-in-law), the last Mowbray Duke of Norfolk.
They also included John Mowbray's elder cousin, John Howard, who
later succeeded to the Norfolk dukedom, and who seems not to have got
on well with Elizabeth Widville.

It is also interesting to note who appears to have been absent. Although
Eleanor's brother-in-law, the Duke of Norfolk, was obliged to take part in
the ceremony, his wife (Eleanor's younger sister) seems not to have been
present. Neither Eleanor's mother, the dowager Countess of Shrewsbury,

nor her aunt, the Countess of Warwick, appears to have attended. The Earl of Warwick himself also chose not to attend the coronation, though some of his relatives, including his brother, the newly appointed Archbishop of York, found themselves forced to attend. It is also interesting to note that, while one of Edward IV's brothers and all three of his sisters were present, his mother – who may have questioned the validity of the Widville marriage – is not mentioned as having been there.

Chapter 10

Learning the Truth

Having been publicly acknowledged as Edward IV's consort, basically for the next eighteen years Elizabeth Widville played the role of England's official queen consort. Presumably she had been brought up and trained by her aristocratic French mother. Therefore Jacquette's influence may well account in part for the fact that Elizabeth now seemed to display herself quite efficiently in a rather grandiose royal style. Many people who saw her acting as queen seem to have found her impressive. At the same time, however, her nepotism alienated much of the traditional aristocracy.

Also, she was not so well off in terms of income as her predecessor, Margaret of Anjou, the consort of King Henry VI.

> In 1452–3 Queen Margaret's chamber received just over £1,719 out of a total income for the household of £7,563; in 1466–7 the chamber of Queen Elizabeth Woodville was given just under £919 out of a total income of just under £4,541. ... The most striking contrast between the account books of Queen Margaret and Queen Elizabeth Woodville is the comparative smallness of the latter's income and her much greater parsimony in expenditure.[1]

In fact, even though she was soon producing children for Edward IV (unlike Margaret of Anjou for Henry VI), Elizabeth does not appear to have been well financed in that respect.

> Although Princess Elizabeth had been born in February 1466, the queen does not seem to have been given any special allowance for her maintenance. It was not until

October 1468 that the queen was granted an extra £400 a year for the maintenance of Princess Elizabeth and her sister Mary, who had been born in August 1467.[2]

Nevertheless, an intriguing official royal seal was introduced for Eizabeth in her new capacity as the royal consort (see Plate 13). The grandiose inscription describes her as '*Dei gratia Regina*' ('by the Grace of God Queen'). In the centre, the seal depicts her arms, surmounted by a large and impressive open crown. As for the coat of arms, that is certainly intriguing. As usual for a consort the left-hand side of the shield as seen by the viewer displays the arms of her partner (the royal arms of Edward IV – France quartering England), held up on that side of the shield by the king's own animal supporter, a lion. On the viewer's right the shield displays the arms of Elizabeth herself. But, bizarrely, those are not the simple arms of her father, as would normally be the case. Instead they include the simple arms of Lord Rivers (Sir Richard Widville) submerged amongst all the elaborate Luxembourg / St Pol arms of Elizabeth's mother, Jacquette. That is very odd, because, of course, Jacquette was not the heiress of the Luxembourg/St Pol family.

Also on its right hand side, the shield has a second animal supporter. The creature in question is not a royal lion, but a different animal, chosen

for (or by) Elizabeth. And like the arms displayed on her side of the shield, the animal supporter chosen for her is also very intriguing, because it appears to be a Talbot hound – the emblem of Eleanor's family. No previous writer on the subject of Elizabeth Widville seems ever to have picked up that potentially rather significant point.

Seven years later, when a foreign visitor was being received at court in England, in her chamber Elizabeth reportedly had her attendant

A Talbot hound.

'ladies playing at the morteaulx, and some of her ladies were playing at Closheys of yuery, and Daunsinge. And sum at divers other games accordinge.'[3] 'Morteaulx' (Marteaux) is like a miniature version of billiards, played by four contestants on a small board. It was once popular with the aristocracy of France. 'Yuery' was a game of nine pins.

A house in Smithfield called Ormond's Inn was assigned to the newly crowned queen for her use, and she soon set up an elaborate ménage. At the head of her household was her chamberlain, Lord Berners, who was paid forty pounds a year and a reward of forty marks; but almost equally important, to judge from their salaries, were the master of the horse, John Woodville, who also got forty pounds a year, and the two carvers, Sir Humphrey Bourchier and James Haute, who got forty marks each. There were five ladies in waiting, Anne, Lady Bourchier, and Elizabeth, Lady Scales, who, like the chamberlain and the master of the horse, received forty pounds each, and Lady Alice Fogge [*sic* – see below],[4] Lady Joanna Norreis, and Lady Elizabeth Ovedale, who received twenty pounds each; and in addition to these ladies, there were seven damsels and two other women attendants, whose salaries ranged from ten pounds down to five marks. The queen also had three minstrels who, for ten pounds divided among them, made sweet music for her pleasure; she had her confessor, Edward Story, chancellor of the University of Cambridge and later Bishop of Carlisle, to whom she paid ten pounds a year for shriving her, and her physician, Domenico de Sirego, who got four times that amount for physicking her, her chancellor, Roger Radcliff, her clerk of the signet, John Aleyn, her receiver general, John Forster, who is responsible for the account book from which all these facts about her household arrangements are gleaned, her attorney general and her solicitor, John Dyve and Robert Isham, and, finally, her own council chamber in the New Tower next [to] the Exchequer. It is of some interest to know, too, that the young Duke of Buckingham and his brother, Humphrey Stafford, lived under the queen's roof, and that she hired one John Giles, master scholar, to teach them grammar.[5]

Lord Berners (John Bourchier, 1415–1474), was a son of Anne of Gloucester and thus a second cousin of Edward IV's father, the late Richard, Duke of York. The Earl of Essex and the Cardinal Archbishop of Canterbury[6] were two of his brothers.

Sir Humphrey Bourchier (*c.*1435–1471) was one of Lord Berners' sons. For some reason the Bourchier family seems to have become closely connected with Elizabeth Widville.

Anne (Widville), Lady Bourchier, was Elizabeth's own sister.

Elizabeth, Lady Scales (d. 1473), widow of Henry Bourchier, was the wife of Elizabeth Widville's senior surviving brother, Anthony Widville. It was thanks to his marriage to her – *iure uxoris* – that Anthony had become Baron Scales [*iure uxoris* = 'by right of (his) wife'].

Alice, Lady Fogge (*née* Haute or Hawte), was the second wife of Sir John Fogge of Ashford in Kent, Lord of the manor of Repton, and treasurer of the king's household. She had been born in about 1444, and had married her widowed husband in 1458. Her mother was Joan Widville, a sister of Sir Richard Widville, 1st Earl Rivers. Thus Alice, Lady Fogge, was Elizabeth Widville's first cousin.[7] So too was the second carver at Ormond's Inn, James Haute (one of Alice's brothers).

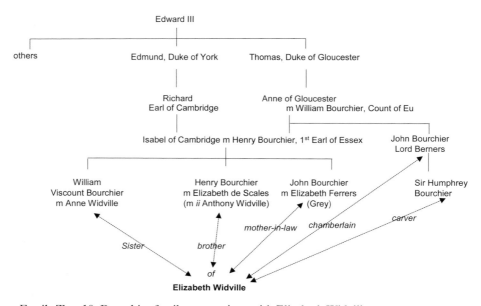

Family Tree 10: Bourchier family connections with Elizabeth Widville.

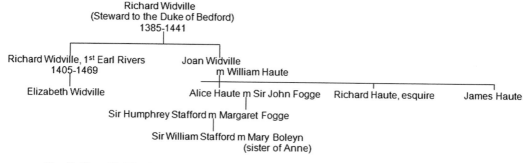

Family Tree 11: The Widville / Fogge / Haute connection.

Domenico di Sirego was a Venetian who also served sometimes as one of the king's physicians.[8] For example, on 1 November 1468 a certificate was issued by William Hatteclyffe, Roger Marchall, and Dominico de Serego,[9] 'the king's physicians', that Joan de Nyghtyngale, of Brentwood in Essex did not have leprosy.[10]

As we can see from some of the above facts in respect of the membership of her household, one of the most speedy outcomes of the public recognition of Elizabeth Widville as Edward IV's consort had obviously been the promotion of her relatives. 'The children of Lord Rivers [were] hugely exalted and set in great honour, as his eldest son made Lord Scales, and the others to sundry great promotions. Then shortly after was Lord Rivers made high treasurer of England, and the queen's eldest son was made Marquis of Dorset. And thus kindled the spark of envy which, by continuance, grew to so great a blaze and flame of fire that it flamed not only through all England but also into Flanders and France.'[11]

Elizabeth herself sometimes received gifts from courtiers, even if they were not really her friends. At that period presents were not traditionally given at Christmas, However, they were exchanged on 1 January ('New Year's Day' – even though that day did not then mark the formal start of a new calendar year in England). For example on 1 January 1464/5 Sir John Howard gave 'New Year's Day' gifts of horses both to Edward IV and to Elizabeth Widville.[12] The horse which he presented to the king was a courser called 'Lyard Duras', valued at £40. However, Elizabeth's present, 'Lyard Lewes', was less valuable (worth a mere £8). It was also possibly an insulting gift (or at least it may have been perceived in that way by Elizabeth). The horse in question was almost certainly Howard's 'grey hobby, Lyard Lowas', whose name had been thus recorded earlier, in the list of Howard's stud which was written down in 1463–64 when he was at Holt Castle with his young cousin, the Duke of Norfolk.[13] Significantly, the word 'Lyard' means 'a grey horse'.[14] In other words, Sir John Howard had apparently chosen to present a grey stud to the woman whom some people have called the king's 'Grey Mare'.

As for Howard himself, he definitely received 'New Year's day' gifts from the king, from the Duke of Clarence, and from Eleanor Talbot's sister, Eizabeth, Duchess of Norfolk, in January 1464/5.[15] However, he received no gift from Elizabeth Widville. Nevertheless, she did give presents herself on some occasions. For example, sixteen and a half years later, on 19 August 1481 she sent the following note, giving a royal buck to Sir William Stonor.

> By the Quene.
>
> We wol and charge you that ye deliver or do to be delivered unto oure trusty and welbeloved Syr William Stoner, knyght, or unto the bringer herof in his name, one buk of this season: to be taken of our gifte within our Forest of Blakmore, any restrainte or commaundement to you directed to the contrary herof notwithstanding. And thise oure letters shalbe your sufficient warrant animpst us in that behalve.
>
> Yeven under oure signet at my Lordes Castell of Wyndesore the xix day of August the xxj yere of my said lordes Reigne.
>
> To our trusty and welbeloved the maistre fforster of oure fforest of Blakmore, and to all other fforsters and kepers there in his absence, and to every of tham.[16]

Earlier, however, it appears that Elizabeth Widville had been 'right greatly displeased with' some female members of the Stonor family.[17] And interestingly, a year after her gift to Sir William Stonor, on 1 August 1482, *he* also found himself in trouble with Elizabeth Widville.

> By the Quene.
>
> Trusty and welbeloved, we grete you wel: and where as we understand by report made unto us at this tyme that ye have

taken upon yow now of late to make maistries withynne our fforest and Chace of Barnewod and Exsille, and þat in contempt of us uncourteisly to hunt and slee our deer withynne þe same to our grete mervaille and displeasir, we wol ye wite þat we entend to sew suche remedy therynne as shall accorde with my lordes laws. And whereas we ferþermore understand þat ye purpose under colour of my lordes Commyssion in þat behalf graunted unto you, as ye sey, hastly to take þe view and reule of our game of dere withyn our said fforest and Chace, we wol þat ye shew unto us or our Counsell your said Cornission, if any suche ye have. And in þe mean season þat ye spare of huntyng withynne our said fforest or Chace, as ye wol answere at your perill. Yoven under our signet at our Maner of Grenewiche the first day of August.

Elysabeth.

To our trusty and welbeloved Sir William Stonor, knyght.[18]

Claims have been put forward to the effect that Elizabeth herself also owned books. She was an intelligent woman, so indeed, she may well have done so. For example, we know that she 'paid ten pounds for a book of some sort not long after she became queen'.[19] Sadly, however, most of the alleged 'evidence' presented in respect of her alleged library has, in effect, been non-existent. For example, a suggestion has been put forward that she might perhaps have owned a book of French romances on the subjects of Sir Launcelot and the quest for the Holy Grail. The reason why that hypothesis was put forward was based upon the fact that the book in question bears 'the signature *E Wydevyll*, followed by a flourished stroke in a fifteenth-century hand in an unobtrusive position on the last flyleaf'.[20] But of course we have no evidence that Elizabeth ever signed her name in that way. Indeed, she would always have been extremely unlikely to have done so. Since the early 1450s her actual surname had not been 'Widville', it had been 'Grey'. In any case, we know that after 1464 she simply wrote *Elysabeth* with no surname (see below). Obviously the most likely owner of the book in question would therefore have been her younger brother, Edward.

The will signature of Elizabeth Widville.

We saw earlier that in 1464 Edward IV is reported to have asked his friend, Thomas Fitzgerald, Earl of Desmond, what people were saying about him. Finally, after several repetitions of that question, the king asked what Desmond himself thought of him. Desmond then revealed to his sovereign that, in his opinion, at any rate, the Widville marriage was a highly questionable relationship for the young monarch.

> Not long after, the said Earl having licence to depart into his country and remaining in Ireland, it chanced that the said king and the queen his wife, upon some occasion, fell at words, insomuch that his grace braste out and said: 'Well I perceive now that true it is that my cousin, the Earl of Desmond, told me at such a time when we two communed secretly together;' which saying his Majesty, then in his melancholy, declared unto her; whereupon her Grace being not a little moved, and conceiving upon those words a grudge in her heart against the said Earl,[21]

Elizabeth began to think of how she could punish Desmond and get her own back on him. More will be said about Elizabeth's subsequent actions in that respect in the next chapter.

Meanwhile, however, the report appears to show that it was at some point in the winter of 1464–5 that Elizabeth had a quarrel with Edward, as a result of which she was then told by the king that the Earl of Desmond did not consider her the genuine royal consort. It is interesting to see that, at an early stage of their union, Edward and Elizabeth were apparently having fights with one another. It is also interesting to note that Edward's reaction when he found himself in a situation of that kind is said to have been the feeling of melancholia.

Eighteen years later, in 1483, Friar Domenico Mancini recorded the fact that the Earl of Desmond was by no means the only peer of the realm who looked down upon Elizabeth, viewing her an unsuitable and inappropriate royal consort. 'By reason of this marriage some of the nobility had renewed hostilities against Edward.'[22] It appears that at least some members of the English aristocracy resented Elizabeth Widville because *her* family was not of aristocratic status. In other words the new queen consort was perceived in some quarters as an interloper.

Moreover, Elizabeth had immediately begun doing everything she could in order to promote the status of her own close relatives. For example, she organised wealthy and high-status marriages for some of her brothers and sisters. As we have seen from the coronation report, one of Elizabeth's younger sisters had been married to Edward IV's cousin, the young Duke of Buckingham, very rapidly indeed. Clearly that second royal alliance had been celebrated before Elizabeth's own coronation took place on 26 May 1465.

The Buckingham marriage is reported by William Worcester to have taken place in February 1465/6, when 'the king made Henry, duke of Buckingham, marry a sister of queen Elizabeth.'[23] But unfortunately William Worcester is by no means to be relied upon in respect of date records.[24] And indeed, in this instance he is certainly mistaken in respect of the year, because we already know that the Buckingham marriage preceded Elizabeth Widville's own coronation, which was celebrated in May 1465. If February is the correct month for the Buckingham marriage, it must therefore have been carried out in February 1464/5.

Presumably the planning of the Buckingham marriage would only have commenced after September 1464, when Elizabeth herself had formally been recognised as the royal consort. Also, given that traditionally the Church did not accept marriage celebrations during the penitential seasons of Advent or of Lent, the periods 2–25 December 1464 and 27 February 1464/5 –14 April 1465 are almost certainly ruled out in this case. In other words, Catherine Widville's marriage to the young Duke of Buckingham must actually have taken place in October or November 1464, in January or early February 1464/5 (the period – but not the year – cited by William Worcester), or in late April or early May 1465.

Moreover, interestingly, in January 1464/5 another significant union took place for one of Elizabeth's siblings. Her brother, John Widville, who was then aged 20, was married to the king's much older widowed aunt, Catherine Neville, dowager Duchess of Norfolk.[25] In other words, more or less immediately after his union with Elizabeth Widville had been publicly acknowledged,

> the king, being too greatly influenced by the urgent suggestions of the queen, admitted to his especial favour all the relations of the said queen, as well as those who were in any way connected with her by blood, enriching them with boundless presents and always promoting them to the most dignified offices about his person: while, at the same time, he banished from his presence his own brethren, and his kinsmen sprung from the royal blood, together with the Earl of Warwick himself, and the other nobles of the realm who had always proved faithful to him.[26]

It also seems that anxiety was felt in certain quarters in respect of the possibility that Elizabeth Widville might have employed sorcery in order to secure her royal marriage. Furthermore, subsequently she found herself both looked down on and to some extent feared in respect of the use which she herself made of royal power in order to punish anyone who either offended her, or whom she perceived as possibly threatening her. As a result, definite anti-Widville events took place in England in the late 1460s, led by the Earl of Warwick and the Duke of Clarence. Details of what precisely was then done in respect of certain members of Elizabeth's family will be examined shortly (see below, Chapter 12).

Initially, of course, the general actions which were then taken 'revived hope among King Henry's party of regaining the crown'.[27] The result was the brief Lancastrian restoration. Nevertheless, by 1471:

> Edward's power in the kingdom was reaffirmed. The queen [Elizabeth Widville] then *remembered* the insults to her family and the calumnies with which she was reproached, namely that according to established usage she was not the legitimate wife of the king. Thus she concluded that her offspring by the king would never come to the throne unless the Duke of Clarence were removed.[28]

Since Mancini employed at this point in his text the Latin word *memor*, he was clearly saying in this account that in 1471 Elizabeth Widville *was remembering* that it had been said that she was neither Edward IV's legitimate wife nor an acceptable royal consort. Obviously, therefore, she must have heard that claim put forward against her *before* the Lancastrian restoration – in other words, in the 1460s.

We have already seen that the first reported statement in that respect had allegedly been made in the autumn of 1464 by the king's own mother. We have also heard that the second reported view – at the most, a few weeks later – was expressed to the king by the Earl of Desmond. Similar comments may well have been made then or subsequently by the Earl of Warwick and others. 'This [union of Edward IV and Elizabeth Widville] the nobility and chief men of the kingdom took amiss, seeing that he [Edward IV] had with such immoderate haste promoted a person sprung from a comparatively humble lineage, to share the throne with him.'[29] But whoever truly voiced objections in respect of the alleged royal marriage, and on precisely what date(s), clearly the case against Elizabeth's union with Edward must have been put forward – and must have reached Elizabeth Widville's own ears – by 1469 at the very latest.

Thus, by 1469 at the very latest – but almost certainly several years earlier – Elizabeth Widville must herself have become well aware of the fact that her status as the legal wife and consort of Edward IV was disputed and contested in some quarters. Possibly that may have influenced her apparent choice of a floral emblem as her symbol.[30] Edward himself had chosen a white rose displayed in a sunburst as his symbol, and he had used that symbol before he gained the crown. Elizabeth seems to have chosen the clove pink (carnation). The flowers in question are displayed around Elizabeth's images, both in the Canterbury Cathedral royal window, and also in the Skinners' Company Book of the Fraternity of Our Lady. It has been suggested that Elizabeth 'chose her clove-pink device because it stood for virtuous love and marriage and was also a devout reminder of the Virgin Mary's own chastity and motherhood'.[31]

Obviously, if Elizabeth Widville had heard, in the course of a 1464/5 dispute with King Edward IV, what the Earl of Desmond had said about her, and if it is true that the king's mother had also told him that he was legally married to another wife, then presumably Edward might additionally have reported Cecily's remarks to Elizabeth. Indeed, maybe it was Elizabeth's influence which then helped remove the dowager Duchess of York from the official requirements in respect of royal prayers which were being commissioned.

Elizabeth's clove pink flower emblems redrawn from the border of her Skinners' Book 'portrait'.

Significantly, however, according to Thomas More's later account, Cecily Neville had actually named – and personally consulted – the woman who was the true legal wife of her son. Of course, as we saw earlier, More refers in that respect to the mythical 'Lady Elizabeth Lucy'. But we have also seen very clearly that More's similar subsequent claim on that point, regarding the 1483–4 legislation in respect of the royal marriage, can be proved false. In other words, if Cecily Neville really did tell Edward IV the name of his legal wife, and consult the woman in question, the name she mentioned must presumably have been the same as the one which was also cited in 1483–4. In other words the probability is that Cecily must also have named Lady Eleanor Talbot (Lady Boteler) as her son's legal wife – and may also actually have talked to Eleanor regarding her relationship with the king.

Since we now know that in the second half of the 1460s Elizabeth Widville already knew that her royal union was disputed, it is therefore plausible that by that time she too had also learnt the name of her rival. Obviously she would also have been well aware of the names of those who were openly and publicly contesting her alleged status as queen consort. The people in question included the king's mother, the Earl of Desmond, the Earl of Warwick, the Duke of Clarence, and others. She may therefore have formulated a list of people she would like to punish or get rid of. Significantly, that list may have included the name of Eleanor Talbot.

Chapter 11

Dealing with the first Problems

Following Elizabeth's coronation as queen consort, the whole Widville family seems to have become rather arrogant in its behaviour. For example, significantly her mother's chosen motto was '*sur tous autres*' – 'above (or on top of) everybody else'.[1] Obviously such arrogance caused great offense in some quarters. 'Nothing that Edward [IV] could do would ever make the Woodvilles popular. They were hated by the lords and by the people. Even his greatest friends, like Hastings, turned from such an alliance; and in 1467 a mob in Kent showed its opinion by despoiling one of River's [sic] manors and slaughtering his deer.'[2]

Evidence in respect of the arrogance does exist. For example, at some point in the second half of the 1460s Elizabeth herself also sent a firm letter to John de Vere, 13th Earl of Oxford, who had served at her coronation, reprimanding him for apparently contesting the inheritance of her 'welbeloved Symon Blyant' to a manor, and tending rather to favour Sir John Paston.

> To oure right trusty and enterly beloved cosyn, th'Erll of Oxon.
>
> BY THE QUENE
>
> Ryght trusty and entierly beloved cosyn, we grete you well, lattyng you wete [know] how it is commen to oure knowlege that where as ze [ye] newly entred upon oure welbeloved Symon Blyant, gentilman, in to the maner of Hemnals in Cotton, descended and belongyng unto hyrn by right of enheritaunce, as it is seid, ze ther upon desired the same Symon to be agreable for hys part to put all maters of variance thenne dependyng atwene hym and oon Sir John Paston,

Knyght, pretendyng a title unto the seid maner into th'award and jugement of two lenered men, by you named and chosen as arbritrours atwene them; and in case that the same arbritrours of and upon the premisses neither yave oute nor made suche awarde be for the brekyng up of Pasche [Easter] terme nowe last passed, ze of your owne offre grauntid and promysid unto the seid Symon, as we be enformed to restore hym forwyth there upon unto hys possession of the seid maner. And how it be that the same Symon, at youre mocion and for the pleasir of youre lordshyp, as he seith, aggreed un to the seid compromyse, and ther upon brought and shewed hys evydence concernyng,and sufficiently provyng hys ryght in the seid maner un to the seid arbritrours and that they have not made nor yolden out betwene the said parties any suche awarde; yet have not ze restored the same Symon unto hys possession of the seid master, but contynuelly kepe hym owt of the same, wich, yf it so be, is not only to hys right grete hurt and hinderaunce, but also oure mervaile. Wherfore we desire and pray you ryght affectueusly that ze woll the rather at the contemplacion of thees oure lettres, shew unto the said Symon, in hys rightfufl interesse and title in the seid maner all the favorable lordshyp that ze goodely may, doyng hym to be restored and put in to hys lawfull and peasible possession of the same, as fer as reason, equite, and good conscience shall require, and youre seid promise, in suche wyse that he may undyrstond hym selfe herynne to fare the better for oure sake, as oure verray trust is in you.

Yeven under oure signet at my Lordes Palois of Westminster, the xxv. day of Juyn

ELEZEBETH [3]

Significantly, but unsurprisingly, 'by early July 1469 Oxford had joined the discontented Yorkists led by his brother-in-law, the Earl of Warwick, and King Edward's brother, the Duke of Clarence.'[4]

One very shrewd and subtle petitioner drew the king's attention to his perception of the arrogance of the Widvilles by offering his discrete and tactful protest in respect of that point to Edward IV in a most astute and perceptive way. When he came to see the king in order to present his petition the man in question arrived

> clad in a short coat, [a] pair of boots upon his legs as long as they might be [and] in his hand a long pike. When the king beheld his apparel he asked him what was the cause of his long boots and long staff. 'Upon my faith, sir', said he, 'I have passed through many counties of your realm, and in places that I have passed the rivers have been so high that I could scarcely escape through them [unless I searched] the depth with this long staff.' The king knew that he meant by it the great rule which Lord Rivers and his blood bore at that time within the realm.[5]

As for Elizabeth Widville's own political involvement, while her activity is sometimes unclear and disputed, she definitely attracted some adverse reactions. One example of that was her involvement in the case involving Sir Thomas Cook, former mayor of London. This was apparently one typical example of her conduct. Cook found himself sent to the Tower of London.

> And fynally, after many persecucious and losses, was compelled as for a fyne sette vpon hym for offence of mysprysion, to paye vnto the kynge. viii. M.*li*. [£8,000] And after he had thus agreed, and was [set] at large for the kynges jnterest, he was thanne in newe trowble agayne the quene; the whiche demaundyd of hym as her right, for euery M.*li*. [£1,000] payde vnto the kynge by waye of fyne, an hondreth marke.[6]

The 'mark' was the gold angel coin worth 13 s. 4 d. Thus the total fine he was required to pay to Elizabeth was 800 marks (about £530). As for Cook's property, that found itself confiscated by Elizabeth Widville's father and his servants. Interestingly this event commenced in 1467 – a year which also seems to have marked the beginning of other manipulative activities on Elizabeth's part. Further evidence showing more details of the possible links between Cook's case and other Widville political machinations will be presented later (see Chapter 14).

The two key examples of major ways in which Elizabeth Widville was reported to have attempted to deal with the problems which were being voiced regarding the validity of her royal marriage, were the execution of the Earl of Desmond and the subsequent execution of the Duke of Clarence. In that respect, it is very interesting to note that Richard, Duke of Gloucester (later King Richard III), the younger brother of Edward IV and of the Duke of Clarence, definitely perceived those two executions as being very clearly connected to one another (see below). It also appears that he must have considered the person responsible for both those deaths as Elizabeth Widville. Richard III's own contemporary statement in respect of those two executions will be presented shortly, but presumably he was not the only person who held the view which he presents.

As we have already seen, before the end of 1467 (and probably earlier, in 1464 or 1465) in a quarrel with Edward IV, the angry Elizabeth Widville had heard that the king had been told by the Earl of Desmond that she was not a suitable person to be his royal consort. She therefore sought – and found – a way of punishing the earl for that remark.

> Her Grace being not a little moved, and conceiving upon those words a grudge in her heart against the said Earl, found such a mean as letters were devised under the king's privy seal, and directed to the Lord Justice or governor of the realm of Ireland, commanding him in all haste to send for the said Earl, dissembling some earnest matter of consultation with him touching the state of the same realm, and at his coming to object to such matter, and to lay such things to his charge, as should cause him to lose his head.
>
> According to which commandment the said Lord Justice addressed forth his messenger to the said Earl of Desmond, and by his letters signifying the king's pleasure willed him with all diligence to make his repair unto him and other of the king's council; who, immediately setting all other business apart, came to them to the town of Droughedda, accompanied like a nobleman with eighteen score horsemen, well appointed after a civil English sort, being distant from his own country above 200 miles. Where without long delay or sufficient matter brought against him, after the order of his Majesty's laws, the said Lord Justice (the rest of the council

being nothing privy to the conclusion) caused him to be beheaded, signifying to the common people for a cloak, that most heinous treasons were justified against him in England, and so justly condemned to die. Upon which murder and fact committed, the king's Majesty being advised thereof, and declaring himself to be utterly ignorant of the said Earl's death, sent with all possible speed into Ireland to the said Lord Justice; whom, after he had well examined and known the considerations and circumstances of his beheading, he caused to be put to a very cruel and shameful death, according to his desert, and for satisfaction and pacifying the said Earl's posterity, who by this execrable deed were wonderfully mated [united], and in manner brought to rebel against the sovereign lord and king. His Majesty, by his letters patent, gave liberty to the Earls of Desmond successively, to remain at home, and not at any time upon commandment to frequent the Deputy and Council, but at such times as they at their own pleasure, for declaration of their duties, should think it so meet. Sithens which licence, so granted, none of them came either to Lord Justice, Deputy or Council.[7]

As we have also seen, in the late autumn of 1464 or the winter of 1464/5, Elizabeth had probably miscarried a royal child. Of course, the baby in question was of unknown gender. Just over a year later, in February 1465/6 she had borne the king a daughter – Elizabeth of York (junior). In August 1467 she produced yet another daughter, Mary of York. Ironically, Elizabeth had previously given birth to two sons by her first husband. However, in February 1467/8 – when she had the Earl of Desmond punished for the things he had said against her status as England's official royal consort – Elizabeth must have appeared to be proving something of a failure in the capacity of producing royal male heirs to the throne. That may have been one of the factors which caused disputes with the king, and which inspired her to take revenge against someone who had spoken against her in terms of her alleged royal status.

Thomas Fitzgerald, seventh Earl of Desmond, the former deputy governor of Ireland, and a friend and ally of Edward IV, found himself beheaded at Drogheda, on Monday 15 February 1467/8. Full research on that event was published earlier in a joint article by the present writer and Annette Carson.[8] His execution was the direct result of actions taken by Edward IV's new governor of Ireland, John Tiptoft, Earl of Worcester. However, Tiptoft was apparently acting on instructions contained in a document which he had received from England, bearing the king's privy seal. In other words, when he had the Earl of Desmond put to death, Tiptoft must have believed that he was following his king's own instructions.

Yet when the news from Ireland reached the king back in England, Edward IV was shocked and appalled. As William Worcester reported in his Annals,

> [1467/8] About the Feast of the Purification of the Blessed Mary [2 February], in Ireland, the Earl of Worcester had the Earl of Desmond beheaded, at which the king was initially displeased.[9]

The king had good reason for feeling angry. Apart from the offensive harm which had been done to his own personal friend, Thomas Fitzgerald, Edward also now discovered that consternation had been caused in Ireland. Thus, in political terms, Desmond's execution proved to be a major catastrophe, sending the surviving members of the formally loyal Fitzgerald family into immediate armed rebellion.

We have also seen that there has been opposition on the part of some historians in respect of the authenticity of the Fitzgerald family's slightly later (sixteenth-century) written account in respect of Thomas Fitzgerald's execution, and the person who is said in that source to have been really responsible for his death. Significantly, however, a surviving fifteenth-century written source does also exist which definitely supports the claim which figures in the Fitzgerald family account, namely that Elizabeth Widville was the key person responsible for the Earl of Desmond's execution.

The fifteenth-century source is in the form of a letter which was penned about sixteen years after Desmond's execution – towards the end of September 1484 – by King Richard III. The letter in question was sent by that king to Thomas Barrett, Bishop of Annaghdown ('Enachden'). Bishop Thomas Barrett was then acting as Richard's messenger to Thomas

Fitzgerald's son and heir, James Fitzgerald, the eighth Earl of Desmond. And the letter which the bishop received from the king contained the latter's instructions:

> the said Bisshope shall on the kings behalve thanke him ... as remembryng the manyfold notable service and kyndnesse by therles fadre unto the famous prince the duc of York the kinges Fader ... Also he shalle shewe that albe it the Fadre of the said Erle the king than being of yong Age was extorciously slayne and murdred by colour of the lawes within Irland by certain persons than havyng the governaunce and Rule there, ayenst alle manhode Reason, and good conscience Yet, notwithstanding that the semblable chaunce was and hapned sithen within this Royaulme of England aswele of his brother the duc of Clarence As other his nighe kynnesmen and gret Frendes the kinge's grace alweys contynueth and hathe inward compassion of the dethe of his [the present Earl of Desmond's] said Fadre And is content that his said Cousyn now Erle by alle ordinate meanes and due course of the lawes when it shalle lust him at any tyme hereafter to sue or attempt for the punysshment therof.[10]

As he reveals very clearly in his letter, Richard III believed that at least two formal executions (those of the Earl of Desmond, and of his own elder brother, George Duke of Clarence) – not to mention the deaths of other unnamed individuals who had been Richard's 'nigh kynnesmen and gret frendes', but who may have been murdered rather than formally executed – had all been brought about in similar ways.

In September 1484, when Richard wrote his letter to the Bishop of Annaghdown, it was definitely believed in other quarters that the person behind the later execution of the Duke of Clarence had been Elizabeth Widville. For example, Domenico Mancini's report establishes that fact absolutely. Mancini wrote towards the end of 1483 that Elizabeth had 'concluded that her offspring by the king would never come to the throne, unless the duke of Clarence were removed; and of this she easily persuaded the king'.[11] Therefore the only possible meaning behind what Richard III wrote in September

1484 is that he also believed Elizabeth Widville to have been the person responsible for the execution of the Earl of Desmond.

Yet, curiously, some historians have argued against that interpretation. Their claim is based upon the fact that Elizabeth is not actually *named* in Richard III's letter. Of course it is true that Richard III does not mention in his letter the name of 'Lady Grey' (Elizabeth Widville). Nevertheless, he clearly blames 'certain persons than havyng the governaunce and rule' in 1467/8 for bringing about the Earl of Desmond's death. Of course, Richard must have known, as others did (see above) that his own brother, Edward IV, had not been responsible for the execution of Desmond. Indeed, Desmond's death had actually shocked the king. However, we have also seen that the year in question was a time when the main problem in England was thought to be the fact that 'rivers have been so high' – indicating very clearly who then would have been acting as the power behind the throne.

However, Richard III then says in his letter 'that the semblable chaunce was and hapned sithen within this royaume of England, as wele of his brother the duc of Clarence.' His reference to the subsequent execution of his brother proves clearly that Richard also cannot possibly have considered John Tiptoft, Earl of Worcester, to have been the key person responsible for the earlier execution of the Earl of Desmond. After all, the Earl of Worcester had definitely played no part in the later execution of the Duke of Clarence. John Tiptoft himself had no longer been alive when George, Duke of Clarence, was put to death. Tiptoft was himself executed by the restored Lancastrian regime in 1470 – seven years prior to the execution of the Duke of Clarence.

In that respect, Richard III also makes it very clear that, in his view, the person responsible for the execution of the Earl of Desmond was still alive in 1484 – and could therefore still be punished. That is why he encourages the existing Earl of Desmond 'to sue' the person who had been responsible for the execution of his father, 'or attempt for the punishment therof'. In other words, the person described as having been in power in 1467/8 must still have been alive in 1484 – but was no longer in power, and could therefore be punished. Obviously therefore the relevant persons 'havyng the governaunce and rule' in 1467/8 cannot possibly have included either John Tiptoft or King Edward IV, both of whom were dead in 1484.

In addition, a few months after the execution of the Earl of Desmond, in the summer of 1468, another death occurred which would certainly have been in Elizabeth Widville's interest – and in the context of which she definitely appears to have played a significant role in at least one respect. This time the death in question was not an execution. It was the death of young Eleanor Talbot – Elizabeth's rival in respect of the status as legal royal consort. In his letter which refers to the deaths of the Earl of Desmond and his own brother, the Duke of Clarence, Richard III also refers to other deaths of other 'nigh kynnesmen' who were put to death for political reasons, but who were not formally executed. It is therefore significant to note the fact that Richard's wife, Anne Neville, was one of the first cousins of Eleanor Talbot. In other words Eleanor was undoubtedly Richard's nigh kinswoman by marriage.

We have already seen that prior to 1468 Elizabeth Widville had become aware of the fact that the legal status of her royal union was in question. She had also probably discovered that Edward IV was said to have contracted an earlier secret marriage. What is more she had probably ascertained that the woman to be identified as his legal consort in that respect was Eleanor Talbot, an aristocratic lady who was descended from Edward I and earlier English kings. Elizabeth must then have become aware of the fact that, even though she was not at court, was making no claims to be acknowledged as queen, and was now focussing her thoughts on a religious life, Eleanor was still alive. By 1468 it seems that Eleanor was living under the protection of her sister and brother-in-law, the Duchess and the Duke of Norfolk, in the vicinity of Norwich. Probably she felt safer there than living alone at her own manor houses in Warwickshire.

Queen Anne Neville, first cousin of Eleanor Talbot.

After Edward IV had publicly recognised his union with Elizabeth Widville in September 1464, Eleanor Talbot seems to have become resident at her sister's dower house, East Hall, at Kenninghall in Norfolk. She seems to have lived there very quietly concentrating on her patronage of Corpus Christi College, Cambridge, and on the development of her religious association with the house of Carmelite friars in Norwich. In fact some historians have claimed that Eleanor became a nun. However, that is not true. Indeed, there were no Carmelite nuns in England at that date.

Instead, like many women at that period, Eleanor remained a laywoman, but became firmly attached to the Carmelite order as a tertiary. If Edward IV heard that news he probably welcomed it. For him it meant that Eleanor obviously had no intention of making a legal claim to be his consort in the church courts. In fact it seems (and Edward was probably already well aware of this) that Eleanor did not wish to live with him. Instead she now wished to develop her own mystic relationship with God.

Since Eleanor was living at East Hall in Norfolk, presumably she also died there. Significantly, in the sixteenth century, John Leland recalled a local tradition which recorded that 'there apperith at Keninghaule not far from the Duke of Northfolkes new place a grete mote, withyn the cumpace whereof there was sumtyme a fair place, and there the saying is that there lay a Quene or sum grete lady, and there dyed.'[12] That account suggests that, in spite of the later attempt made by Henry VII and his government to write Eleanor Talbot out of history, some people must still have remembered that Eleanor had actually been officially recognised in 1483–5 as the legal wife and consort of King Edward IV.

Interestingly, it was during the summer of 1468 that Eleanor died at a comparatively young age. In fact she was probably about a year older than Elizabeth Widville. Compared to her family evidence (see below), Eleanor appears to have had an unusually short life. Significantly, the only immediate relatives who died at similar ages had all died unnaturally (been killed).

The date of Eleanor's death is also significant in two other ways. Firstly there is the chronological link to the execution of the Earl of Desmond. Secondly there is the link to a prominent royal event which was taking

The average age at death of members of this family who died naturally was 61-62

Name	born	died	age	natural / unnatural death
John Talbot, Earl of Shrewsbury	1387	1453	66	unnatural (in battle)
Margaret Beauchamp, Countess of Shrewsbury	1404	1467	63	natural
John Talbot, Lord Lisle	1426	1453	27	unnatural (in battle)
Sir Louis Talbot	1428	1459	30	unnatural? (injured in conflict?)
Sir Humphrey Talbot	1433	1492	59	natural
Eleanor Talbot	1436	1468	32	unnatural?
Elizabeth Talbot, Duchess of Norfolk	1442/3	1506	63	natural

The length of life of members of the Talbot Family.

place in the summer of 1468. That summer's grand royal occasion was the marriage of Edward IV's youngest sister, Margaret, to Charles the Bold, Duke of Burgundy. It comprised an alliance which, though being opposed by the Earl of Warwick, had definitely been pushed forward by Elizabeth Widville and her family. After all, through Jacquette (her mother) Elizabeth had connections with the Duchy of Burgundy.

And when the plans were made for Margaret's journey across the Channel, a very significant choice was made in terms of the noble woman who was officially honoured by being appointed as the head of Margaret's entourage. The person selected for that key role was Eleanor's sister, Elizabeth Talbot, Duchess of Norfolk. Moreover, arrangements were also made for the Duchess to be accompanied by all the other living members of her own family – with just one exception. Elizabeth Talbot's brother, Sir Humphrey Talbot, went with her to Flanders, and so did her nephew and nieces, the young Lisles. Yet significantly just one key member of the Duchess of Norfolk's immediate family was left behind in England. The person in question was Elizabeth's sister, Eleanor Talbot. As a result, Eleanor suddenly found herself alone in Norfolk.

Elizabeth Talbot and the other living family members only actually left England – sailing with Margaret of York from Margate – on Thursday 23 June 1468. However, they must all have been involved in preparatory wedding events in the London area earlier in June, before they actually left the country. For example, Margaret's formal departure from the English capital had taken place five days earlier, on Saturday 18 June. Subsequently, the Duchess of Norfolk only set off back to England from Flanders on Wednesday 13 July.[13] In other words the Talbots had probably found themselves tied up in royal events for more than four weeks.

Thus, on 30 June, when Eleanor Talbot died in Norfolk, in family terms she was all alone. Her close living blood-relatives were all away in the Low Countries. Indeed, one significant outcome of the Talbot absence abroad was the fact that initially the legal requirements which arose from Eleanor's death could not be started. That process only began two weeks after Eleanor's demise, when her sister, the Duchess of Norfolk, had finally arrived back in England.

It does seem probable that Eleanor was aware that she might possibly be dying earlier in June. For example, on Saturday 4 June she made a significant deed of gift in favour of her sister.[14] If she was to be killed it therefore seems that arrangements must have been made to poison her. That same methodology was also reported later in the case of another alleged victim, Eleanor's first cousin, Isabel Neville, Duchess of Clarence, and also of the latter's baby son, Richard. In both of the two Clarence cases the killing by administration of poison seems to have taken about two weeks (see below, Chapter 14).

Eleanor's death in June 1468 could well have made things potentially less worrying for the king. But in fact Edward always seems to have thought that he had nothing to fear in respect of Eleanor and her conduct. Thus he appears to have remained supportive of her and those close to her. But the person whose fear of Eleanor must have been much greater than Edward's is Elizabeth Widville. That point, together with Eleanor's early death in unusual circumstances, some of which Elizabeth Widville had been involved in arranging, makes it possible that Eleanor may have died unnaturally. In that case, once again, the individual most likely to have been responsible for planning Eleanor's death would have been Elizabeth Widville.

Obviously no firm proof exists for the hypothesis that young Eleanor Talbot was killed, and that her murder was planned by Elizabeth Widville. However, we do know for cetain that in 1467–68 Elizabeth Widville was involved in operations against some people. Moreover, it appears that the motivation behind her earlier organised execution of the Earl of Desmond had definitely been her anxiety regarding the questions raised in respect of the validity of her royal marriage.

Chapter 12

Losing the first Relatives

As we saw earlier, when Edward IV's cousin, Richard Neville, Earl of Warwick, first heard of the young king's union with Elizabeth Widville, he was appalled. 'The nobility and chief men of the kingdom took [the marriage] amiss, seeing that he [Edward] had with such immoderate haste promoted a person sprung from such a comparatively humble lineage.'[1] Nevertheless, together with Edward's younger brother, George, Duke of Clarence, Warwick then found himself obliged to formally present Elizabeth Widville to the nation as its queen at Reading Abbey, on Michaelmas day (29 September) 1464.

It seems that probably Edward, aware of Warwick's hostility in respect of the Widville family, was seeking to assert his authority by forcing him – together with the king's own younger brother, George, Duke of Clarence

Reading Abbey.

(then the heir presumptive to the English crown) – to act as patrons and sponsors on behalf of the consort whom he himself had now publicly acknowledged.

In the end, though, that probably proved to be a mistake. Warwick, some other nobles, and even members of the royal house of York itself, began to feel that Edward was no longer truly acting as a 'Yorkist' because he was listening too much to the opinions of Elizabeth Widville, was promoting the interests of *her* immediate family members, and was giving them far too many gifts. At the same time the king was distancing himself, both politically and physically, from his own immediate family (including his cousin, the Earl of Warwick), and from those members of the aristocracy who had previously been his supporters.[2]

Indeed, the situation had become bizarre. After all, in the person of Edward IV's late father, the house of York had originally claimed the English crown on the grounds of its own strictly legitimate royal descent. Yet by now embarking publicly on a questionable partnership, Edward IV was potentially undermining the future of Yorkist legitimacy. Even people who were not aware of the young king's earlier Talbot marriage (and the consequent Widville bigamy) nevertheless shared the view expressed by the Earl of Desmond in respect of Edward's union with a widow of insignificant family background. Moreover, it was a union which had been conducted secretly and without parliamentary approval.

It was noted earlier that on the occasion of Elizabeth's subsequent coronation Warwick definitely appears to have remained absent. However, George, Duke of Clarence, was once again required to play an important role in his capacity as Steward of England. Thus, Edward IV seems in some ways to have been extraordinarily insensitive. After all, hitherto, ever since 1461, George had not only been the king's senior surviving brother, but also the heir presumptive to his throne. Obviously he might now expect to be replaced as the royal heir sooner or later by new royal children produced by Elizabeth Widville. In other words, the subsequent animosity between the Duke of Clarence and Elizabeth was probably almost inevitable. Moreover, it also led to the growth of a major alliance between George and his older cousin, the Earl of Warwick. Those two men now found themselves united in their opposition to the entire Widville family. To cement their alliance, Warwick proposed a marriage between his own elder daughter, Isabel, and the Duke of Clarence.

Edward IV initially opposed that royal marriage project. However, as we have seen, inspired by Elizabeth Widville, he worked on a different royal marriage, aimed at joining his youngest sister, Margaret of York, with the son and heir of the Duke of Burgundy. The celebration of that royal marriage, in the summer of 1468, coincided, as we have seen, with the mysterious death of Eleanor Talbot, at a time when all her close relatives had been shipped out of the country in attendance on the royal bride. As for Warwick, for his part he would definitely have preferred Margaret to marry a more authentic French prince. He had therefore opposed the Burgundian marriage proposal. In other words, in every way, in the 1460s, royal marriages seemed to prove divisive for the house of York.

Possibly the king's ongoing quarrel with his cousin, Warwick, delighted Elizabeth Widville, given that, as she must have known, Warwick had always looked down on her family. The growing animosity between Edward IV and the Earl of Warwick produced various consequences. For example, Warwick's younger brother, the Archbishop of York, who had been Edward IV's chancellor, suddenly found himself dismissed from that post. As for Warwick himself, when the Burgundian royal marriage took place, once again he found himself compelled by Edward IV to publicly accept and endorse the royal event in question.

There is not much doubt that Elizabeth Widville was ambitious and power-hungry. As we shall see later, that point is proved clearly by the action she took in 1483, following Edward IV's death (see below, Chapter 14). As for Warwick, although he has become known as 'the Kingmaker', that appellation is misleading. His initial aim was simply to bring down that inappropriate royal consort and her intrusive family, and to restore Edward IV to what he himself perceived as true Yorkism. His principle ally in that respect was the king's brother, George Duke of Clarence, and the two of them continued to seek a formal union in the planned royal marriage between George and Warwick's daughter, Isabel.

That planned marriage, though initially opposed by Edward IV, had been supported by his mother, who may even have been present when it was finally celebrated at Calais in 1469.[3] Warwick and Clarence were themselves then using Calais as their base for opposition to Edward and his policies. However, Warwick also had a rebellion incited against Edward IV in the north of England. The figurehead leader of that rebellion was known as 'Robin of Redesdale'. Probably, in reality, he was

Sir William Conyers of Marske, but the false name he used was based upon that of the legendary 'Robin Hood'.[4] Naturally, one of the chief demands of 'Robin of Redesdale' and his rebels was that all the Widvilles should be removed from power.

So although, unfortunately, as part of the mythology of 'history', Warwick has become widely known as 'the Kingmaker', originally neither he nor his son-in-law, George, Duke of Clarence, had any plan for *dethroning* Edward IV in 1469 and substituting another sovereign. Basically they were not anti-Edward, they were merely anti-Widville. In other words, their aim was to restore Edward IV to a true Yorkist stance as they perceived it. Thus, presumably, the logical outcome of the Widville removal would have been for Warwick and Clarence to take on the role of the king's chief advisors, thus making those two politically correct Yorkists the new power behind the throne.

The Earl of Warwick and his new son-in-law publicly sided with the ongoing uprising in the north of England by issuing their own joint manifesto against the Widvilles and their 'deceivable covetous rule' of England.[5] They also sailed home from Calais to Sandwich. They then rode to Canterbury, where they invited the men of Kent to support their anti-Widville movement. As for the king himself, based on the advice he received from various lords (Lord Hastings, Lord Mountjoy, Sir Thomas Montgomery and others) – who probably understood very well what was going on, and Warwick's motivation – he himself took no direct action against 'Robin of Redesdale'.

Warwick and Clarence progressed from Canterbury to London. They then continued towards Coventry. On Wednesday 26 July 1469 they fought the battle of Edgecote Moor against forces loyal to Edward IV. Their opponents in the battle included two members of the Widville family. They were Elizabeth Widville's father, Richard, Lord Rivers, and his second surviving son, John Widville. Both men were captured and taken prisoner.

They were then given a speedy show trial. Richard Neville, Earl of Warwick, finally had his long-term enemy namesake, Richard Widville, executed at Kenilworth on 12 August 1469. Elizabeth's younger brother, John Widville, who had rather bizarrely become Warwick's youthful uncle (being the husband of Warwick's aunt, the much older Catherine Neville, dowager Duchess of Norfolk) was also beheaded alongside his father.

Father – Richard Widville, 1st Earl Rivers – executed Kenilworth, 12 August 1469

2nd brother - Anthony Widville, 2nd Earl Rivers – executed Pontefract, 25 June 1483

3rd brother - John Widville - executed Kenilworth, 12 August 1469

Son – Sir Richard Grey – executed Pontefract, 25 June 1483

Brother-in-law – Henry, Duke of Buckingham – executed Salisbury, 2 November 1483

Executed relatives of Elizabeth Widville.

Their execution was followed by the capture of Edward IV himself. The king was staying at Olney when he suddenly found himself taken prisoner.

> The king … felt that he had been betrayed, and prepared all his men to go and confront his brother the Duke of Clarence and his cousin of Warwick, who were coming before him. They were between Warwick and Coventry when they received the news that the king was coming to see them. … it was not then to be believed that his brother of Clarence, nor his cousin of Warwick would think of treason when meeting him in person; wherefore the king proceeded to a village nearby and there he lodged all his men not far from the place where the Earl of Warwick was staying. At about midnight the Archbishop of York came to the king with a large party of armed men. He went right up to the king's lodging, saying to those who guarded his person that he needed to speak to the king, to whom they announced him; but the king sent him a reply that he was resting and that he should come in the morning when he would be happy to receive him. Which response did not please the archbishop, so he again sent his messengers to the king a second time, to say that he had to speak to him. When they did this the king ordered that he should be allowed in, in order to hear what he wanted to say, for he had no doubts regarding his loyalty. When the archbishop had entered the chamber, where he found the king in bed, he quickly said to him 'Sire, get up', from which the king wished to excuse himself, saying that he hadn't yet had any rest. But the archbishop, false and disloyal as he was,

said to him a second time: 'You must get up and come to my brother of Warwick, for you cannot resist this.' And the king, thinking that nothing worse could happen to him, got dressed, and the archbishop led him without making much noise to the place where the said earl and the duke of Clarence were, between Warwick and Coventry.[6]

As a result, Edward IV found himself detained at Warwick Castle. Meanwhile it must have looked as though the Earl of Warwick and his son-in-law the Duke of Clarence had now achieved their aim and become the effective power behind the throne.

However, Warwick and his son-in-law had so far only got rid of two members of Elizabeth Widville's family. There remained many others to remove. Amongst the most important of them were Elizabeth herself and her mother. Of course, Jacquette had now become a widow once again. In September 1469 she clearly found herself targeted as the next intended victim of the anti-Widville campaign. Thomas Wake, one of the Earl of Warwick's followers, produced a significant piece of material evidence against her, in the form of an 'image of lede made lyke a man of armes, conteynyng the lengthe of a mannes fynger, and broken in the myddes, and made fast with a wyre.'[7] Clearly the alleged descendant of the water-fay, Melusine – who owned a book by Jean d'Arras on the subject of her reputed sorcerous ancestress[8] – was now finding herself publicly accused of sorcery.

Clear evidence certainly exists to show that in fifteenth-century England there was belief in magic. For example, in the first half of that century the Queen dowager, Joanna of Navarre (widow of King Henry IV) found herself accused of committing witchcraft against him by her stepson, King Henry V, and subsequently Joanna's step-daughter-in-law, the childless Eleanor Cobham, Duchess of Gloucester (sister-in-law of Jacquette de St Pol and her first husband, the Duke of Bedford), seems to have begun taking magic potions which were produced for her by the London potion maker Margery Jourdemayne. Henry V's accusation against his step mother may merely have been a political manoeuvre on his part. As for Eleanor Cobham, her simple aim was to attempt to conceive an heir for her husband (Henry VI's uncle).

However, Margery Jourdemayne was also believed to have other talents, including the ability to foretell the future. For example, she is reported to have told Edmund Beaufort (who later became Duke of Somerset) that he would die at 'the Castle', and he was eventually killed at the first battle of St Albans, at that town's 'Castle Inn'.

As a result of Margery Jourdemayne's reputation for fortelling of the future, in a hostile political environment Eleanor Cobham had found herself accused of having consulted Margery, not only in respect of possible childbirth, but also regarding the death-date of King Henry VI. Margery Jourdemayne was then arrested. She was searched, and it was claimed that amongst her possessions a small and partially melted wax image of a man was found. That was alleged to be a wax figure of the young king, and its partial melting was said to mean that Margery had been using spells to make the king ill.

Margery was therefore tried, found guilty of witchcraft, and burnt at the stake on 27 October 1441. As for her client, Eleanor Cobham, she was

Witchcraft, using a figurine.

also arrested. Although she admitted using Margery's skills in an attempt to help her conceive, she denied the treasonable charges in respect of the king's life. Nevertheless, she was found guilty of treason, was forced to do a public walk of penance through the streets of London, and was then imprisoned for the rest of her life.

One less widely-known piece of evidence of witchcraft in fifteenth-century England is that in 1466–67 the town of Colchester had its own mysterious *sortilega* (fortune teller) living within the medieval town walls in the parish of St Martin.[9] Of course, Colchester cannot have been unique in that respect. As in the case of 'Margery Jourdemayne', the name of the Colchester fortune teller seems rather unusual. She was called Jeweyn Blakecote. Unfortunately it appears that, like Margery, she cannot have been able to predict her own future, because Jeweyn's surviving records reveal her prosecution and heavy fining for what she had been doing.

In fact, all the surviving evidence in respect of the sorcery of Margery Jourdemayne, Eleanor Cobham and Jeweyn Blakecote comprises records of the legal proceedings which were brought against those three women. We also have similar extensive surviving evidence in respect of the case which was then brought against Jacquette de St Pol. And a few years after the case against Jacquette, some associates of George, Duke of Clarence, also found themselves condemned in respect of magic processes which they had allegedly used against the king. Once again it is the legal issue involved which has preserved the evidence.

Obviously the casting of the sovereign's horoscope – or any other use of magic against the king – was condemned by the medieval English state as treasonable activity. As for the Church, until the fifteenth century that body seems generally to have taken a fairly tolerant view of some supernatural activities, such as the casting of horoscopes, endeavours to produce gold, attempts to recover items which had been lost, and seeking to improve the weather. But in respect of love spells, because some of those had apparently started to include the misuse of Church sacraments coupled with the employment of menstrual blood, the Church, despite earlier tolerance, was beginning to condemn them.[10]

The fifteenth century also appears to show an increase in alleged attempts to harm or destroy enemies through the use of figurines. The small human figurines used for such casting of spells were often made of wax. But in fifteenth-century England it seems that lead figurines were sometimes employed. In every case of this sort the figurine in question represented the person who was being subjected to spellcasting. It was thought that magic could either be used to harm a person via a figurine or to influence their conduct. For example, sometimes the use of such figurines might form part of any attempt to snare a victim into a love affair. As we have seen, it was alleged in England that, with her mother's help, Elizabeth Widville may have used love spells to entrap Edward IV.

Obviously, however, the lead figurine which Thomas Wake produced as a solid piece of evidence against Jacquette had not been used for the working of love spells. The image in question must have been employed in an attempt to cause harm, because it had been broken in the middle, and ensnared in wire. Possibly, the intended victim had been the Earl of Warwick, though the surviving records of the case brought against Jacquette actually contain no evidence specifying the identity of the person in question.

However, Thomas Wake also claimed that he had other evidence to offer. He cited John Daunger, a parish clerk from Northamptonshire, whom Wake declared would certify that Jacquette had also made images of Edward IV and of her own daughter, Elizabeth. In other words the case brought against Jacquette definitely included the allegation that spells had been cast to unite the king with his Widville consort, and that figurines had formed part of that spell-casting process.

At the time when the case was initially brought against Jacquette it must have seemed that the Earl of Warwick was winning his attempt to oust the Widvilles and to restore himself as the power behind the throne. But eventually, of course, he failed. Although he was briefly held in the custody of his cousin, Warwick – and also his middle brother, George, Duke of Clarence – subsequently, supported by his incredibly loyal (and apparently less anti-Widville) younger brother, Richard, Duke of Gloucester, Edward IV regained both his own freedom and his royal power. On Tuesday 6 March 1470 he met his middle brother, the Duke of Clarence at their mother's London home – Baynard's Castle.[11] Probably, their mother was attempting to reconcile her two sons. The meeting of those two brothers appeared to be friendly on that occasion. Indeed, following the meeting they left their mother's abode together and walked the very short distance to St Paul's Cathedral, where the two brothers made a joint offering. Unfortunately, however, conflict still existed between them and both brothers were still seeking supporters.

It was when Edward IV had reclaimed royal power and independence that Jacquette submitted her petition to him in respect of the witchcraft accusation brought against her while Warwick had been holding power. The text of her petition to the king, and the judgement which was then reached will be presented shortly. Meanwhile, finding himself categorised as a traitor by Edward IV, Warwick deserted the house of York and then tried to restore King Henry VI. Ultimately he was to find himself defeated and killed at the battle of Barnet. As a result, *his* original records in respect of the evidence used against Jacquette have not survived.

Thus the only evidence which we have surviving is the evidence which was cited in the context of Jaquette's subsequent petition to Edward IV for the case brought against her by Warwick to be quashed. Sadly, we also have no precise record of how far the case against Jacquette had actually been taken under the Earl of Warwick. Obviously, Jacquette had not been burnt at the stake – though that could well have been what Warwick was hoping for. However, it certainly cannot have been the case that under Warwick Jacquette had been formally judged to be innocent. Indeed, the fact that Jacquette later felt that she had to submit a petition to Edward IV makes it appear likely that judgement against her may more or less have been reached by the judges working on her prosecution under Warwick, even though no precise record survives in that respect.

But of course, because the political situation had then changed once again, Jacquette's subsequent petition to Edward IV proved successful. By the judges appointed by Edward she was officially cleared of all the charges which had been made against her. Edward IV would always have been extremely unlikely to support the view that Elizabeth's mother had seduced him by sorcery into his union with her daughter.

Naïvely, however, that final outcome has often been seen by historians as revealing the truth – rather as Henry VII's later judgements in respect of Richard III have been so perceived. In reality the only thing which can be said for certain is that Edward IV's clearing of Jacquette was carried out when he was in power, and that it was then politically correct from his point of view.

In other words it is actually impossible now to accurately evaluate the case brought against Jacquette by Warwick. The casting of love spells to unite Edward and Elizabeth had definitely been considered a possibility ever since the autumn of 1464, when the union of that couple had been publicly recognised. What is more, the same view was voiced again later, in 1483 and 1484, as part of the official evidence which was then brought against the union in question. Thus, in spite of her eventual, unsurprising vindication by Edward IV when he had regained power, one cannot simply assume that the case brought against Jacquette by Warwick had all merely been invented.

On 19 January 1469/70, however, Jacquette found herself formally exonerated in respect of the charges which had been made against her. The two key witnesses had then been made to effectively withdraw their earlier evidence. On 10 February 1469/70 the final official verdict was communicated to the Lord Chancellor, Bishop Robert Stillington, as follows:

> Edward by the grace of God, kyng of Englond and of Fraunce, and lord of Irland, to the reverent fader in God Robert byshope of Bathe and Wells, oure chaunceller, greting. Forasmoche as we send unto you within these oure lettres the tenure of an acte of oure grete counsail, amonge othir thinges, remaynyng in thoffice of oure prive seal, in fourme as folowith.
>
> In the chambre of the grete counsaill, callid the parliment-chambre, within the kyngs paleis att Westminster, the x day of Februarie, the ix[th] yere of the regne of oure Soveraygne Lord the Kyng Edward the IIIIth, in the presence of the same oure soveraigne lord, and my lordis of his grete counsail, whos names ben under writen, a supplicacion addressed unto oure said soveraygne lord, on the behalf of the high and noble princesse Jaquet Duchesse of Bedford, and two sedules in papier annexed unto the same supplicacion, were openly, by oure saide soveraygne lordis commaundement, radde; and aftirward his highnes, by thavis of my said lordis of his grete counsaill, acceptyng eftsones the declaracion of my said lady specified in the said supplicacion, accordyng to the peticion of my said lady, commaunded the same to be enacted of record, and therupon lettres of exemplification to be made under his grete seal in due fourme; the tenure of the supplicacion and cedules, wherof above is made mention, hereafter ensue in this wyse.[12]

The official signature of King Edward IV, in the form 'R E' (*Rex Edwardus*).

The petition received by the king from Jacquette states her identity and her Christian faith. It then cites the case brought against her earlier by Thomas Wake, with the rather strange assertion that he was thereby breaking the law. It also states that Wake asked John Daunger to submit additional evidence against her, but claims that Daunger would not do so. The petition is quoted by the king as follows:

> To the kyng oure soveraygne lord;

> Shewith and lamentably complayneth unto your highnes your humble and true liegewoman Jaquet Duchesse of Bedford, late the wyf of your true and faithfull knyght and liegeman Richard late Erle of Ryvers, that where shee at all tyme hath, and yit doth, truely beleve on God accordyng to the feith of Holy Chirche, as a true cristen woman owith to doo, yet Thomas Wake squier, contrarie to the lawe of God, lawe of this land, and all reason and good consciens, in the tyme of the late trouble and riotous season, of his malicious disposition towardes your said oratrice of long tyme continued, entendyng not oonly to hurt and apaire her good name and fame, but also purposed the fynall distruccion of

her persone, and to that effecte caused her to be brought in a comune noyse and disclaundre of wychecraft thorouout a grete part of this youre reaume, surmytting that she shuld have usid wichecraft and sorcerie, insomuche as the said Wake caused to be brought to Warrewyk atte your last beyng there, soveraigne lord, to dyvers of the lords thenne beyng ther present, a image of lede made lyke a man of armes, conteynyng the lengthe of a mannes fynger, and broken in the myddes, and made fast with a wyre, sayyng that it was made by your said oratrice to use with the said wichcraft and sorsory, where she, ne noon for her ne be her, ever sawe it, God knowith. And over this, the said Wake, for the perfourmyng of his malicious entent abovesaid, entreted oon John Daunger, parishe clerk of Stoke Brewerne, in the counte of Northampton, to have said that there were two other images made by your said oratrice, oon for you, soveraygne lord, and anothir for oure soveraigne lady the quene, wherunto the said John Daunger neyther coude ne wolde be entreted to say. Wheruppon it lykid your highnesse, of your noble grace, atte humble sute made unto your highnesse by your said oratrice, for her declaracion in the premisses, to send for the said Wake and the said John Daunger, commaundyng them to attende upon the reverent fadir in God the bishop of Carlisle [Edward Story, formerly Chancellor of the University of Cambridge, and Elizabeth Widville's confessor], the honorable lord therle of Northumberland [Henry Percy, 4th Earl], and the worshipfull lords lord Hastyngs and Mountjoye [Walter Blount, 1st Baron Mountjoy], and mayster Roger Radclyff, to be examined by them of such as they coude allegge and say anenst your said oratrice in this behalf; thaxaminacions afore them had apperith in wrytinge herunto annexed; wherof oon bill is conteyning the sayings of Wake, and writte with his owne hand; and anothir shewyng the saiyngs of the said Daunger, and wrete in the presence of the said lords; which seen by your highnesse, and many othir lords in this your grete councell, the xx day of January last passed, then beyng there present, your said oratrice was by your grace and theime takyn clerid and declared of the said noises and disclaundres, which as yet remaygneth not enacted; forsomuch as divers your lords were then absent. Wherfor please it your highnesse, of your most habundant grace and grete rightwisnesse, tenderly to consider the premisses, and the declaracion of your said oratrice had in this behalf, as is afore shewid, to commaunde the same to be enacted in this youre said grete counsaill, so as the same her declaration may allway remaigne there of record, and that she may have it exemplified undir your grete seall: And she shall continually pray to God for the preservacion of your most royal estate.[13]

In her petition Jacquette states clearly that Edward IV has had Thomas Wake and John Daunger re-examined by the Bishop of Carlisle (who happened to be Elizabeth Widville's chaplain), the Earl of Northumberland and others. Thus the evidence from Wake and Daunger which is then included in the record of Jacquette's acquittal, is not what either of them had said originally. Instead, it is an updated version, which had been produced as a result of their investigation by the bishop, who also happened to be the chaplain of Jacquette's daughter.

The updated evidence of Thomas Wake is presented as follows:

Thomas Wakes bille.

Sir, this ymage was shewed and left in Stoke [Stoke Bruerne, a mile to the east of Shutlanger – see below] with an honest persone, which delyverid it to the clerk of the said chirche, and so shewid to dyvers neighbours, aftir to the parson in the chirche openly to men both of Shytlanger [Shutlanger, a small village in south Northamptonshire, five miles east of Towcester, 7 miles south of Northampton, 11 miles north of Milton Keynes, and less than 2 miles north of the Woodville manor at Grafton Regis] and Stoke; and aftir it was shewed in Sewrisley a nounry [Sewardsley Priory – originally a small but independant house of Cistercian nuns in Showsley, just north of Shutlanger, but from 1460 a cell of the Cluniac abbey of St Mary de la pré, Northampton], and to many other dyvers persones, as it is said, &c. And of all this herd I nor wist no thyng, till after it was sent me by Thomas Kymbell

Stoke Bruerne.

from the said clerc, which I suppose be called John Daunger, which cam home to me, and told me as I have said to my lord of Carlille and to your maistershipp, from which saying as by herdsay I neither may nor will vary. And yf any persone will charge me with more than I have said, I shall discharge me as shall accord with my trouthe and dutee.[14]

Thomas Wake makes it clear that the evidence which he presented in respect of the figurine genuinely was what he had heard about it – though of course he does not specifically name Jacquette as the owner on this occasion. In other words he is not actually withdrawing his former case, but for the sake of his own safety he is now being rather careful in respect of what he says.

Wake also reveals that he did not actually know Daunger personally. Moreover, he himself had had no prior awareness of the existence of the broken lead figurine which he had presented as physical evidence until the object in question had been sent to him by his bailiff, Thomas Kymbell. Wake's evidence also reveals that from Kymbell he heard that a number of people in Shutlanger and the surrounding area were aware of the existence of the figurine. Moreover, the object in question had reportedly been examined both by the local parish priest and by the nuns of Sewardsley Priory. It is also interesting to observe that Wake makes no mention in his surviving evidence of the existence of other figurines representing Edward IV and Elizabeth Widville. Thus, in reality, the only person who referred to two such figurines in the presence of those who were rejudging the case under Edward IV was actually John Daunger – in spite of the fact that his mention of them was actually in the form of a denial that he had ever mentioned them.

Next the evidence of John Daunger is cited:

> John Daungers bille.
>
> John Daunger, of Shetyllanger [Shutlanger], sworn and examined, saith, that Thomas Wake send unto hym oon Thomas Kymbell, that tyme beyng his bailly, and bad the said John to send hym the ymage of led that he had, and so the said John sent it by the said Thomas Kymbell, att which tyme the same John said that he herd never noo wichecraft of my lady of Bedford. Item, the same John saith, that the said ymage was delyvered unto hym by oon Harry Kyngeston of Stoke; the which Harry fonde it in his owne hous after departyng of soudeours. Item, the same John saith, that the said Thomas Wake, after he cam from London, fro the kyng, send for hym and said that he had excused hymsylf and leyd all the blame to the said John; and therfor he bad the said John say that he durst not kepe the said image, and that he was the cause he send it to the said Thomas Wake. Item, the same John saith, that the said Thomas Wake bad hym say that ther was two othir ymages, oon for the kyng, and anothir for the quene; but the said John denyed to say soo.[15]

Obviously John Daunger is behaving more cautiously and carefully in the current situation than Thomas Wake. Daunger states that although he had handling of the lead figurine he does not know that it had belonged to Jacquette. However, it does seem that John Daunger was personally acquainted with Jacquette, whose manor of Grafton Regis was located less than two miles away from his own home in Shutlanger. Also, as his bill shows, Daunger does now refuse to speak of images of Edward and Elizabeth. Moreover, he asserts that Wake had invented the story of those other figurines. However, we have also seen that Wake's testimony (or lack thereof) did not accord with Daunger's in that respect.

In effect it appears that, in the new political situation, the two key witnesses against Jacquette had been effectively dissuaded and prevented from making a case against her. However, why are there only two cited witnesses? The key person who made the connection between Jacquette, the broken lead figurine and the sorcery allegation appears to have been Thomas Kymbell. After all, it was Kymbell who had the evidence sent to Wake. It therefore seems to be a highly suspicious point that apparently Thomas Kymbell was never interrogated by Edward IV's judges.

Finally, those present when Jacquette was found innocent are listed as follows:

> Present my lords whos names foloweth; that is to say, my lordis the cardinall and archebishop of Caunterbury [Thomas Bourchier], tharchebishop of York [George Neville – Warwick's brother], the byshops of Bathe, chauncellor of Englond [Robert Stillington – who had married Edward IV to Eleanor Talbot], Elye, tresorer of Englonde [William Grey], Rouchester, keper of the privie seal [Thomas Rotherham, *alias* Scott], London [Thomas Kempe], Duresme [Lawrence Booth], and Karlill [Edward Story]; therls of Warrewyk, Essex, Northumberland, Shrewsbury, and Kent; the lords Hastings, Mountjoye, Lyle, Crowmell, Scrope of Bolton, Say, &c.[16]

Significantly, Warwick and his younger brother, George, Archbishop of York, had apparently both been present. Elizabeth Widville, who had recently lost her father and her brother, John, must have been relieved to see her mother made safe.

Although her reputation had now officially been restored, it is possible that Jacquette may already have been feeling unwell in 1470. At all events, she did not long survive the judgement which was reached in her favour. She died two and a quarter years later, on 30 May 1472. So, in the end, Elizabeth did also lose her mother – albeit not in the manner which the

Earl of Warwick might possibly have had in mind. Incidentally, it is not known where Jacquette's body was buried and although she seems to have made a will, the text of that document does not survive.

Nevertheless, eleven years after her death, in 1483, the witchcraft accusation against Jacquette was voiced again. It was referred to then in connection with the formal recognition of Edward IV's earlier marriage to Eleanor Talbot and the consequent questioning of the validity of his subsequent secret Widville marriage. Obviously the Talbot marriage issue had not been mentioned at the earlier court hearings, in 1470, when Jacquette was still alive. But in 1483 the accusation of sorcery was specifically linked with the theory that Jacquette had wished to secure her daughter's union with the king.

In the end it is impossible to judge now whether Jacquette may ever have used sorcery. Her own claim of innocence could just be seen as partisan, likewise the accusation made against her by Warwick could be seen in the same light. Although no clear evidence exists in either direction in respect of her case, it is clear on the basis of other evidence (presented earlier) that the possibility of attempting to use the power of the occult was by no means unheard of in fifteenth-century England. Thus if Jacquette had heard from her daughter that the young king fancied her, but that for her own part Elizabeth was unwilling to become his mistress, then using spells to try to win over Edward IV into making an offer of marriage might well have seemed a logical way forward. Also, there is no surviving evidence to show that Jacquette ever acted maliciously in any way. Of course, when she had experienced nearly ten years of family insults from the Earl of Warwick, she would probably not have liked him much. If she then heard that he had put her husband and one of her children to death, she might possibly have tried using a figurine of him in order to attempt to punish him a bit for what he was doing to her family.

Chapter 13

The first Crown Loss

Although initially he appeared to have regained royal power, by the autumn of 1470 Edward IV had lost it again, and found himself fleeing with his younger brother, the Duke of Gloucester, to the Low Countries. Elizabeth Widville had obviously not been with Edward when he had found himself imprisoned by his cousin, Warwick. But she manifestly had been with him around the time when her mother was officially being judged innocent, because in about February 1469/70 she began another pregnancy, which was to have the significance of seeming to produce a male heir for Edward IV (see above, Chapter 7, for Elizabeth's list of royal conceptions).

However, from September 1470 until March 1470/71 Edward was in exile. During those months Elizabeth Widville was not with him. She was alone in the London area. And since London had once again acknowledged the Lancastrian King Henry VI and was expecting the eventual return of *his* queen consort, Margaret of Anjou, Elizabeth had obviously ceased to be able to claim royal rank. At this period she was merely referred to as 'the Qwen that was'.[1] Thus, Elizabeth felt obliged to seek sanctuary in Westminster Abbey.

Of course, when she claimed sanctuary she did not sleep within the abbey church itself. Nor did she live with the Benedictine monks of Westminster in the domestic buildings of their religious house. Unfortunately the sanctuary building in which she must have lodged is now no longer in existence. It was pulled down in the eighteenth century.

> The Broad Sanctuary is the name applied to that short portion of the public street which passes to the north and west of the Abbey, continuing onward under the name of Victoria

Street: and reminds us of the right of Sanctuary which once belonged to this monastery, ... and of the very strong stone fortress which once stood here, ... called The Sanctuary, a house of refuge for the distressed. It was a massive, gloomy stone fortress built by the Confessor, strong enough to withstand a siege. It had a cruciform chapel attached to it, which those who sought refuge here were expected to attend. ... Near by the Sanctuary stood the old Belfry Tower in which the Abbey bells were hung.[2]

Thus, while Elizabeth may not have attended the Benedictine religious offices in the abbey church itself, and may not have met most of the Westminster monks, she must have heard all the bells ringing to call those Benedictines to their hours of prayer.

She went to the Westminster Abbey sanctuary accompanied by her re-widowed mother, and by her three young daughters, Elizabeth (aged 4), Mary (aged 3) and Cecily (aged 18 months). It was in that location – in the vicinity of the present street bearing the name Broad Sanctuary – that the restored Lady Grey then found herself giving birth to a son (christened Edward, after his father) early in November 1470. The precise date of that birth is slightly unclear, and fifteenth-century documents exist citing both 2 November and 3 November. At his baptism, Thomas Millyng, Abbot of Westminster, and the Westminster Prior, John Estney, were the little boy's two godfathers, and Lady Scrope (see below) was his godmother. Later, as we have seen, all Elizabeth Widville's royal children were officially judged to be illegitimate. Ironically, however, not only was little Edward (later 'Edward V') born a bastard – he was also born as a commoner, since on the date of his birth his father was not England's king. Indeed he was not even the Duke of York or the Earl of March.

The new Lancastrian government commissioned Elizabeth, Lady Scrope (*née* St John – one of the older half-sisters of Lady Margaret Beaufort, Countess of Richmond, Lady Stafford) to keep an eye on Lady Grey, her mother and daughters in the Abbey sanctuary. She was paid £10 for that service.[3] Probably Lady Scrope was not pestilential in her supervision, because food was provided for the group (see below). Subsequently Lady Scrope was pardoned for the role she had fulfilled in that respect by Edward IV when he was restored to power.[4]

After his return Edward also gave the following reward to the London butcher, William Gould, who had supplied Elizabeth with meat while she has been in the sanctuary at Westminster.

By the King.

RIGHT reverend fadre in God, right trusty and welbeloved, We grete you well; lating you wit that for the grete kyndnesse and true Hert that oure welbeloved William Gould, citezen of London, bocher, shewed unto us and unto oure derrest wife the Quene, in our last absence out of this oure Roialme, every weke, than yeving unto hir for the sustentacion of hir houshold half a beef and ij. motons; and also aftir oure Feld of Tewkysbury, at her being in the Towre, brought C. oxen into a medow beside our said Towre for the [ki]lling of the same, wherof the Kentishmen, and other at tymes, oure rebells, shipmen, toke of the saide bests I. and ledde away . . . an to his great hurt and damage, We have yeven and graunted unto the saide William, in recompense of his said hurts, and for other causes us moeving, our Letters of licence, that he by himself, his factours, or attorneys, maye charge a Ship called the Trynyte of London, of the portage of xxx. ton or within, in any porte or place of this oure Roialme, with oxe hids, ledde, talowe, and alle other merchandises except staple ware, and the saide Ship, so charged and defensibly araied for the defense of the same, with suche a maistre and nowmbre of mariners as the saide William, his factours or attornes, shall name unto you in oure Chancerye, to goo out of this oure saide Roialme into what parties by yonde the Sea it shall like him or theim; and there to discharge and recharge the same Ship with all maner goods and merchandises leefull; and retourne into this oure saide Roialme, and all other places under oure obeissance: and so to discharge and recharge the saide Ship, with the saide goods, wares, and merchandises, and goo and corn as often as it shall please him or theim, during con hoole yere, without any lett or impediment of us or eny of oure officers and ministres; paing unto us therfor all maner costumes, subsides, and duetees unto us for the same due and apperteynyng, any act, statute, ordinance, provision, or restraint hadde or made into the contrarye notwithstanding. Wherfore we wol and charge you that undir oure Prive Scale, being in youre ward, ye do make herupon our Letters to be directed unto oure Chancellor of England, commaunding him by the same to make herupon our Letters Patentes undir oure Great Scale in due forme, and thies our Letters shal be your warrant. Yeven undir oure Signet at our Palois of Westminster the xxiiij. day of Feverier ... of our reign.

FREMAN.

To the reverend fadre in God our right trusty and welbeloved the Bishop of Rochester, keper of our Prive Seale.[5]

However, it seems rather strange that Elizabeth and her companions were said to have been supplied with half a beef and two muttons *every week* during their stay in sanctuary. After all Wednesday 27 February 1470/1 had been Ash Wednesday, the fast day which marks the commencement of Lent. And Edward IV had only returned to London – and visited Elizabeth at Westminster – four days before the end of Lent. Thus for the last six weeks of her stay in sanctuary Elizabeth should not have been eating any meat. What is more, a virtuous woman would probably also have avoided – or at least minimised – the eating of meat earlier, during the penitential season of Advent which led up to Christmas. If she did eat meat regularly during Advent, and more notably if she ate *any meat at all* during Lent (when it was forbidden), Elizabeth Widville obviously cannot have been virtuous, faithful or well-behaved from a religious point of view.

Contemporary evidence for other households confirms clearly that religious observances in respect of diet were well maintained in the fifteenth century. For example, the Howard accounts for January and February 1465/6, clearly mark the beginning of Lent by showing that Sir John (later Lord) Howard and his family abstained from meat on Ash Wednesday. On that day they ate salt fish, white herring, plaice and fresh cod.[6] Further evidence for the observance of Lent can be found later in Howard's career. For example, during the period 20–24 March 1480/1 records survive of purchases of food which include shellfish

Pope Sixtus IV.

(whelks and oysters), salted fish (including eels) and a variety of fresh fish, comprising salmon, herring, plaice, eels, cod, and 'stokfish' (dried fish). Nuts, spices and dried fruit were also purchased during that Lenten period, but no meat.[7] Similarly the surviving household book of Dame Alice de Bryene of Acton (near Sudbury in Suffolk), covering the year 1412–13, shows clearly that her household ate no meat from Ash Wednesday (8 March 1412/3) until Easter Sunday (23 April 1413). At the end of Lent, on the Feast Day of the Resurrection, beef, pork, bacon and pigeons were eaten. But throughout the intervening weeks of the penitential period only fish, including herrings, haddock, cod, plaice, turbot, salt fish and stockfish [dried fish], shellfish, including oysters, whelks and mussels, and eels were purchased.[8]

Curiously, however, it does seem that Elizabeth Widville may later have been influential in promoting the use of the rosary, and in introducing the praying of the *Angelus*, in England. Both of those prayer patterns focus on the easily memorisable recitation of the 'Hail Mary'.[9] On 2 January 1480/1, at St. Peter's, Rome, Pope Sixtus IV issued the following ruling in respect of correspondence which he had apparently received from Elizabeth.[10]

The pope lately ordered the feast of the Visitation of St. Mary the Virgin to St. Elizabeth, and its octave, to be everywhere celebrated annually on 6 *Non. Julii* (2 July), and the newly instituted office to be recited, and granted certain indulgences. It has been recently set forth to him by Elizabeth, queen of England, that within the octaves of the said feast there are other very solemn feasts in England, which are very devoutly kept by both clergy and people, so that the said office cannot be sung on those feasts.

The saints whose feasts would actually have been celebrated during the octave in question were: 2 July, St Swithin; 3 July, St Thomas (apostle); 4 July, St Martin; 5 July, St Ireneus; 6 July, St Seburga; 7 July, St Thomas Becket (secondary feast marking the translation of his relics); 8 July, St Grimbald (French); St Margaret, Anglo-Saxon princess, Queen of Scotland; 9 July, St Everilda (Anglo-Saxon); 10 July, St Canute of Denmark. It is therefore rather difficult to see how those feasts would have been a major problem. Nevertheless,

> At the petition, therefore, of the said queen, containing that she has a singular devotion for the feast of the Visitation, the pope, in order that she and the faithful of those parts may not be deprived of the said indulgences on the said feasts, hereby ordains that all the faithful of the realm who, in addition to the recital of the office usually recited on the said feasts within the said octave, recite also in choir or privately the office of the octaves of the feast of the Visitation, or are present at the recital thereof, shall, being penitent and having confessed, gain the same indulgences as they would gain if they recited the office of the said octaves as the principal office of the day,[11] or were present thereat. Moreover, seeing that, as the pope has learned, there is observed in divers parts of the world a certain new way of praying, newly and not without great devotion invented, called the Psalter of the Blessed Virgin Mary,[12] to wit, that any one wishing to pray in this way daily says, to the honour of the same Blessed Virgin Mary and against the threatening perils of the world, as many times the Angelical Salutation 'Ave Maria' as there are psalms in the Psalter of David,[13] namely, a hundred and fifty times, saying the Lord's Prayer once every ten salutations,[14] the pope, approving the said way of praying, hereby grants to all the faithful of the realm, present and future, each time they pray in the said way, for each fifty [psalms] of the Psalter a relaxation of five years and five quarantines of enjoined penance. Furthermore, seeing that both in those parts and throughout almost the whole of Christendom the bells are wont to be rung for the Salutation of the Virgin Mary at dawn and noon and sunset, in order to stir up the devotion of the faithful to salute Her,

and seeing that the queen desires the devotion of the faithful of the realm for the said Salutation to be increased more and more, the pope grants by these presents (which shall hold good in perpetuity as far as regards all the aforesaid) to all of the said faithful who, being penitent and having confessed, when the bells are rung at dawn or noon or eventide[15] for the said Salutation, kneel and devoutly say, at least once, the Angelical Salutation,[16] a hundred days of indulgence for each time they do so. Moreover, inasmuch as it would be difficult for these presents to be borne to all places in which there would be need of them, the pope hereby decrees that a notarial copy, bearing the seal of an ecclesiastical court or of a bishop or other prelate or ecclesiastical dignitary, shall receive the same credence as if the present original letters were exhibited.

Overall, the role of religion in Elizabeth's life remains unclear, despite the fact that attempts have been made in the past to advance certain claims in that respect.[17] For example, we know that 'on 12 July 1466 the city of London agreed that she should have a piece of land at Tower Hill, next to the Postern, on which to build a chapel or college as she thought best.'[18] But no evidence exists to indicate what – if anything – she ever founded there.

Later, in the 1470s she did found a chapel of St Erasmus beside the Lady Chapel at Westminster Abbey to act as a chantry for the royal family. The chapel had been completed before the first anniversary of the execution of George, Duke of Clarence, because on 13 January 1478/9 Edward IV issued a charter in respect of it.[19] The function of that chapel was to offer prayers for the good estate of Edward and Elizabeth while they were alive, and to pray for their souls – and those of their children – when they were dead.

Mysteriously, David Baldwin has claimed that 'she [Elizabeth Widville] and the King went on pilgrimage to the shrines of St Mary [*sic*] of Walsingham (Norfolk) and St Thomas of Canterbury on a number of occasions.'[20] As his alleged evidence for that claim he then cites 'see for example [Gairdner,] *Paston Letters*, v, p.112'.[21] Genuine evidence certainly does exist to show that Edward IV himself made at least two pilgrimages as the reigning monarch to the shrine of Our Lady of Walsingham in Norfolk. For example, in June 1469 he rode from Norwich to Walsingham

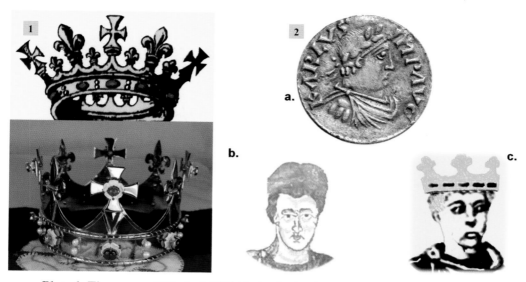

Plate 1: The crown of Elizabeth Widville (as depicted on her seal) compared with the somewhat similar open crown commissioned by the author in 2013 for the subsequent reburial of Richard III, and made by George Easton.

Plate 2: Contemporary 8th- and 9th-century images of Elizabeth Widville's imperial ancestors: a) Charlemagne as depicted on one of his coins; b) Louis the Pious, redrawn from a manuscript illustration; c) Charles the Bald, redrawn from a manuscript illustration.

Plate 3: Elizabeth Widville's alleged ancestress, the water fay Melusine, as depicted in the church at Pucé in the Gironde.

Plate 4: Some of Elizabeth Widville's close male relatives: a) her maternal grandfather, Pierre I, Count of St Pol; b) her maternal first cousin, Pierre II, Count of St Pol; c) her second (and eldest surviving) brother, Anthony Widville, 2nd Earl Rivers (who appears to have resembled his cousin, St Pol) – all redrawn from contemporary manuscript illustrations. They all have dark hair.

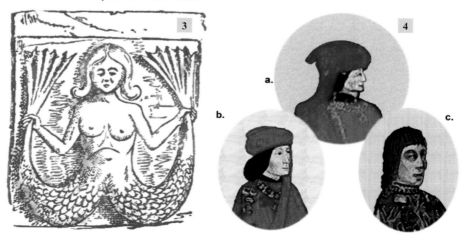

Plate 5: The arms of the house of St Pol.

Plate 6: The first husband of Elizabeth Widville's mother – John of Lancaster, Duke of Bedford (nineteenth-century engraving).

Plate 7: Elizabeth's paternal great grandfather, John Widville, from his tomb slab at St Mary the Virgin Church, GraftonRegis.

Plate 8: The arms of Elizabeth's father, Richard Widville, Earl Rivers.

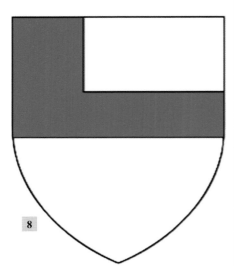

Plate 9: Astley Castle, home of Sir John Grey. (The Creative Commons Attribution-Share Alike 3.0 Unported license.)

Plate 10: Edward Grey, later Viscount Lisle, younger brother of Sir John Grey and brother-in-law of Elizabeth Widville. From his tomb at St Mary's Church, Astley.

Plate 11: A nineteenth-century engraving of a depiction of Elizabeth Widville in a fifteenth-century stained glass window.

Plate 12: Elizabeth Widville depicted in about 1466. Like her maternal line male relatives she appears to have been a brunette with reddish brown hair and brown eyes. (Modern copy of her Queens' College Cambridge portrait, commissioned by the author and presented to Middleham.)

Elizabeth Widville.

Plate 13: Elizabeth Widville's seal as Queen Consort. She displays all her mother's arms as well as her father's. Also she appears to have chosen as her own personal heraldic supporter a *Talbot* hound.

Plate 14: Elizabeth Widville as depicted in a stained glass window at Canterbury Cathedral in about 1480 (redrawn, with the later damage removed).

Plate 15: The arms used by Elizabeth Widville. Ironically her mother's Luxembourg arms have taken the prime position and her father's arms have been moved to the place usually used for female line ancestral arms. Yet her mother had not been the Luxembourg heiress.

Plate 16: Jacquette Widville, Lady Strange, younger sister of Elizabeth, from her brass, St John the Baptist Church, Hillingdon.

Plate 17: The young, tall, slim King Edward IV in about 1461 (nineteenth-century engraving based on the Rous Roll).

Plate 18: The fattening King Edward IV in the 1470s, redrawn from a portrait of that period.

Plate 19: The ailing King Edward IV in the 1480s, as depicted the Royal Window at Canterbury Cathedral.

Plate 20: A young knight and his lady in the 1460s (after German Master E.S.). This suggests how Edward IV might have looked with Eleanor Talbot in 1461 - or with Elizabeth Widville in 1464.

Plate 21: A late eighteenth-century engraving showing an imaginery image of the first meeting of Lady Grey (Elizabeth Widville) with Edward IV. Her father's Widville coat of arms is depicted on the wall above the door.

Plate 22: The main problem: Eleanor Talbot, Lady Boteler. An image commissioned by the author, based on facial reconstructions of the Norwich CF2 skull.

Plate 23: Eleanor's sister, Elizabeth Talbot, Duchess of Norfolk, from the window she gave to Long Melford Church, Suffolk.

Plate 24: Eleanor Talbot as a Carmelite tertiary, from the Coventry Tapestry (courtesy of St Mary's Guildhall and Coventry City Council).

Plate 25: Eleanor Talbot's niece, Elizabeth Talbot, Viscountess Lisle, who married Elizabeth Widville's brother-in-law. A modern copy of Staatliche Museen Preussischer Kulturbesitz, Gemäldegalerie, Berlin, no. 532, commissioned by the author, and presented to Middleham. The original portrait seems to have been painted in Flanders in 1468 by Petrus Christus.

Plate 26: The friend? Elizabeth Lambert, Mistress Shore, as depicted on her brass memorial at Hinxworth Church, Herts.

Plate 27: Other enemies: the arms of Thomas Fitzgerald, Earl of Desmond.

Plate 28: Other enemies: George, Duke of Clarence and his wife (Eleanor Talbot's first cousin), Isabel Neville. Images commissioned by the author from Mark Satchwill, based on contemporary evidence - a painting of George from Wavrin's *Chronicle*, *circa* 1475, and the image of Isabel from the sanctuary arch, Toller Porcorum Church, Dorset.

Plate 29: Elizabeth's royal sons: Edward V and Richard of Shrewsbury, both redawn from images produced in the 1490s.

Plate 30: Richard III (from Coventry Tapestry, courtesy of St Mary's Guildhall and Coventry City Council).

Plate 31: Elizabeth's royal daughter and namesake, Elizabeth of York junior, consort of Henry VII (nineteenth-century engraving).

Plate 32: Henry VII (nineteenth-century engraving).

accompanied by his brother, the Duke of Gloucester, by Sir Thomas Montgomery, Sir John Howard and other courtiers, and by Lord Rivers (Richard Widville), Lord Scales (Anthony Widville) and Sir John Widville.[22] However, Elizabeth Widville was not with the royal party on that occasion. Later, in September 1482, a possibly sickly Edward IV made another pilgrimage to the Norfolk shrine.[23] But again there is no sign that Elizabeth accompanied him.

As for the source cited by Baldwin, that merely says 'the Kyng, and the Qwyen, and moche other pepell, ar ryden and goon to Canterbery, nevyr so moche peple seyn in Pylgrymage hertofor at ones, as men seye.'[24] The event in question apparently took place in September 1471, and it sounds to have been not so much a religious event in terms of its motivation, as a rather grandiose ceremonial royal procession. Of course the surviving Paston letter is simply referring to a single visit to Canterbury. Moreover, there is no mention of a visit of Elizabeth Widville to the Walsingham shrine in this or in any other surviving Paston letter. Thus the claim made by Baldwin in respect of Elizabeth's alleged pilgrimages appears to be totally groundless.

Chapter 14

Dealing with more problems

As we saw earlier, Eleanor Talbot had died at quite a young age in the summer of 1468, and probably her death was to the advantage of her rival, Elizabeth Widville. In the second part of the reign of Edward IV, in the 1470s, several more deaths took place which were also probably to the advantage of Elizabeth Widville in various ways. One of them – the execution of the Duke of Clarence – she is definitely stated to have brought about by at least one contemporary source. It has also been suggested that she was behind the poisoning of the Duchess of Clarence and one of her children. In the present study the hypothesis will also be explored that Elizabeth Widville may have been behind the sudden and unexpected death of Eleanor Talbot's brother-in-law, John Mowbray, Duke of Norfolk, and also behind the executions of various Mowbray and Clarence retainers.

Eleanor Talbot had died at a time when the government had separated her from all her close relatives. In July, when her sister, Elizabeth Talbot, returned to England from Margaret of York's wedding celebrations, as well as having to deal with the legal issues that arose from Eleanor's passing, she also found herself dealing with the government prosecution of certain members of her household.

Of course Elizabeth Talbot's husband was John Mowbray, fourth Duke of Norfolk. He was a cousin of King Edward IV, and a high-ranking nobleman, who, however, was not always in a very stable situation financially. Both his mother, Eleanor Bourchier (died 1474), and his grandmother, Catherine Neville (died 1483) – the two dowager Duchesses of Norfolk – needed support. Moreover, his grandmother had also been given a young husband – John Widville – to support.

It had been on Wednesday 13 July 1468 that Elizabeth Talbot had set off on her crossing from Flanders back to England. She was accompanied by:

> two young gentlemen, that one named John Poyntz, and that other William Alsford, the which were arrested because, in the time of the 'foresaid marriage, they had familiar communication with the Duke of Somerset and his 'complices there, in the which they were both detected of treason: whereupon one Richard Steris [Steers], skinner of London, with those two were beheaded at Tower Hill the 21st day of November.[1]

The claimed reason for the punishment of Elizabeth Talbot's two gentlemen was that contact had been made by them in the Low Countries with the political exile, Edmund Beaufort, who claimed to be the fourth Duke of Somerset. But of course Edmund Beaufort was Elizabeth Talbot's first cousin (their mothers had been sisters), and she had probably always kept in contact with her Beaufort cousins – particularly Edmund's sister Anne, who was residing in the Duchess of Norfolk's own county, and who had recently married a Paston.[2]

The particular contemporary account quoted above states that the two Norfolk servants were called John Poyntz and William Alsford. However, as we shall see, other contemporary sources give slightly different versions of their surnames. Poyntz is elsewhere cited as 'Pounyngys', 'Poynes' and 'Poiner, while the surname Alsford is given as 'Alphey', and 'Alford' (see below). The above account also attributes their execution at Tower Hill to Monday 21 November 1468, in the form of a beheading. As we shall see, other contemporary sources are slightly less precise in terms both of the date and of their fate.

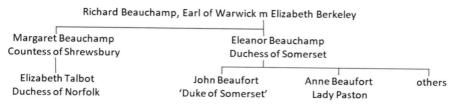

Family Tree 12: Elizabeth Talbot's Beaufort cousins.

An account in Gregory's Chronicle presents the story of this execution of Elizabeth Talbot's two gentlemen within the wider context of a period of various troubles in London. According to Gregory's account, various other people were also being executed in London at that time, or were having their property confiscated.

> That yere [1468] were meny men a pechyd of treson, bothe of the cytte and of othyr townys. Of the cytte Thomas Goke, knyght and aldyrman [Sir Thomas Cook, former mayor of London], and John Plummer, knyght and aldyrman, but the kyng gave hem bothe pardon. And a man of the Lorde Wenlockys, John Haukyns was hys name, was hangyd at Tyburne and beheddyd for treson.
>
> And Umfray Hayforde, the Scheryffe of London, was a pechyd and loste hys cloke for the same mater; and many moo of the cytte loste moche goode for suche maters. Ande that same yere the Kyngys suster, my Lady Margerete, was weddyd unto the Duke of Burgon; and she was brught thedyr with many worschypfulle lordys, knyghtys, and squyers. And the Byschoppe of Salysbury [Richard Beauchamp] resayvyd hyr, for he hadde ben in that londe many dayes before. And sum gentylly men that brought hyr there bare hem soo evylle in hyr gydynge, that they loste hyr heddys at London sone after that they come home. One Rychard Skyrys, squyer, Pounyngys, and Alphey, the iij were by heddyd at the Towre Hylle.[3]

Interestingly, we have already seen that Elizabeth Widville and members of her family were apparently involved in the case against Sir Thomas Cook (see above Chapter 11). There is therefore definite evidence which specifically links the Widville family – and its ambition – to *one* of the legal cases ongoing in London at this point in time. That significant fact raises the question of whether Elizabeth Widville might also have been somehow involved in the contemporary prosecution of other people, including two members of Elizabeth Talbot's entourage, not to mention the possibility that she may somehow have been behind the surprisingly early death of Eleanor Talbot herself, at a moment when Eleanor had found herself completely separated from her closest relatives.

Two other sources exist, which, while they suggest that Elizabeth Talbot's servants, John Poyntz (Pounyngys), and William Alsford (Alphey), were prosecuted, go on to suggest that even though those two men found themselves sentenced to death, they were not actually executed.[4] The two sources in question may well contain errors. For example, they seem confused in respect of the date. Nevertheless, it is worth considering one of them. That is because the source in question makes a link between the actions which were taken against Elizabeth Talbot's servants and other contemporary actions – including the subsequent executions of Elizabeth Widville's father, Earl Rivers, and her brother, John Widville (who, as we have seen, intriguingly happened to have been married to the much older dowager Duchess of Norfolk – Elizabeth Talbot's grandmother-in-law).

> This yere [1468? 1469?], the thursday after Martilmas day [St Martin's Day, 11 November – i.e Thursday 17 November 1468?], Richard Steeres, a seruaunt of the Duke of Excetir, was dampned, and drawyn through the Cite, and behedid at the Tower hill. And vpon the next day [Friday 18 November? – but see the above account which refers to Monday 21 November] wer Alford and poynes drawen to Tybourn there to be hanged and quartered [the above account refers to beheading], but they were pardoned and lived. And sone after was therle of Oxenford arrested for treason. And on Monday the xxj[th] [xxj[st]] day of Novembre[5] the merchauntes Esterlinges were condempned to merchaundes Englissh in xiij m[l] vc. xx li. The same yere [*sic*] the lord Ryvers was beheded, and his son Sir John Wodevyle w[t] hym [actually they were executed in August 1469].[6]

In other words it appears that in some quarters it was thought that the cases brought by the king (or the powers behind his throne) against Elizabeth Talbot's servants were linked in some way to the subsequent campaign which was launched against members of Elizabeth Widville's own family, led by the Earl of Warwick and his son-in-law, George, Duke of Clarence. And of course those two anti-Widville campaigners were respectively Elizabeth Talbot's uncle and cousin by marriage.

119

May it therefore be that the motivation which led to the launching of an attack on members of Elizabeth Talbot's household was actually something which had been done by Elizabeth Talbot herself? If so, the most likely explanation would seem to be that the Duchess of Norfolk had actually been deeply shocked to find her beloved sister dead when she returned home after Margaret of York's Burgundian marriage. Possibly she had therefore been heard voicing her suspicions as to the cause of Eleanor's death and she might have voiced her suspicions to her cousin by marriage, the Duke of Clarence (ally of herself and her husband – see below), and also to her uncle, the Earl of Warwick. If the Duchess of Norfolk had behaved in that way, presumably the other side would then have decided that action of some sort should be taken quickly to warn her off and to silence her.

Moreover, there is further significant evidence which suggests that in the second half of 1468, Elizabeth Talbot must have done something which caused concern in government quarters. The evidence in question is the fact that about five months later on 8 December 1468, Edward IV granted a 'general pardon to Elizabeth, wife of the king's kinsman John, Duke of Norfolk, of all offences committed by her before 7 December.'[7] As usual, of course, that grant of a pardon does not specify what the recipient may have done wrong. Indeed, often, for men, such pardons were issued simply in order to clear the ground for them before they took on a new government post. But such cannot have been the motivation for the grant of a pardon in the case of Elizabeth Talbot – so why did she require one? What is more, significantly, just over a month later, on 28 January 1468/9, a similar pardon was granted to her (and Eleanor's) surviving brother, Sir Humphrey Talbot.

Partly because the Duke of Norfolk was not a hugely wealthy man, in the August of the following year (1469) – at around the time when Elizabeth Widville's father and brother were executed – he besieged Caister Castle in Norfolk. For John Mowbray that was part of an inheritance dispute which had already been ongoing for some years. His opponents were the Paston family. However, there does not seem to have been any personal animosity between the two sides. Normally the Pastons were retainers of the Duke of Norfolk (see below). The siege of Caister Castle continued for two months and the Duke of Norfolk had a much larger force on his side, so probably he was always bound to win.

However, the most interesting point about the Caister Castle siege in this present context is the fact that, during the siege, John Mowbray was in close touch with his cousin, the Duke of Clarence, and also with the Earl of Warwick's younger brother, Archbishop George Neville. This was the time at which the Duke of Clarence and his father-in-law, the Earl of Warwick appeared to be the power behind the throne and, as we have seen they were then openly engaged in strong anti-Widville activity.

In September 1469, the Pastons were also well aware of the fact that the Duke of Clarence was one of the powers behind the throne, because then they also appealed to him. By that time it was clear that the Pastons had been defeated, and on Tuesday 26 September 1469, at the request of the Duke of Clarence, the Duke of Norfolk granted them a safe conduct permitting all the living Paston defenders to safely retreat out of Caister Castle.

Later, after the Lancastrian restoration and Edward IV's return to the throne, although the Duke and Duchess of Norfolk had been married for more than 20 years, they still had no children. It seems that, like her sister, Eleanor, and their first cousin, Anne Neville, (who subsequently became the wife of Richard, Duke of Gloucester, and who later became his queen consort, when he was made King Richard III), Elizabeth Talbot may have had some problem with conceiving children. For that reason she and her husband made a pilgrimage to Walsingham in September 1471, travelling virtuously on foot from Framlingham Castle. Their pilgrimage appears to have worked for them, because the following year Elizabeth finally found herself pregnant and in December 1472 she gave birth to a daughter, Anne Mowbray, following which, despite the fact that it was winter, her virtuous husband, the Duke, made a rapid thank-you pilgrimage to Walsingham.

In March 1475 the Norfolks made another pilgrimage to Walsingham. This time they travelled from their house in Norwich. Subsequently, in the summer of 1475, Elizabeth found herself pregnant yet again. It seems that in the winter of 1475 the Duke and Duchess of Norfolk spent Christmas together at their home in Norwich. Then, after Christmas the duke departed southwards returning to his principal official residence, Framlingham Castle in Suffolk. But because Elizabeth was pregnant – and both she and her husband were hoping that she would at last give birth to a son and heir – she remained behind in Norwich.

Sir John Paston II joined John Mowbray at Framlingham, and it is one of his surviving letters which reports for us the dramatic news of what happened next:

> It is so fortunyd that wher as my lorde off Norffolke yisterdaye beyng in goode heele, thys nyght dyed a–bowte mydnyght; wherffor it is alle that lovyd hym to doo and helpe nowe that that may be to hys honoure and weel to hys sowele.[8]

Paston offers no explanation regarding the cause of John Mowbray's sudden and unexpected death, early on the morning of Wednesday 17 January 1475/6. But since he states clearly that on the previous day the duke had been in good health, obviously that event must have come to Paston – and others – as a shock.

So could it possibly be that, like his sister-in-law, Eleanor Talbot, and like two of his retainers, the Duke of Norfolk had now been got rid of? Might his unexpected death – followed by the subsequent miscarriage of his distressed widow – have been part of a complex plan of dubious legality formulated in certain quarters for securing the Mowbray inheritance for the recently born second son of Elizabeth Widville and Edward IV (see below)?

Overall, the sum of all the evidence in respect of Elizabeth Talbot and her husband, John Mowbray, appears to suggest that they must have been suspicious in respect of Eleanor Talbot's sudden death. What is more, they appear to have been closely linked to their close relatives,

Isabel Neville, Duchess of Clarence, from the sanctuary arch of Toller Porcorum Church, Dorset.

the leading anti-Widville campaigners, George Duke of Clarence and Richard Neville, Earl of Warwick. As a result, following the restoration of Widvillism in 1471, the Norfolk couple must have found themselves on the wrong side politically. That fact may account for the sudden and apparently unexpected death of John Mowbray.

Eleven months later, in December 1476, another unexpected death took place – a death which was definitely considered in some quarters to have been a murder. The victim on this occasion was yet another close relative of Eleanor Talbot – her first cousin Isabel Neville who was, of course, the wife of the Duke of Clarence.

Since March 1475/6, two months after the death of the Duke of Norfolk, Isabel had been pregnant. The following account presents her subsequent death as usually reported – though as we shall see it contains various inaccuracies.

> The Duchess of Clarence brought her third [*sic* – fourth] child Richard into the world on October 6 [*sic* – 5 October], 1476, in a new chamber of the infirmary of Tewkesbury Abbey, but no reason is given by the chronicle for her residence in the monastic buildings at the time. The infant was baptized the next day '*in ecclesia parochiali*', that is, in the nave of the abbey, and on a later day was confirmed at the high altar. The Lord George (as the duke was called) and the Lady Isabel removed to Warwick on November 12, and it is noted that she was then in mortal sickness [*infirmata*], though nothing is said of the common belief that both she and her infant were suffering from poison. Whether they were poisoned or not, both died very shortly afterwards, the duchess on December 12 [*sic* – 22 December]. Then the fair young mother of twenty-five was brought back again to the abbey on January 4, 1477, and after lying under a hearse in the midst of the choir for thirty-five days, was buried in a vault which was made eastward of the high altar.[9]

It has sometimes been suggested that during the birth of her son Richard, Isabel had found herself under the care of a lady called Ankarette Twynyho (*née* Hawkeston). Ankarette definitely played some role in caring for Isabel

123

after the birth. However, there is no reason for believing that she had been directly involved in any way in the birth itself. As we have seen, the birth took place at Tewkesbury Abbey. But it was a few weeks later, at the Clarence family home of Warwick Castle, that Ankarette seems to have acted as one of Isabel's attendants. Certainly no evidence exists suggesting that she had acted as a midwife – or that she acted as nurse to the newborn baby.

Born probably in about 1412, Ankarette would have been in her sixties in 1476. Probably, therefore, she would have been rather too old for acting as nurse to the new baby. Her maiden name of Hawkeston suggests that she may have come originally from Cheshire or Staffordshire. But she had then married William Twynyho, who held an estate at Keyford in Somerset. Ankarette bore her husband at least three children. She was a widow by 1476 but she and her family were definitely in the service of the Duke and Duchess of Clarence.

After giving birth to Richard, 'Lady Isabel, the late wife of George, duke of Clarence, was … physically healthy, on 10 October in the sixteenth year of the reign of King Edward IV since the conquest [1476].'[10] There is therefore no reason to suppose that her subsequent death came about as a result of the childbirth. The duchess appears to have returned from Tewkesbury to Warwick Castle on 12 November. It seems likely therefore that, in the trial which occurred some months later, a slight error may have been made in recording the alleged date of her poisoning – because the surviving records of her trial state that it was on 10 October 1476 that Ankarette:

> falsely, traitorously and feloniously gave the same Isabel a venomous drink of ale mixed with poison to drink, to poison and kill the same Isabel; of which drink the said Isabel sickened from the aforesaid 10 October until the Sunday next before the following Christmas; on which Sunday the aforesaid Isabel then and there died because of it.[11]

The issue in respect of the date which has been recorded will be examined in greater detail shortly (see below).

Following the unexpected death of his wife, the Duke of Clarence found himself initially preoccupied with arranging her burial at Tewkesbury Abbey. Suddenly, however, he then found himself confronting a second family death – that of his newly-born son, Richard. The little boy was less elaborately buried than his mother – and in Warwick. The death of little Richard also seemed to be due to the administration of poison. In his case, however, the person responsible appeared to be another Clarence servant, John Thursby.

George must have been suspicious about the cause of those two demises in his family when they occurred. However, he took no immediate action in respect of prosecution. One possible reason may have been that he needed to seek for evidence in respect of what had taken place. Another reason was that probably he himself felt greatly disturbed, and possibly afraid that other murders would take place in his family. Certainly it seems that he felt very anxious about the future of his surviving elder son, Edward, Earl of Warwick. George seems to have wished to ensure that this one surviving son and heir was not also murdered. As we shall see later, George was subsequently accused of having plotted to smuggle young Warwick out of England, to the safety either of Ireland or of Flanders.

Manuscript illustration which shows Anthony Widville presenting a book to Edward IV.

George, Duke of Clarence was the English lieutenant of Ireland, having been confirmed in that role by Edward IV for the next twenty years in 1472[12] and intriguingly an eighteenth-century account reports that he paid a visit to Ireland in 1477.

The account in question describes the manuscript illustration which shows Anthony Widville presenting a book to Edward IV.

> It represents Anthony Woodville, earl of Rivers, presenting the book, and Caxton his printer, to king Edward the Fourth, the queen and prince. The portrait of the prince (afterwards Edward the Fifth) is the only one known of him, and has been engraved by Vertue among the heads of the kings. The person in a cap and robe of state is, probably, Richard duke of Gloucester, as he resembles the king, and as Clarence was always too great an enemy of the queen to be distinguished by her brother. The book was printed in 1477, when Clarence was in Ireland, and in the beginning of the next year he was murdered.[13]

Since his whereabouts are known to have been Warwick in April 1477, and subsequently London from May onwards (where he found himself imprisoned at the Tower), a visit to Ireland by George could only have taken place before April. He must therefore have gone there in February or March 1476/7, just after the murders of his wife and younger son, and significantly, at precisely the time when he was later accused of having been trying to smuggle his son and heir out of England to safety.

Some historians have proposed that George thought Elizabeth Widville had been responsible for the poisoning of Isabel and of young Richard. Actually no surviving fifteenth-century source makes that allegation. Nevertheless at least two of the three people accused of the Clarence family poisonings appear to have had potential Widville connections. The first of the two is Ankarette Twynyho, because her son, John Twynyho, can later be found working with Elizabeth Widville's brother, Anthony, Earl Rivers, with Eizabeth's son, Sir Richard Grey, and with her first cousin, Richard Haute (see above, Chapter 10, Family Tree 11).[14]

The second of the two accused who appears to have had Widville connections is Sir Roger Tocotes. He was appointed by Elizabeth Widville to the stewardship of some of her West Country properties.[15] Roger Tocotes was a prominent member of the Wiltshire gentry. His wife,

Elizabeth, had previously been married to Sir William Beauchamp (the brother of the Bishop of Salisbury and a cousin of the Duchess of Clarence). Sir Roger had served in France with George and his father-in-law, the Earl of Warwick. But when George was reconciled with his brother, King Edward IV, Tocotes followed the Duke of Clarence. Later (from 1475) he served as a member of George's council.

The three accused of poisoning the Duchess of Clarence and her newly born son, Richard, were Sir Roger Tocotes, Ankarette Twynyho and John Thursby. The last of those three was a local yeoman in George's service. George had Ankarette seized in April 1477 at the manor of Keyford, at Frome in Somerset.[16] She was then conveyed to Warwick, where she was placed on trial on the morning of Tuesday 15 April. John Thursby had also been arrested and stood beside Ankarette in the dock. As for Sir Roger Tocotes, he was also accused. Indeed, George appears to have believed that he had acted as the organiser of the family murders. However, Tocotes did not figure with the other two in the dock in Warwick because apparently he had not been arrested.

The most direct surviving evidence of the court case which was heard in Warwick regarding the alleged murder of Isabel, Duchess of Clarence, and her baby, Richard, is preserved in the *Baga de Secretis*, Bundle 1 (records of court cases from the reign of Edward IV)

> Tuesday next after the Clause of Easter [15 April], 17 Edw. 4 [1477].
>
> Warwickshire Indictment taken before the Justices of the Peace, whereby it is found that Ankerett Twinnewe, otherwise Twymowe, late of Warwick, widow, late servant of George, Duke of Clarence and Isabella his wife, did on 10th October [*sic* – see below], 16 Edw. 4 [1476] at Warwick give to the said Isabella poisoned ale, of which poison she died on Sunday next before the then following Christmas [22 December 1476].
>
> Also against Roger Tocotes, late of Warwick, Knight, servant of the said Duke and Duchess, for that on the said 10 October, he abetted the said Ankarett to commit the said felony.
>
> Also that John Thuresby, late of Warwick, yeoman, late servant of Richard Plantagenet, second son of George Duke of Clarence, compassing the said death of the said Richard,

gave him, on [Saturday] 21st December 16 Edw. 4 [1476], certain poisoned ale, of which poison he died on [Wednesday] 1st January then next ensuing [1476/7].

And furthermore that the said Roger Tocotes, otherwise Tokettes, late of Warwick, Knight, on the said [Saturday] 21st December, procured and abetted the said John Thuresby to commit the said felony.[17]

As was observed earlier, the above evidence is intriguing in respect of the dates as they are recorded. Young Richard is said to have first been given his poison on Saturday 21 December, following which the little boy died on Wednesday 1 January. In other words the poisoning of Richard took eleven days to bring about his death. However, Isabel is said to have first been given poison on 10 October, and to have died on 22 December, suggesting that in her case it took 73 days to kill her. Also her poisoning on 10 October is said to have taken place in Warwick. However, on that date Isabel had still been at Tewkesbury. The obvious solution would be that the date recorded as 10 October is actually a mistake. Presumably it should actually have been recorded as '10 December'. In that case Isabel's poisoning to death would have taken twelve days – just a few hours longer than it took to kill her son.

In respect of the court case, however, there is no indication that anything was done improperly. Evidence was presented to the Warwick court, based upon which it found both Ankarette Twynyho and John Thursby guilty of murder. Ankarette was to 'be led from the bar to the said lord king's gaol of Warwick aforesaid, and drawn from that gaol through the centre of that town of Warwick to the gallows at Myton, and be hanged there on that gallows until she is dead.'[18] Thursby was likewise sentenced to death. Both sentences were carried out.[19]

Shortly after the executions, on 20 May 1477 the king requested that the records of the Twynyho trial should be submitted to him.[20] Clearly either he or the power behind the throne had some interest in what George had done to substantiate the claim that his wife and son had been murdered. In addition, Ankarette's grandson presented a petition to the 1478 Parliament. He requested – successfully – that the verdict against his grandmother should be overturned. That was rather similar to the action taken earlier by Jacquette, Duchess of Bedford – and the result produced on that occasion.

Nevertheless, Ankarette Twynyho's trial and execution were never included by Edward IV as part of the case which was subsequently brought by him against his brother – possibly because including that material might have risked focussing attention on the fact that Elizabeth Widville had been thought to be inculcated in political killings. Certainly the official record in the Rolls of Parliament in respect of the case which was actually brought against George, Duke of Clarence, appears to have been edited rather carefully.

The account written in 1483 by the Italian Friar Domenico Mancini reports that, in the early 1470s, after Edward IV's restoration,

> The queen then remembered the insults to her family and the calumnies with which she was reproached, namely that according to established usage she was not the legitimate wife of the king. Thus she concluded that her offspring by the king would never come to the throne unless the duke of Clarence were removed; and of this she easily persuaded the king.[21]

What actually focussed Elizabeth Widville's fears on George in the 1470s may well have been the fact that 'there was a kind of prophecy' which became current at that time in a manner which will be explored shortly. The prophecy stated 'that after E., that is, after Edward the fourth, G would be king – and because of its ambiguity – George Duke of Clarence (who was between the two brothers, King Edward and King Richard) on account of being Duke George, was put to death.'[22]

A slightly later source – the account written by Polydore Vergil – records that, in respect of the Duke of Clarence, the chief cause of his arrest by his brother, the king, was the fact that 'loe sudaynly [Edward IV] fell into a fact most horrible, commanding rashly and upon the suddane his brother George of Clarence to be apprehendyd.'[23] The fact in question had to do with the trial and execution of George's servant, the Warwickshire esquire, Thomas Burdet, together with his two associates, the Oxford astronomers – and astrologers – Dr John Stacy (Stacey; Stace) and Thomas Blake.

All three of those men were arrested in 1477. Thomas Burdet was accused of publishing and distributing in Holborn and Westminster verses which challenged the accession rights to the throne of Edward IV's son by

Elizabeth Widville. The publication and distribution of that material had taken place on 6 March 1476/7, and again on 5 and 6 May 1477.[24] No record survives of what precisely the verses in question contained. Nevertheless, it is clear that poems were employed politically during the so-called 'Wars of the Roses'[25] and the probability is that what Burdet had published and given out was a poem containing the prophecy of 'G', and highlighting George, Duke of Clarence, as the true legal heir to the throne of England.

At about the same time Dr John Stacy of Merton College Oxford, and his colleague Thomas Blake, Chaplain of the same college, were both arrested for misusing magic. And Thomas Burdet is known to have had dealings with Stacy and Blake at Westminster, three years earlier, on 20 April 1474.[26] Stacy and Blake were both accused of having used magic to help in the murder of Lord Beauchamp.[27] As reported about ten years later by the continuator of the Crowland Abbey Chronicle,

> A certain Master John Stacey, called the Astronomer, though he had rather been a great necromancer, examined together with one Burdet, a squire in the duke [*of Clarence*]'s household, was accused, among many charges, of having made lead figures and other things to get rid of Richard, Lord Beauchamp, at the request of his adulterous wife and during a very sharp examination he was questioned about the use of such a damnable art; he confessed to many things both against himself and against the said Thomas [*Burdet*]. He and Thomas were therefore arrested together. Sentence of death was eventually passed upon them both in the King's Bench at Westminster in the presence of almost all the lords temporal in the kingdom along with the justices. They were drawn to the gallows at Tyburn and permitted to say anything they wished, briefly, before they died; they declared their innocence, Stacey, indeed, faintly, but Burdet with great spirit and many words, as though, like Susanna, in the end he was saying 'Behold I die, though I have done none of these things.'[28]

But curiously Stacy and Blake only found themselves arrested two years after Lord Beauchamp's death. It may therefore be the case that, as academic astrologers, they had more recently helped Burdet produce his published verses on the prophecy of 'G'.

Stacy found himself questioned under torture. Not surprisingly he therefore confessed that he had also sought to kill the king and his eldest son by using black arts against them. Moreover, he admitted casting their horoscopes to learn their likely death dates. Stacy's confession also specifically implicated Thomas Burdet. However, the subsequent case against Burdet also accused him of inciting rebellion against Edward IV by publishing and circulating treasonable writings. The verses in question were said to have aimed at dethroning the king and also removing his eldest son from the order of succession.

It therefore seems probable that the poems in question may well have contained specific reference to the fact that Edward IV's 'marriage' to Elizabeth Widville was bigamous, followed by allegations of bastardy in respect of Elizabeth Widville's royal progeny. Presumably the verses – whose aim was to promote the cause of Burdet's master, George, Duke of Clarence – ended with the statement that Edward IV's heir on the throne of England would therefore bear a name beginning with the letter 'G'.

Thomas Burdet (c.1425–1477) had been the landowner of Arrow in Warwickshire. Left fatherless as a child, he had been the ward of Humphrey Earl of Stafford until 1446.[29] He had then served John, first Lord Beauchamp of Powick (to whose wife, he was probably related). Subsequently, however, he had served Lord Sudeley – the father-in-law of Lady Eleanor Talbot. It is therefore probable that Burdet had known Eleanor. Possibly he had therefore been aware of her secret marriage with Edward IV. Later he had entered the client network of Richard Neville, Earl of Warwick. And following Warwick's death he had entered the service of George, Duke of Clarence.[30]

On 12 May 1477 the king appointed a commission of *oyer* and *terminer* to try Burdet, Stacy and Blake.[31] The commission was presided over by Elizabeth Widville's eldest son, Thomas Grey, Marquess of Dorset. It also included her brother, Anthony Widville, Earl Rivers, and Henry Bourchier, Earl of Essex, who had various connections with her (see above, Family Tree 10). The most complete surviving account of the trials of Burdet, Stacy and Blake reports as follows:

> Jurors present, that THOMAS BURDET esquire, late of ARROW, in the county of WARWICK, not having God before his eyes, and thinking little of the debt owed to his

allegiance, seduced by the instigation of the devil, on the twentieth day of April in the fourteenth year of the reign of KING EDWARD THE FOURTH, after the Conquest, and at various times thereafter, in the town of WESTMINSTER, in the County of MIDDLESEX, falsely and treacherously, against the debt of his allegiance, plotted to encompass the death of the king, and he falsely and traitorously proposed to kill the king himself, then and there, and to fulfil his false and nefarious purpose, he falsely and treacherously laboured and procured one JOHN STACY, late of OXFORD, in the county of OXFORD, a gentleman, and THOMAS BLAKE, late of OXFORD, in the county of OXFORD, cleric, in the aforesaid town of WESTMINSTER, on the twelfth day of November next following, to calculate and work on the birth of the said lord king and of EDWARD his first-born son, Prince of Wales, and on the death of the same lord king and prince, to know when the same king and his son Edward shall die. And as for the said JOHN STACY and THOMAS BLAKE, knowing the false and wicked purpose of the aforesaid THOMAS BURDET, the same JOHN STACY and THOMAS BLAKE, on the twelfth day of November, in the aforesaid town of WESTMINSTER, falsely and treacherously planned to encompass the death of the king and prince, and then and there plotted to kill the same king and prince. And afterwards, on the sixth day of February, in the same fourteenth year, in the said town of WESTMINSTER, the aforesaid JOHN STACY and THOMAS BLAKE to fulfil their false and treasonous purpose, falsely and traitorously laboured to calculate by means of the magic art, the black art, and astronomy, the death and final destruction of their king and prince. And afterwards, to wit, on the twentieth day of May, in the fifteenth year of the reign of the said king, in the said town of WESTMINSTER, the aforesaid JOHN STACY and THOMAS BLAKE falsely and traitorously laboured by the above-mentioned arts, which is forbidden by the laws of Holy Church, by the teaching of various doctors, by the fact that each of them was bound to the lord king, and by the fact that the investigation of kings and princes, in the form described above, is not permitted without their consent. And afterwards, the same JOHN STACY, and THOMAS BLAKE, and the aforesaid THOMAS BURDET, at the above-mentioned town of WESTMINSTER, on the twenty-sixth day of May, in the same fifteenth year, falsely and traitorously expressed themselves to a certain ALEXANDER RUSSETON, and to other subjects of the lord king, saying 'that by means of the aforesaid calculation and arts, carried out in the said form by the said JOHN STACY and THOMAS BLAKE, the same king and prince will not live long, but should die within a short time', with the intention of that by the revelation of this information, the people of the king should withdraw their heartfelt love from the king, and that the same lord the king, on perceiving this, might fall into sadness, and his life be cut short. And that the aforesaid THOMAS BURDET, to the death and destruction of the said king, his sovereign lord, and the said lord prince, and to subvert their rule by war and discord between the king and his lieges in the aforesaid realm, on the sixth day of March, in the seventeenth year of the reign of the said king, in HOLBORN, the County of MIDDLESEX, falsely and treacherously plotted, conspired, and went about to kill the same king and prince. And to fulfil that false, heinous end, the aforesaid THOMAS BURDET composed and made various notes and writings in seditious rhymes and ballads inciting treasonable riots, made in HOLBORN, and in the said town of WESTMINSTER. These he falsely and traitorously gave out, scattered abroad, and sowed on the said sixth of March, and on the fifth and sixth days of May, in the said seventeenth year, with the intention that the people of the king should withdraw their heartfelt love from the king, and should desert him, and war should break out against the same king, to the final destruction of the king himself and of lord prince and all their supporters, as well as against the crown and dignity of the king himself.[32]

Although they had claimed to be innocent, on Monday 19 May 1477, Stacy, Blake and Burdet were all found guilty of high treason. The next day Stacy and Burdet were both taken to Tyburn and hung, drawn and quartered.[33] On the scaffold Burdet protested against his condemnation. Curiously, however, despite having been condemned, Thomas Blake was not executed. On the 3 June he was pardoned thanks to a request made on his behalf by James Goldwell, Bishop of Norwich,[34] who – perhaps significantly – had studied at Oxford. Incidentally it was also Goldwell who had finalised the planned link between the Duke of Clarence and the Earl of Warwick by obtaining the papal dispensation for the marriage of the Duke and Duchess of Clarence.

> The next day the duke of Clarence came to the council chamber at Westminster bringing with him the famous doctor of the Orders of the Minors, Master William Goddard,[35] to read out the confession and the declaration of innocence before the lords assembled in the council – which he did and then retired. At this time the king was at Windsor. When he heard the news he was greatly displeased and recalled information laid against his brother which he had long kept in his breast; the duke was summoned to appear, on a fixed day, at the royal palace of Westminster in the presence of the mayor and aldermen of the city of London and the king, from his own lips, began to treat the duke's action already touched upon [i.e. causing Burdet's statement to be read to the council], *amongst other things* [not specified], as a most serious matter, *as if* it were in contempt of the law of the land and a great threat to the judges and jurors of the kingdom. What more is there to say? The duke was placed in custody and was not found at liberty from that day until his death.[36]

Thus George, Duke of Clarence was arrested and imprisoned at the Tower of London in June 1477. He was detained there for six months. During that time Edward IV and Elizabeth Widville were busy planning the wedding of their second son, Richard of Shrewsbury, to Eleanor Talbot's niece, Anne Mowbray, who, given her mother's miscarriage following the curious sudden death of the Duke of Norfolk, had definitely become her father's heiress. Although Anne's mother – Elizabeth Talbot, dowager Duchess of Norfolk – 'was entitled to divers possessions by reason of her dower and jointure', she found herself persuaded 'to forbear and leave a great part thereof, and it was appointed between the king and herself that she should have divers specified possessions for life.'[37]

The marriage of the two children was splendidly celebrated on Thursday 15 January 1477/8, at the Palace of Westminster. However, Anne's own mother seems to have played only a very small part in the little girl's nuptials. 'Despite her recorded presence at the wedding banquet, Elizabeth Talbot, Duchess of Norfolk, seems to have taken little part in the wedding festivities. At no other stage of the proceedings is her name so much as mentioned.'[38] Nevertheless, members of the

George, Duke of Clarence.

royal family and relatives of Elizabeth Widville played prominent rôles in the celebrations.

The following day Parliament was opened at Westminster. In respect of his younger son, Richard – now Duke of York and Norfolk and Earl Marshall of England – Edward IV had a dubious law enacted, stating that if Anne Mowbray 'should happen to decease without issue by the said Richard the latter should have for life divers specified possessions and reversions.'[39] About a month later questions were asked about that act by Lord and Lady Berkeley, who would normally have figured prominently amongst the Mowbray co-heirs if young Anne were to die childless.

In parliament Edward IV also began putting the case against his brother. The king reportedly began by recalling how he had confronted various earlier attempts to overthrow him. It was then claimed that there was now a new plot against him, which also focussed specifically on Elizabeth Widville and their offspring. It was asserted that this new plot was being led by George, Duke of Clarence. Thus, in spite of their close blood relationship, given George's alleged plotting Edward IV argued that he was now forced to seek his brother's conviction for treason.

The claim was then made that, although Edward IV had always been kind to his brother, George had now protested that his own servant – Thomas Burdet – had wrongly been put to death. George was also said to be protesting that Edward had deprived him of his livelihood. The aim adopted by the Duke of Clarence was therefore said to be to place himself upon the throne.

Incidentally, George was also said to have retained a document issued to him by the restored Lancastrian King Henry VI, in which Henry stated that if both the Lancastrian monarch and his alleged son, Edward of Westminster, happened to die without leaving direct heirs, then George would be the legal Lancastrian heir.

Also George was said to have plotted with the abbot of Tewkesbury and others. The aim of the plot in question had been to smuggle his surviving son and heir, Edward of Clarence, Earl of Warwick, out of England, to the alleged safety of either Ireland or Flanders. As we saw earlier, George had apparently made a trip to Ireland in February/March 1476/7, just after the death of his wife and younger son.

The resulting Act of Attainder against George clearly states that his intended victims included Elizabeth Widville, and the children she had borne to Edward IV. It also states that George had made his servants spread seditious stories in order to help him achieve his alleged aim. Thomas Burdet is mentioned, after which the seditious stories are stated to have been spread by George's servants 'of similar disposition' – though no other names of servants are actually cited, nor is any precise evidence presented in respect of what seditious stories they had propagated.

Although George is accused of possessing a grant issued by Henry VI, in which George himself was acknowledged as the heir to the throne if both Henry and Edward of Westminster died (which they had done), he is not actually accused of having *used* that document in any way. Mention of it therefore appears to have merely constituted part of an attempt to focus the evidence brought against George on points which it would be safe to place on public record.

Similarly, George was alleged to have accused Edward of being a bastard. Why would Edward IV have mentioned that in Parliament? The obvious hypothesis is that Elizabeth Widville may have pointed out to Edward that he would easily be able to disprove the point in question. On the other hand, equally significantly, the Act of Attainder never mentions that George had accused his brother of bigamy. Yet, in reality, all the evidence which is available clearly indicates that George had apparently never claimed the throne *itself*. He had merely claimed consistently to be the legal *heir* to the throne. That was why the prophecy had asserted that Edward IV would be *succeeded* by someone named 'G...'. In other words, George had not been acting against his *brother*. He had been acting against Elizabeth Widville and her children. The basis behind such a political position must obviously have been that the '*marriage*' of Edward and Elizabeth had never been legal. And as Mancini reported about five years later, Elizabeth Widville was well aware of that as George's contention. But of course, in respect of the legal documentation of the case brought against him, if George had presented any evidence to show that her marriage to the king was bigamy, Elizabeth Widville would then have made sure that the evidence in question was not placed on record.

It is commonly asserted that the Act of Attainder was passed on Friday 16 January 1477/8. Parliament had certainly been opened on that date. However, the text of the Act itself mentions no date. Subsequently, however, on Saturday 7 February, Edward IV appointed his cousin – Elizabeth Widville's brother-in-law – Henry, Duke of Buckingham, to the post of Steward of England. In the grant which was issued, that appointment was specifically connected to the recent judgement against the Duke of Clarence.

> despite the close blood ties and the inner feelings of love, which We had and practiced to the aforesaid George in his tender age, and which naturally move Us in a contrary direction, as We understand it, the Office of the Steward of England (whose presence is required here for the execution of a Judgement which has yet to be carried out) is currently vacant.[40]

As the new Steward of England, Buckingham then found himself required to execute the recent judgement against George by putting him to death.

Chapter 15

Losing Edward IV

Popular accounts of Edward IV suggest that he was always besotted with making love, and that he had innumerable mistresses. If that was true, obviously, in effect, Elizabeth Widville would have lost him from the very start of their relationship. Instead of spending time with her, he would have spent much of his time in bed with other women, and begotten heaps of bastards.

However, as was seen earlier, Edward's own contemporary, the Italian poet Cornazzano clearly denies that story.

> da credere è che spesso occultamente
> Si trastullasse in qualche concubina.
>
> (there is make-believe that he secretly
> would play around with some concubine.)[1]

The Great Seal of Edward IV.

Moreover, in recently published research the present writer has shown that Edward only seems to have recognised a maximum of two bastard children in his own lifetime. Although subsequently the regime of Henry VII appears to have recognised two or three more bastard children of Edward IV, it is not certain whether real evidence for some of those claims existed.

After all, the government of Henry VII – like many other

governments, unfortunately – did not always tell the truth. And it found itself dealing with a population in England which had recently been told officially – and a significant proportion of which may always have suspected – that all the children borne for Edward by Elizabeth Widville were actually bastards. Of course Henry VII's government was frantically trying to brush questions in respect of the legitimacy of the Widville royal offspring out of history because Henry himself had chosen to marry one of them. Suggesting that Edward had always had mistresses and produced bastards – though they did not include his Widville progeny – may have helped in that respect. In fact it would have been a government technique very similar to the invention of the name of 'Elizabeth Lucy', which appears to have been carried out in order to ensure that the many people in England who must have remembered that the throne had been offered to Richard III because Edward IV was discovered and proved to have committed bigamy nevertheless became confused in respect of the identity of Edward's real consort and forgot the name of Eleanor Talbot. Moreover, even if the necessary evidence actually did exist in respect of the newly acknowledged bastard children of Edward IV, it seems that the total number of such children fathered by him would still definitely remain a single-figure.[2]

In respect of the alleged bastardy issue, the present writer also demonstrated that apart from Eleanor Talbot (who has actually often been overlooked or ignored in the past) and Elizabeth Widville, in reality it is extremely difficult to actually name any other female sex partners of Edward IV. Traditional accounts have claimed 'Elizabeth Lucy', Catherine de Clarington, a girl from the Hampshire Wayte family, and Elizabeth ['Jane'] Shore (*née* Lambert). But, as we have seen, 'Elizabeth Lucy' appears to be a completely mythical being invented by the government of Henry VII in order to help ensure that the name of Eleanor Talbot would be forgotten. Even a modern account of her to be found on the internet, while continuing to claim that a woman of that name may have been a mistress of Edward IV, and may have borne him children, makes it clear that no authentic contemporary evidence exists in respect of her. It also shows that the later accounts written about this alleged woman contradict one another in various respects.[3]

As for Catherine de Clarington, it is not certain that she really existed. Her name is only mentioned by a much later source (George Buck –

early seventeenth century), and no contemporary evidence can actually be found in respect of her. While Elizabeth Lambert/Shore definitely did exist, and is stated in surviving contemporary sources to have been the mistress of both Elizabeth Widville's eldest son (the Marquess of Dorset)[4] and of his stepfather-in-law, Lord Hastings,[5] there is absolutely no authentic evidence to link her sexually with the king himself.

Thus, apart from Eleanor Talbot and Elizabeth Widville, the only authentic female sexual partner of Edward IV for whom we have part of a name appears to have been a Miss Wayte. It has been alleged that her first name was Elizabeth – part of an attempt to link her with the mythical 'Elizabeth Lucy' – but that does not appear to have been the case. There is a good deal of surviving contemporary evidence in respect of the fifteenth-century Wayte family of Hampshire, but it has not been possible to identify a daughter called Elizabeth in the right period. Thus Miss Wayte's first name remains unknown.[6]

What is more Miss Wayte appears likely to have been Edward's mistress only very briefly, at the time when he was experiencing the problem of losing power, and when he also found himself separated from Elizabeth Widville (i.e. *circa* 1470). At other times the pattern of her pregnancies obviously indicates that Edward IV must have been in regular sexual partnership with Elizabeth Widville. What appears to have existed between the couple is a partnership pattern which closely resembled that of Edward's own parents, Richard Duke of York and Cecily Neville.[7] In the case of Edward IV's father there never seems to have been any marital infidelity. In other words, although before he met Elizabeth Widville, Edward may occasionally have tried sex elsewhere, and although he may have repeated that when he found himself separated from her, for the most part the king seems to have been a fairly faithful partner. He was faithful to Elizabeth Widville even if (as we saw earlier) that caused him conflict with his mother, and with other blood relatives.

Thus it appears that Edward and Elizabeth were mostly close to one another, and truly cared for each other. Of course they may have argued on occasions, after all, they were both normal human beings. But on the whole they were genuinely affectionate partners. Unfortunately for Elizabeth, however, Edward had misbehaved in another way. His secret marriage with her had been bigamous, and although she had not been aware of that at the time she accepted and entered into their own secret union, subsequently, when she discovered what Edward had done, it caused

Elizabeth years of stress in respect of her own status and that of her royal children. But of course none of that was in any way her own fault.

Based on what has now been revealed by the present writer in respect of Edward IV's movements it seems that it was probably when he was struggling against his cousin, the Earl of Warwick, and his brother, the Duke of Clarence, that Edward found himself alone in Hampshire and slept on at least one occasion with Miss Wayte. It would then have been nine months later, when Edward was in exile in the Low Countries, that Miss Wayte produced a bastard son, who was christened Arthur. However, it seems probable that Edward may never actually have seen the little boy in question. Certainly he never formally recognised him. Initially Arthur was apparently brought up by his mother's family, under the surname of Wayte. It was only years later, when his father was dead, that the boy found himself formally recognised by Henry VII as a bastard son of Edward IV. However, he was then allowed to use the royal arms and also the surname Plantagenet, and he received letters from the surviving daughter of George, Duke of Clarence which addressed him as her cousin.[8]

It seems possible that a few months after begetting Arthur, when he himself was in exile in the Low Countries, Edward may also have produced another bastard son. This time one whom he himself later had sent to him in England, when he had regained his throne, and whom he then formally recognised as 'my Lord the Bastard'.[9] It is even possible that the boy in question was the famous individual who later called himself 'Richard of England', but whom Henry VII named as 'Perkin Warbeck'.[10]

However, significantly, both of those engenderings of bastard sons appear to have occurred at a time when Edward found himself forcibly separated from Elizabeth Widville. Meanwhile she herself was hiding from her family's enemy, the Earl of Warwick, in the security of Westminster Abbey. She had claimed sanctuary there. Thus it was in that location that she too finally gave birth to a son fathered by Edward IV. When he returned to England, and was shown that son, the king was clearly delighted. 'She had browght into this worlde, to the Kyngs greatyste joy, a fayre sonn, a prince, where with she presentyd hym at his comynge.'[11]

Ironically, one of the finest surviving sources for proving that Edward personally declared that he loved and trusted Elizabeth is probably the will which he wrote on 'the xx day of Juyn, the yere of oure Lord God M.cccc.lxxv, and the yere of oure Reigne the xvth, beeing in helth of body and hole of mynde, thanked bee his Grace, at oure Towne of Sandwich', before he left England for France. In it Edward speaks of 'oure said derrest and moost entierly beloved wiff Elizabeth the Quene'.[12] He states that:

> we wol that oure said wiff the Quene have and enjoye all her owne goods catelles stuff beddying arrases tapestries verdours stuff of houshold plate and jouelx and all other thing which she now hath and occupieth, to dispose it freely at her will and pleaser without let or interruption of oure Executours; and for the perfite execution of this oure last Wille and testament we ordeigne and make oure said derrest and moost entierly beloved wiff Elizabeth the Quene, the Reverende Faders in God William [Grey] Bisshop of Ely [died 1478], Thomas [Rotherham] Bisshop of Lincoln [later Archbishop of York], John [Alcock] Bisshop of Rochestre [later Bishop of Worcester], William Lord Hastynges oure Chamberleyn, Maister John Russell Clerk Keper of oure Prive Seall [later Bishop of Rochester, then Bishop of Lincoln], Sr Thomas Mountgomery Knight, Richard Fowler oure Chaunceller of the Duchie of Lancastre [died 1477], Richard Pygot oure Sergeant, and William Husee oure Attourny, oure Executours, praieing and requiring and also straitly charging thaim and specially oure said derrest Wiff in whom we moost singulerly put oure trust in this partie, that she and thay put thaim in thair uttermast devoirs to see this oure last wille and testament bee truely executed and perfourmed in all things in manere and fourme afore declared as oure singler trust is in her and thaim and as she and thay wil answere afore God at the day of dome.[13]

However, possibly Edward did not really understand Elizabeth and how things were for her. After all, one of her colleagues named in the royal will as a co-executor is Lord Hastings. It seems that he was the person who had initially arranged for Elizabeth to meet the young king in order to petition his assistance. Yet ultimately Hastings proved not to be Elizabeth's friend. By February 1461/2 Hastings had found himself married by Richard Neville, Earl of Warwick, to the latter's recently widowed young sister, Catherine Neville (Lady Bonville). The fact that Warwick obviously then perceived Hastings as an ally may explain why (like Warwick) Hastings apparently did not ultimately take a friendly view of the Widville family.

It is also reported – probably correctly – that in accordance with England's standard practice at that time, in 1482/3, when he found himself dying, leaving his son and heir a minor, Edward expected his own surviving younger brother, Richard, Duke of Gloucester, to act as lord protector of the realm. However, it seems that Elizabeth Widville would have preferred to follow what she probably saw as the Continental norm – and act herself as the regent for her young son. Of course, as Edward IV must have known, that was something which had never been done in medieval England.

Edward appears to have died early in April 1483. However, the precise date on which Elizabeth Widville finally lost her royal partner is unclear. Normally modern historians rather naïvely claim that Edward IV died in the early hours of the morning on Wednesday 9 April 1483.[14] Certainly 9 April 1483 was the date on which Edward IV's death was officially *announced* in public.[15] Unfortunately that in no way proves that he actually passed away early on the morning in question. For example, the contemporary diary, written in Rome by Jacopo Gherardi da Volterra, apostolic secretary and 'secret chamberlain' to Pope Sixtus IV, records both the English royal demise and its officially announced date. However, intriguingly, it then questions the authenticity of that alleged date.

A. 1483, 9 aprile: Eduardus Britannie insule rex inclitus per hos dies moritur apud Londonas; dictum est ad nonam presentis mensis, pro vero affirmare non ausim.

1483, 9 April: Edward, renowned king of the British island at this time, died in London; it is said on the ninth of the present month, I would not dare to affirm that for the truth.[16]

In that context it is intriguing to note that, sixty-eight years later, when Edward IV's great grandson, King Edward VI, died in July 1553, clear evidence exists to prove that the death of that young king was then kept hidden for four days. On that occasion the concealment of the royal demise formed part of an attempted coup. When the death of Edward VI occurred, John Dudley, Duke of Northumberland, who had been acting as regent on behalf of that boy king, wished to ensure that he himself remained in power. His plan in that respect was to change the succession in favour of his own daughter-in-law, the late young king's cousin, Lady Jane Grey – a descendant of both Elizabeth Widville and her brother-in-law. Obviously, Dudley felt he needed a little time in order to succeed in bringing about the move which he planned. So that was why the death of Edward VI was initially concealed. In 1553 the death dissimulation actually did lead initially to the proclamation of 'Queen Jane' – though in the long term Dudley's plan did not prove to be a success.

Intriguingly, the possibility is that something very similar may have taken place in 1483 in an attempt to protect the future of Elizabeth Widville and ensure that she and her family remained in power. The fact is that a considerable amount of contradictory evidence exists relating to the date upon which Edward IV passed away. Contemporary York Records definitely imply that the king must have died before 9 April. A Requiem Mass was offered for the repose of Edward's soul at York Minster on 8 April, and offering Requiem Mass for a living person is a sin. The most obvious traditional dates for the offering of such a mass would have been the seventh day after the death or the third day after. Thus, based on the York evidence it seems possible that Edward IV may have died either on Tuesday 1 April or on Saturday 5 April. But either way, the available evidence definitely suggests that the king must certainly have died before 9 April.[17]

Official local government records also survive in both the east of England and in the west of the country which report death dates in respect of Edward IV. The record in the east of England is the Colchester Oath Book. That contains official annual reports, each of which was written up just after Michaelmas – at the end of September, or the beginning of October of the year in question. The Oath Book year heading written up in September 1483 refers to

> Anno domini Edwardi quarti nuper Regis anglie, iam defuncti, vicesimo secundo, usque octavum diem Aprilis tunc primo sequentem
>
> (the 22nd year of the reign of the Lord Edward IV, late king of England, now deceased, up until the 8th day of April first following)[18]

Thus it implies that Edward IV died on 8 April. As for the west country record, that relates to Bristol, and it also states that on 'the viij th day of Aprile the king Edward the iiij th dyed at Westminster.'[19]

There are also three interesting contemporary French sources in respect of Edward's death date. The chronicler Jean Molinet, states in his history that Edward IV 'died on the fourth day after Easter'.[20] The date of Easter Sunday is variable, of course, but in that particular year the major feast-day in question fell on 30 March. Thus Molinet was saying that the death occurred on Thursday 3 April. That death date would be consistent with the subsequent offering of a requiem mass at York Minster, and a further piece of evidence in strong support of Molinet's date will be presented shortly (see below). As for the Bishop of Lisieux (Thomas Basin), he stated in his account that Edward fell ill on Good Friday (28 March) and died within a week. Basin's account therefore states no precise death date. Nevertheless, it clearly means that Edward must have been dead by Friday 4 April.[21] Therefore he could well have died on 3 April as recorded by Molinet. The third French source is the report written in 1483 by Friar Domenico Mancini. That claims that the king died on Monday 7 April.[22]

Obviously therefore, while it offers no precise solution, the sum of the contemporary evidence available strongly implies that Edward died before 9 April. Nevertheless, it is clearly the case that the news of his death was only made public on 9 April. That strongly suggests that in 1483 something very similar was done in respect of the news of the sovereign's demise as the event which took place seventy years later, in 1553.

In other words, when Edward IV – who may have been unwell for some weeks, or even a few months – actually passed away, his manipulative partner, Elizabeth Widville, aided by some of her close relatives and certain other political supporters, kept his passing concealed for a short time in order to try to set her own plans for the future in motion. She had long been worried about the future of her royally fathered children, and her prime aim was therefore to ensure that her son, Edward, Prince of Wales should succeed his father on the English throne.

She had already worked hard in that respect, even persuading Edward IV to put his own brother, George, to death. Thanks to her influence the boy had been placed at Ludlow Castle under the guardianship of her own brother, Anthony Widville, Lord Rivers. Thus the boy had probably been brought up as a strong supporter of his own mother's family, as he himself made clear when he told his uncle, the Duke of Buckingham, that 'as for the government of the kingdom, he had complete confidence in the peers of the realm and the queen.'[23]

When their father died the two living sons of Edward IV and Elizabeth Widville were not together, of course. As we have seen, Edward, Prince of Wales dwelt at Ludlow Castle, under the care of his maternal uncle, Anthony Widville. However, Richard of Shrewsbury, Duke of York and Norfolk, was apparently residing at the Palace of Westminster together with his parents and his five surviving sisters.

Because she needed to ensure that the Prince of Wales was proclaimed and crowned as England's new reigning monarch, one of the first things which Elizabeth Widville probably did following the death of Edward IV would have been to dispatch news of the death to her trusted brother at Ludlow. However, the same news was kept concealed elsewhere. At that stage her planned date for the boy's coronation was Sunday 4 May.[24] In all probability, of course, it seems *that* date may well be significant in respect of the potential evidence which it offers regarding the concealed death date of Edward IV. After all, a plan for crowning his successor on the earliest date possible would have needed to pin-point the date which lay precisely one month and one day ahead of his father's demise. Otherwise the court would still have been in mourning, so that celebrating a coronation would not have been considered fitting. In other words Elizabeth Widville's planned date for the coronation of her son appears to back up the death date of 3 April which Molinet recorded for Edward IV.

Presumably Elizabeth also passed on the information of Edward IV's death in secret to her other younger brothers, including Lionel, Bishop of Salisbury, and Sir Edward Widville. Doubtless the members of the royal council were also already aware of the king's demise. Indeed, they must have agreed with Elizabeth Widville that the news should not immediately be made public. However, it seems probable that their joint agreement in that respect must have been arrived just a fraction too late to prevent Archbishop Thomas Rotherham of York from dispatching the news to his Dean at York Minster, together with orders for the celebration of a royal requiem mass in that cathedral. However, Elizabeth would probably not have seen that as a major catastrophe – assuming that she heard of it. After all, York was far away from the capital, and the plan was only to keep the king's death concealed for a short time.

As for the object of that plan, it must have been to try to ensure that, in spite of English precedents in respect of regencies for minor sovereigns, on this occasion the person wielding that power would eventually be the new king's mother. That was seen as the normal procedure in France. In England the normal precedent in the case of the succession to the throne of a child king had been to assign regency powers (for which the title 'lord protector' had evolved) not to the little boy's mother, but to the closest living mature prince of the blood royal. Such action had been taken in the cases of the fourteenth- and fifteenth-century child kings Edward III, Richard II and Henry VI. The logical sequence in the case of the new boy king, Edward V, was that his only surviving paternal uncle, Richard, Duke of Gloucester, should now be appointed his 'lord protector'.

On Wednesday 9 April Edward IV's death was formally announced and Edward V was proclaimed king. However, no announcement was made appointing a lord protector. Nevertheless, government continued, led by members of the royal privy council and by Elizabeth Widville. The head of the privy council would have been the Lord Chancellor. Edward IV had appointed Thomas Rotherham, Bishop of Lincoln, to that post in 1475, and in 1480 Rotherham had become Archbishop of York. Rotherham obviously sided with Elizabeth Widville. As a result he later found himself dismissed from the post of chancellor when the late king's brother, Richard, Duke of Gloucester, found himself officially appointed lord protector.

Another obvious member of the privy council would have been the Keeper of the Privy Seal – John Russell, Bishop of Lincoln. Since Russell subsequently succeeded Rotherham in the post of chancellor, presumably his stance had been less obviously pro-Widville in the weeks of April 1483. Lord Hastings had been Edward IV's chamberlain, and so he too would presumably have been a member of the privy council. However, he clearly did not support Elizabeth Widville's aim for the powers of regent. As we have seen, a marriage had been negotiated for him in 1461 by Richard Neville, Earl of Warwick (enemy of the Widvilles), with Warwick's own sister Catherine Neville. Hastings' connection with Warwick may thus explain why he initially proved not to be a Widville friend and supporter. His Neville marriage seems to have ceased producing children in about 1470, and it was presumably after Edward IV's return from exile to the throne of England that Lord

Hastings became involved with Elizabeth Lambert (Mistress Shore) as her lover. Subsequently, however, Elizabeth Lambert was apparently also adopted as his mistress by Elizabeth Widville's eldest son, the Marquess of Dorset, thus causing more hostility between Hastings and Elizabeth Widville's family. As a result, in April 1483 he found himself in open conflict with her and her ambitions. Indeed, it seems that it was Hastings who notified the Duke of Gloucester, in the north of England, as to what was going on in London. Moreover, in the capital Lord Hastings appears to have led the opposition to the plans of Elizabeth Widville. The Crowland Chronicle continuator makes it clear that two opposing factions now existed in London. 'Some collected their associates and stood by at Westminster in the name of the queen, others at London, under the protection of Lord Hastings.'[25]

The late king's surviving executors when he died were also potentially significant figures in respect of the way forward. They included Archbishop Rotherham, Bishop Russell and Lord Hastings, whose political stances have been explored. They also included Bishop John Alcock of Worcester. He may well have been a Widville supporter. However, he does not appear to have been in the capital when Edward IV died, because he was serving the Prince of Wales at Ludlow. Therefore it does not seem possible that he could have played any significant role in respect of government support for Elizabeth Widville. However, another executor, the attorney general, William Huse, had worked with Elizabeth Widville on a previous occasion, when Edward IV had been in France. On that occasion the Prince of Wales had been proclaimed 'keeper of the realm', but the little boy was left in the care of his mother. It is therefore possible that Huse supported the moves of Elizabeth Widville in April 1483. Another surviving executor was Sir Thomas Montgomery. However, he was a close relative by marriage of Eleanor Talbot, so he seems unlikely to have been pro-Widville.

Nevertheless, in practical terms government of the realm had to continue. Thus on Monday 21 April various government appointments were made in London.[26] About a week later, on Sunday 27 April, that was followed by the issue of a number of royal commissions. Elizabeth Widville's eldest son by her first marriage, Thomas Grey, Marquess of Dorset, together with her eldest surviving brother, Anthony Widville, Earl Rivers, both figured prominently in those royal commissions.

Curiously, however, although the late Duke of Norfolk's cousin, Lord Howard, was named in respect of the royal commission for the county of Kent, his title as 'Lord' was omitted. Apparently he was now simply identified as 'Sir John Howard, knight'.[27] As we saw earlier, the conduct of Edward IV and Elizabeth Widville in respect of the Mowbray inheritance had been to oust the late Duke of Norfolk's two surviving cousins, Lord Howard and Lord Berkeley, from the Mowbray inheritance as far as possible, in favour of their own younger son, Richard of Shrewsbury. It may therefore be the case that by now omitting Howard's lordly title he was actually being insulted, marking the fact that Elizabeth was aware that Howard was not one of her supporters. After all, he was a cousin of the late Duke of Norfolk, he seems to have acted earlier for his cousin's sister-in-law, Eleanor Talbot,[28] he was still the friend of Eleanor's sister, the dowager Duchess of Norfolk, and he was also in the close service of Cecily Neville, who may have questioned the authenticity of her son's Widville 'marriage' in 1464.

Elizabeth also seems to have chosen to ignore another key official role. Richard, Duke of Gloucester, had been appointed by his late brother as the Lord Admiral of England, Ireland and Aquitaine. Thus theoretically he was in official command of the English navy. Nevertheless, the man who put to sea on Tuesday 29 April in command of a fleet of twenty vessels – also making off with part of the royal treasure – was not Gloucester. The commander of the fleet in question was Elizabeth Widville's own younger brother, Edward.[29]

> No sooner had the death of King Edward [IV] become known, than the French not only made the seas unsafe, but even bore off prizes from the English shores. … Therefore in the face of threatened hostilities a council, held in the absence of the Duke of Gloucester, had appointed Edward [Widville]: and it was commonly believed that the late king's treasure, which had taken such years and pains to gather together, was divided between the queen, the marquess [of Dorset] and Edward [Widville].[30]

As Armstrong noted, Mancini's report of the Widvilles making off with some of the royal treasure comprised a serious offence – and damaging evidence against Elizabeth and her family.[31]

Since she and at least two of her brothers, together with various supporters were already in the capital, planning the new regime as they hoped to see it, Elizabeth Widville did not urgently require the physical presence of her son, the new king. Therefore it was only after St George's day had been duly celebrated in Ludlow that Earl Rivers set off with his royal nephew on their trip to London. They travelled via Northampton, presumably with the deliberate intention of meeting the boy king's surviving paternal uncle, the Duke of Gloucester in that vicinity.

Chapter 16

Losing more relatives

While she sent information in respect of the death of Edward IV and plans for the future to her own brother, Lord Rivers, at Ludlow Castle, it seems that Elizabeth Widville sent nothing to Edward's brother, Richard, Duke of Gloucester, at Middleham Castle. Lord Rivers and his nephew and ward, the new king, had apparently heard the news by Monday 14 April, though, as we have seen, they did not rush off to London, but remained at Ludlow for another ten days in order to celebrate there the feast of St George.

As for the Duke of Gloucester, it seems the news of Edward's demise only reached him about a week after it arrived at Ludlow, on Sunday 20 April. Apparently it came to him in the form of a letter from Elizabeth Widville's enemy in London, Lord Hastings. Obviously Gloucester was not invited to his brother's funeral. When Edward's body was interred at St George's Chapel, Windsor, on Saturday 19 April,[1] the leading male relative at those ceremonies had been the late king's eldest nephew, John de la Pole, Earl of Lincoln, who was married to Elizabeth Widville's niece, Margaret Fitzalan – though that little girl had not yet reached her teens, so of course their marriage had not been consummated, and never was. However, excluding the Duke of Gloucester from his brother's interment was not a unique act as far as Elizabeth Widville was concerned. After all she herself seems not to have attended the late king's burial.

Nevertheless, when he heard the news of his brother's passing, Gloucester rode from Middleham to York, where he required oaths of fealty to be offered to his nephew, the new king, Edward V, by the city magistrates.[2] Also, in spite of the fact that he had apparently heard nothing from Elizabeth Woodville, 'Gloucester wrote the most pleasant letters to console the queen.'[3] Maybe he also had correspondence with Lord Rivers.

Edward IV's burial at St George's Chapel, Windsor, as discovered in 1789.

No such correspondence has actually survived, but the evidence in favour of it lies in the fact that the young king's party, travelling from Ludlow with the boy's maternal uncle, appears to have arranged to meet up with the young king's paternal uncle in the vicinity of Northampton.

So what precisely was the relationship between Rivers and Gloucester? They had certainly found themselves together – and working on the same side – on a number of earlier occasions. For example, in June 1469 they had both accompanied Edward IV on his pilgrimage to Walsingham.[4] Subsequently the two of them had accompanied the king into exile in the Low Countries.[5] When Rivers commissioned an illustration of himself presenting a book to Edward IV, he had the Duke of Gloucester included in the illustration, and shown standing beside him (see illustration page 125).

Moreover, subsequently, in respect of their journeys to London, both Gloucester and Rivers arrived at Northampton on the same day – Tuesday 29 April.[6] That implies strongly that they must have made firm plans for the meeting in question. Unfortunately, however, the continuator of the Crowland Chronicle has slightly clouded the situation which then arose by presenting an account of precisely what took place which seems confusing in one key respect. He states that:

> When he [Gloucester] had reached Northampton, where the duke of Buckingham joined him, there arrived to pay their respects, Anthony, earl Rivers, the king's maternal uncle,

Richard Grey, a very honourable knight, uterine brother to the king and others who had been sent by his nephew the king to submit everything that had to be done to the judgement of his paternal uncle, the duke of Gloucester. When they first arrived they were greeted with a particularly cheerful and merry face and, sitting at the duke's table for dinner, they passed the whole time in very pleasant conversation. Eventually Henry, Duke of Buckingham also arrived, and because it was late, they went off to their various lodgings.[7]

The confusion relates to the precise order of arrivals. Because the Duke of Buckingham is mentioned early in this account, that could be taken to mean that actually Buckingham had been the first associate to join the Duke of Gloucester at Northampton. However, later it is clearly stated that 'eventually' Buckingham arrived. Thus in reality it appears that Buckingham must actually have been the *last* to join the others. It therefore seems that much earlier in the day Earl Rivers had met up with the Duke of Gloucester. Presumably their meeting must therefore have been pre-planned. Moreover, when the two lords did meet up in Northampton, Gloucester then found himself enjoying a 'cheerful and merry' time dining and conversing with Rivers and his companions.

In other words it seems that initially Gloucester himself had received Rivers in an entirely friendly way, and that they had got on well together. Obviously, however, that then raises the question as to why on earth Gloucester subsequently had Rivers, Sir Richard Grey, and others arrested the following morning, when all of them, together with the Duke of Buckingham, had made their way from Northampton to Stony Stratford to meet the young king. The obvious answer would be that, following his own late arrival, and the subsequent departure of the group which had travelled from Ludlow with Lord Rivers, Buckingham had completely maligned Gloucester's perception of Rivers. After all, as Mancini reminds us, 'the duke of Buckingham ... loathed her [Elizabeth Widville's] race',[8] in spite of (or possibly because of) the fact that arrangements had been made for him to marry one of them. So it seems that Buckingham – not Gloucester – must actually have been the key person behind the subsequent plans which were made for the destruction of Elizabeth's brother, Anthony, together with one of her sons.

Of course, the following day, when the news reached Elizabeth Widville in respect of what had happened to her brother and her son, Sir Richard Grey, at Stony Stratford, it sent her into a panic. She had been hoping to be appointed as regent for her son, King Edward V, and to preserve the future of her family. But it now looked more likely that the normal English pattern in respect of minor kings would be followed and that the boy's paternal uncle would be created lord protector – with the backing of her brother-in-law and enemy, the Duke of Buckingham.

Nevertheless, she appears not to have given up her planned project immediately. Initially, she and her eldest son, Thomas Grey, Marquess of Dorset,

> who held the royal treasure, began collecting an army, to defend themselves, and to release the young king from the hands of the dukes.[9] But when they had exhorted certain nobles who had come to the city, and others, to take up arms, they perceived that men's minds were not only irresolute, but altogether hostile to themselves. Some even said openly that it was more just and profitable that the young sovereign should be with his paternal uncle than with his maternal uncles and uterine brothers.[10]

Thus, in the end, Elizabeth finally abandoned the Palace of Westminster that evening. Once again she now felt herself forced to take sanctuary at Westminster. With her she took her brother Lionel, Bishop of Salisbury, her eldest son, Thomas, Marquess of Dorset, and all of her royal daughters, together with her younger son by Edward IV – Richard of Shrewsbury, Duke of York and Norfolk.[11]

Some other Widvilles also now perceived their family's attempted retention of power as having failed. Apparently they also felt that their situation in England was now potentially perilous. Thus, Edward Widville – Elizabeth's youngest brother – whom she had placed in command of a naval force, and to whom she had assigned part of the royal treasury – now fled to Brittany, together with his ships and that part of the royal treasury which had been placed in his custody. In Brittany he joined the entourage of the self-styled 'Earl of Richmond' (later King Henry VII).

Back in England, however, Elizabeth Widville's son, Edward V, now found himself in the care of his paternal uncle, the Duke of Gloucester, and his paternal cousin (and maternal uncle by marriage), the Duke of Buckingham. Escorted by those two dukes he was brought on to London. He arrived at the capital on the afternoon of what had originally been his intended coronation day – Sunday 4 May. But of course he was not crowned on that date, and he did not meet his mother when he reached London. However, he was duly welcolmed into the city, and taken to the Bishop of London's palace, next to St Paul's Cathedral,[12] where the Duke of Gloucester once again ensured that oaths of fealty were taken to the boy king. Clearly Gloucester then had no thought of claiming the throne of England for himself, despite later mythology in that respect. He was simply appointed as lord protector of the realm for Edward V when they reached the capital, significantly, he definitely 'does not appear to have assumed [the] office [of lord protector] until chosen and appointed by the council after his arrival in London with Edward V.'[13]

Edward V remained at the Bishop of London's palace for several days. Then:

> there was talk in the Great Council about the removal of the king to some other, more spacious, place; some suggested the Hospital of St John, some Westminster, but the duke of Buckingham suggested the Tower of London.[14]

So the young king was installed there in the King's Lodging, which was a traditional residence for sovereigns awaiting their coronation.

Meanwhile, the necessary planning for Edward V's crowning was still under way. Amongst many other things, that work included the very important need to persuade the young boy's mother to leave the sanctuary at Westminster Abbey. Obviously if she and her family came out they would be able to attend her son's forthcoming coronation. Thus, on Friday 23 May:

> an oath was read of Richard, Duke of Gloucester, Protector of England, Thomas, Archbishop of Canterbury, Thomas, Archbishop of York, Henry, Duke of Buckingham, who had lately been given charge of our lord the King.
>
> Item: oath that, if the same lady is willing, the said lords wanted the lady Elizabeth, Queen of England, who is now living in the sanctuary of St Peter of Westminster, to give up the privileges of that same place.[15]

In other words, on 23 May at the latest (though he may actually have sent messages to her earlier), the Duke of Gloucester definitely contacted Elizabeth Widville – whom he then still recognised as a queen – at the abbey and asked her to come out. Probably the invitation in question was conveyed to her on Gloucester's behalf by the two archbishops. Unfortunately, in spite of receiving the invitation, Elizabeth chose not to emerge from the sanctuary in May.

In the end, even if she herself planned not to attend the coronation of her son, Edward, it was important to ensure the presence at that ceremony of Edward's younger brother, Richard of Shrewsbury, because he was a very significant peer of the realm, holding the two important duchies of York and Norfolk. Therefore on Monday 16 June, a delegation led by Cardinal Bourchier was dispatched by boat up the River Thames from London the very short distance to Westminster. The delegates accompanying the cardinal then requested Elizabeth Widville, 'in her kindness, to allow her son Richard, duke of York, to leave and come to the Tower for the comfort of his brother, the king. She willingly agreed to the proposal.'[16] Her action in that respect appears to show very clearly that she trusted the lord protector and the government which he headed; that she still fully expected the coronation of Edward V to take place, and that she wished her youngest son – a peer of the realm – to be present at that event.

Thus, on Monday 16 June Elizabeth Widville handed her son, Richard of Shrewsbury, into the custody of Cardinal Bourchier. He and the other delegates then returned by boat westwards, to the Tower of London. Thus young Richard must have entered the Tower via the river gate which was then known simply as *Porta Aque* or *la Watergate*. Later, of course – in the sixteenth century or early in the seventeenth century – that riverside entrance acquired the sinister name of 'Traitor's Gate' or 'Traitors' Gate'.[17] But it was not called that in 1483. In the Tower young Richard joined his brother in the King's Lodging.

Presumably Elizabeth was not then aware of the fact that, as we saw earlier, one week previously, 'gret besyness ageyns the Coronacione'[18] had emerged at a meeting of the royal council which had been working on the ongoing plans for that event. But she must have learnt that news later. There was also other distressing news for her. As we saw earlier, her brother, Anthony Widville, Earl Rivers, had found himself arrested at Stony Stratford, together with his nephew – Elizabeth's second son, Sir Richard Grey (the younger of the two Grey half-brothers of Edward V), and also

The signature of Elizabeth's brother, Anthony, Earl Rivers, from his will.

Sir Thomas Vaughan. Despite their arrest, initially Anthony – and the others – had remained alive. All three men had simply been taken north and imprisoned. However, two months later they found themselves placed on trial at Pontefract Castle. They were then executed there towards the end of June 1483. Some sources date the execution of Earl Rivers to 20 June.[19] The more widespread belief claims that he was executed on 25 June 1483. However, in either case, given that the Duke of Gloucester did not agree to receive the crown until 26 June, presumably Rivers must technically have been executed during the reign of his nephew, Edward V.

Writing his account a few years later, in the reign of Henry VII, John Rous reported:

> at the time of his death, Lord Antony Woodville, Earl Rivers, was found to be wearing sackcloth next to his bare flesh, as he had done long before that. Moreover, at the time of his imprisonment in Pontefract, he wrote a poem, which was shown to me, in English in the following words:

> Somewhat musyng and more mornyng,
> In remembring the unstydfastnes,
> This world being of such whelyng,
> Me contrarieng, what may I gesse?
> I fere dowtless remediles,
> Is now to sese my wofull chaunce.
> Lo in this staunce, now in substance,
> Such is my dawnce.
> Wyllyng to dye methynkys truly
> Bowndyn am I, and that gretly.

157

To be content.
Seyng plainly that fortune doth wry
All contrary from myn entent.
Hytt is ny spent
Welcome, Fortune.
But I ne went,
Thus to be shent.
But sho hit ment,
Such is huz won.

and so the aforementioned lords were sentenced to death –
and to a conspirators death – by Richard, Duke of Gloucester,
then Protector of England. Thus, innocent of all that had not
been invented by their executioners, peacefully and humbly
they submitted to the cruel torment of their enemies.[20]

The curious assertion by Rous that Anthony Widville was condemned
to death by Richard, Duke of Gloucester, is clearly nonsense. Although
Gloucester must eventually have agreed to his arrest, we have already
seen that such does not appear to have been his idea initially, when he
received Rivers at Northampton in the most friendly way. It appears more
likely that Anthony Widville's brother-in-law, Henry Stafford, Duke of
Buckingham, was the person who pushed for his arrest. It is also clear that
the subsequent trial and execution of Anthony Widville, of his nephew,
Richard Grey, and of Sir Thomas Vaughan were all carried out by the
Earl of Northumberland. Nevertheless, the result for Elizabeth Widville
was that she now received the news that she had lost yet another of her
brothers. Moreover, this time she had also lost one of her sons.

Chapter 17

The second Crown Loss

About three years after the alleged event, on about 30 April 1486, the Crowland Abbey Chronicle continuator wrote a report which stated that in the end, in the early summer of 1483,

> Richard [Duke of Gloucester] the protector claimed for himself the government of the kingdom with the name and title of king. ... It [the alleged claim] was put forward, by means of a supplication contained in a certain parchment roll, that King Edward's sons were bastards, by submitting that he had been precontracted to a certain Lady Eleanor Boteler before he married Queen Elizabeth and, further, that the blood of his other brother, George, Duke of Clarence, had been attainted, so that, at the time, no certain and uncorrupt blood of the lineage of Richard, Duke of York, was to be found except in the person of the said Richard, Duke of Gloucester.[1]

In reality, however, the claim in question was not actually put forward by Richard, Duke of Gloucester. Ever since they had arrived in London he had simply been acting as lord protector on behalf of the young King Edward V, and planning that boy's coronation. However, as we saw earlier, one of the bishops who normally finds himself required to fulfil an official role at an English coronation is the Bishop of Bath and Wells. Thus, as part of the preparations for crowning Edward V on the new planned date of 24 June, Bishop Robert Stillington had been summoned to London.

When he arrived there, around the end of the first week of June, Stillington approached the royal council and informed them that, in his view, the coronation of Elizabeth Widville's son could not proceed, because before Edward IV's secret marriage to Elizabeth he himself had secretly married that same king to Eleanor Talbot (Lady Boteler). Thus the subsequent Widville marriage was illegal and the royal children of Elizabeth Widville were, in reality, all bastards. It was on Monday 9 June, after the royal council had met, that Canon Simon Stallworth(e), a priest in the service of the chancellor, Bishop Russell, wrote his important surviving letter to Sir William Stonor in which he reported that there was now 'gret besyness ageyns the Coronacione'.[2]

In his letter, however, Canon Stallworth(e) does not specifically refer to Bishop Stillington. Interestingly, the earliest source which does now survive in respect of the fact that it was Bishop Stillington who produced the key evidence in question can be found in Henry VII's legal records of January 1485/6:

> *Reversel d'un Act. Touts les Justices de l'Exchequer Chambre primo die Termini par le commandement le Roy communerent pour le reversel del bil et Act qui bastard les enfants le Roy E.iv et Eliz. sa femme. ... fuit mouve per ascun deux qu'il serait bon ordre, q' cestui q' fist ceo faux bill, refomera c': et disoient q' le Evesque de B fist le bil, et les Seigniors vouloient avec lui in le Parlement Chambre.*

> Reversal of an Act. All the Justices of the Exchequer Chamber the first day of the [Michaelmas] Term, by the command (of) the King discussed the reversal of the bill and Act which bastardised the children of King E.IV and Elizabeth his wife. ... there was a move by some of them that it would be good for the person who had brought about this false bill to reform it: and they said that the Bishop of B made the bill, and the Lords wanted to have him in the parliament Chamber.[3]

In the fifteenth century the only episcopal see in England whose place name began with the letter B was the diocese of Bath and Wells, and Robert Stillington held that bishopric from 1465 until his death, in May 1491.

As for the royal council, in June 1483, when it heard from Bishop Stillington, it decided that, since, as yet, no official parliament had been opened, but given that the prospective members of such an assembly had been summoned to the capital for the intended official opening of a new parliament after the planned coronation, those prospective members of the planned – but as yet unopened – new parliament should be asked to meet at the London Guildhall and listen to the evidence which the bishop was presenting. Their meeting in that location would not be called a parliament, of course. Instead it would be referred to under the heading of 'the three estates of the realm'. At the Guildhall the evidence of Bishop Stillington would be presented to the meeting in question, and the three estates would then make the decision as to what should be done.

Thus the three estates met at the Guildhall. They heard Stillington's evidence, and on that basis they decided that the legal wife of Edward IV had been Eleanor Talbot, that his subsequent alleged marriage to Elizabeth Widville had not been valid, and that all of the late king's children were therefore bastards (since his legal wife, Eleanor, had borne none). Given the earlier act of attainder against the Duke of Clarence, they also saw *his* surviving children as legally excluded from succession to the throne. They therefore decided that the legal heir to the English crown was currently Richard, Duke of Gloucester. They then produced a petition to Richard, asking him to accept the role of king. *Their* document was therefore the 'supplication' subsequently referred to by the Crowland Abbey Chronicle continuator (see above).

The full text of their petition survives, and it was presented earlier (see above, Chapter 8). First it spoke of 'the ungracious, pretensed marriage (as all England hath cause so say) made betwixt the said King Edward and Elizabeth (sometyme wife to Sir John Grey, Knight), late nameing herself (and many years heretofore) "Queene of England".' It then went on to say that 'we considre howe the said pretensed marriage betwixt the above-named King Edward and Elizabeth Grey was made of grete presumption, without the knowyng or assent of the lordes of this lond, and alsoe by sorcerie and wichecrafte committed by the said Elizabeth and her moder, Jaquett, Duchess of Bedford (as the common opinion of the people and the publique voice and fame is through all this land).' Speaking of the fact that it had been a secret ceremony, the three estates then went on to state very clearly that 'at the tyme of contract of the same pretensed marriage (and bifore, and longe tyme after) the said King Edward was, and stoode, marryed, and trouth-plyght, to oone Dame Elianore Butteler [*née* Talbot] (daughter of the old Earl of Shrewesbury [John Talbot]) with whom the saide King Edward had made a precontracte [earlier contract][4] of matrimonie longe tyme bifore he made the said pretensed mariage with the said Elizabeth Grey in manner and fourme aforesaide.'

The logical conclusions reached by the three estates of the realm were therefore

a) 'the said King Edward (duryng his lyfe) and the said Elizabeth lived togather sinfully and dampnably in adultery, against the lawe of God and his church',
b) 'all th'issue and children of the said king beene bastards, and unable to inherite or to clayme anything by inheritance, by the lawe and custome of England.'

They also decided that Elizabeth Widville had never really been queen, and in future she would once again be known as Lady Grey.

In 1483 the loss of an English queen consort's crown, which was then formally suffered by Elizabeth, was actually by no means unique. In fact such had theoretically been the fate of all the three preceding fifteenth-century royal consorts of England, despite the fact that, just like Elizabeth Widville, all three of them had earlier been crowned.

For example, the first Lancastrian consort, Joanna of Navarre, had married the recently enthroned King Henry IV on 7 February 1402/3 at Winchester Cathedral. She then made her state entry to London on 26 February and was crowned as queen consort at Westminster Abbey. After her husband died, his son, King Henry V did accuse her of witchcraft against him, and she found herself imprisoned for a while. Nevertheless, she remained a titular English 'queen' until her death, in 1437, and was buried at Canterbury Cathedral in that capacity. It was only about a quarter of a century after her death – when Edward IV acquired the English crown – that her husband was officially declared to have been *rex de facto, non de iure* ('king in fact but not in law'),[5] thereby placing Joanna's official queenly status also in question.

Next, in her own homeland, in June 1420, Catherine of France had married Henry V. Later the couple travelled to England. There Catherine was crowned as queen consort at Westminster Abbey on 23 February 1420/1. In 1422 Henry V died and Catherine became the queen mother. Despite her subsequent involvement in love affairs, theoretically she retained her official queenly status until her own death in January 1436/7, when she was buried as Henry V's consort in his chantry at Westminster Abbey. But in her case too, it was about a quarter of a century after her death, following the accession of Edward IV, that her husband was officially declared to have been *rex de facto, non de iure* ('king in fact but not in law')[6] – thus making Catherine's queenly rank also questionable.

As for Margaret of Anjou, as we have seen she married Henry VI in 1445. She was then crowned as his queen consort at Westminster Abbey on 30 May 1445. But in her case her husband lost the throne in 1461. He regained it briefly nine years later, in 1470, but then lost it again, after which Margaret of Anjou found herself imprisoned for four years in the Tower of London. Thus she did not die as queen on 25 August 1482, and was never buried as queen. Indeed, she is officially referred to by name in the parliamentary records of Edward IV as 'Margaret late called queen of England.'[7]

What had happened in respect of the three Lancastrian queens, following the Yorkist takeover, makes the subsequent fate of Elizabeth Widville in no way unusual. Also, given her own earlier anxiety regarding the validity of her royal union, the decision reached in the summer of 1483 cannot possibly have surprised her. It was a decision which she had apparently been fearing to hear for almost nineteen years, and of course, there was nothing she could do about it. She simply had to accept the situation. Likewise the loss of royal status on the part of her children – including 'Edward V' – was simply a potential outcome which she had long feared.

Thus, in March 1483/4, when the former Duke of Gloucester – who had now been persuaded to accept the crown, becoming King Richard III – was once again in contact with her, and was once more seeking to persuade her to leave the sanctuary at Westminster Abbey, and to bring out her daughters, she would not have been the least bit surprised to find him addressing her as 'dam Elizabeth Gray late calling her self Quene of England.'[8] However, when Richard promised her that he would secure suitable marriages for the daughters whom she had borne to his brother, King Edward IV, it also seems that she had no difficulty in believing his promise.

> Memorandum that I Richard by the grace of God king of England and of Fraunce and lord of Irland in the presens of you my lords spirituelle & temporelle and you Maire and

Aldermen of my Cite of London promitte & swere *verbo Regio* & upon these holy evangelies of god by me personally touched that if the doghters of dam Elizabeth Gray late calling her self Quene of England that is to wit Elizabeth Cecille Anne Kateryn and Briggitte wolle come unto me out of Saintwarie of Westminstre and be guyded Ruled & demeaned after me than I shalle see that they shalbe in suertie of their lyffes and also not suffer any maner hurt by any maner persone or persones ... And that I shalle do marie sucche of theim as now bene mariable to gentilmen borne and everiche of theim geve in mariage lands & tenementes to the yerely valewe of CC marc for terme of their lyves and in like wise to the other doghters when they come to lawfulle Age of mariage if they lyff and suche gentilmen as shalle happe to marie with theim I shalle straitly charge from tyme to tyme loyngly to love & entreat theim as their wiffes & my kynneswomen As they wolle advoid and eschue my displeasure ... In witnesse wherof to this writing of my othe & promise aforsaid in your said presences made I have set my signemanuelle the first day of Marche the first yere of my Reigne [Monday 1 March 1483/4].[9]

Elizabeth Widville's decision in respect of leaving sanctuary herself at that point is not known for certain. But she definitely sent her daughters out to Richard, and probably she came out too.[10] In other words, the surviving evidence in terms of her actual conduct suggests that she apparently trusted Richard III completely. Also his subsequent conduct in respect of her daughters proves that she had been quite correct in that respect.

Later that year (1484), Richard arranged a suitable marriage for Elizabeth Widville's third (and second surviving) daughter, Cecily, who was then married to Ralph Scrope (the younger brother of Thomas, 6th Baron Scrope).[11] The following year, after his loss of his own consort, Anne Neville, Richard III negotiated a royal match for himself, with the Infanta Joana of Portugal. His Portuguese negotiations also included a planned marriage for his eldest illegitimate niece, Elizabeth of York. Richard's plan for that niece was apparently to restore her to royal status by uniting her with a junior cadet member of the Portuguese royal family.[12] The two planned Portuguese royal marriages would almost certainly have taken place if Richard III had not then been defeated and killed at the battle of Bosworth.

Unfortunately, unlike his mother, Elizabeth's senior son, Thomas Grey, Marquess of Dorset, appears not to have trusted Richard III. He became involved in the subsequent rebellion which is named after that major traitor, the Duke of Buckingham. When that rebellion failed Thomas fled from England and he then joined the so-called 'Earl of Richmond' in France. Curiously, however, Elizabeth obviously felt that was not a wise move on her son's part.

> By secret messengers [she] advised the marquise her soon, who was at Parys, to forsake erle Henry, and with all speede convenyent to returne into England, wher he showld be sure to be caulyd of the king unto highe promotion.[13]

The conduct of Elizabeth Widville as subsequently reported in that respect by Polydore Vergil makes it seem very hard to believe that she could possibly have perceived Richard III as the person who had been responsible for the executions of her brother, Lord Rivers, and of her second son, Sir Richard Grey. It also makes it difficult to believe that in her view Richard III had in any way harmed her two sons fathered by Edward IV.

It seems impossible now to ascertain what precisely she believed in respect of those boys. Possibly she knew that one of them ('Edward V') had died naturally – like three of her other royal children (Mary, Margaret and George).[14] She may also have heard that men from Kent – including her own cousins, Richard Haute, and his brother-in-law, Sir John Fogge (see above, Chapter 10, Family Tree 11 'The Widville / Fogge / Haute connection') – apparently took part in an 'entreprise' [abduction][15] which might have illegally extricated young Richard of Shrewsbury from the Tower of London in July 1483.[16] It is even conceivable that the boy then secretly grew up, lived and ultimately died and was buried in their county.[17] If so, however, despite Richard III's detailed ensuing proclamation of instructions to 'his true subgiettes of this his Countie of Kent',[18] that boy's subsequent whereabouts then appear to have remained unknown, both by the king and by Elizabeth.

Nevertheless, she cannot possibly have thought that Richard III had harmed her two sons by Edward IV in any way. If she had thought that

Richard III had harmed them, then her reported recommendation to her eldest son that he should trust the new king would have been ludicrous. It is significant that apparently it was Elizabeth's message to him which convinced the Marquess of Dorset. 'Cauled home of his mother … [and] subornyd by king Richerds fayre promyses',[19] as soon as he received his mother's advice Thomas Grey attempted to abandon France and return to England. Unfortunately, however, he then found his plan in that respect was blocked by 'the Earl of Richmond'.

It is also interesting that the only surviving source which claims that it was Elizabeth Widville who urged her eldest son to abandon the 'Earl of Richmond' (later Henry VII) and to work with Richard III is Polydore Vergil, who was writing for King Henry VII. The fact that Vergil recorded that point appears to imply that he – and therefore also, presumably, Henry VII and his government – did not view Elizabeth Widville in a very favourable light, in spite of the fact that they found themselves forced to acknowledge her as Edward IV's queen consort in order to promote the claim that her eldest daughter was the Yorkist heiress.

Further significant evidence in respect of the apparently critical view of Elizabeth Widville which was held by Henry VII and his regime will emerge in the next chapter. Vergil will then be shown to have also reported that her son-in-law eventually punished her for having surrendered her daughters to the care of Richard III (see below).

Chapter 18

The Queen's Mother

The question as to what was Elizabeth Widville's view of King Richard III – and what was his view of her – is very intriguing. Earlier, during the reign of Edward IV, her relationship with the king's youngest brother – Richard, Duke of Gloucester, as he then was – though it may not have been particularly close, does not ever appear to have been difficult, unlike her relationship with their middle brother, George, Duke of Clarence. We saw earlier that subsequently, when he had become King Richard III, Gloucester wrote a letter to the Earl of Desmond in which he implied (without naming her specifically) that Elizabeth Widville was responsible for the deaths of his brother, George, of the previous Earl of Desmond, and of other friends and relatives. Yet his personal reaction in that respect appears to have been erroneously evaluated by some historians.

For example, one published account claims that:

> It is significant that Gloucester, who blamed the Woodvilles for Clarence's murder in a letter, was now [c. 1478] exclusively based in the north (wearing black mourning clothes and hinting in a letter to the Earl of Desmond [written in 1484] at his alienation from his brother's court).[1]

But the account in question is inaccurate in a number of ways. First, the quote refers to 'Clarence's murder', when it should use the word execution. Also in this instance, as I have shown, the relevant dates do not correspond. Moreover, in reality Mancini does not in fact assert that Gloucester wore continuous mourning for George following the execution of that particular brother. Referring simply to the period of April–May 1483, Mancini states that, following his arrival in London and his appointment as lord protector, Gloucester:

> iam pullas vestes ponit, quas post mortem fratris semper induerat.

> (now set aside the sombre / mournful garments, which after the death of his brother, he had always been wearing).[2]

Since Mancini certainly does not mention George, Duke of Clarence, in this context, presumably the brother's death to which he refers was simply the passing of Edward IV in April 1483. In other words Gloucester had worn dark clothes for a month or so – not for five years. Moreover the clothes in question had simply been standard mourning on his part – not a symbol of his hostility in respect of Elizabeth Widville.

Of course the death of Edward IV may eventually have forced Elizabeth Widville to think of Richard as her potential rival (on the basis of English precedents in terms of who should exercise regency powers for her son, the new boy king, Edward V). Although that did cause a kind of remote and impersonal conflict with the Duke of Gloucester, which eventually led her to reclaim sanctuary at Westminster Abbey, her subsequent behaviour in terms of actually dealing with Richard showed no sign of enmity on her part in respect of the man himself.

As we have seen, first of all she was perfectly happy to hand over her younger son, Richard of Shrewsbury, to join his elder brother in the King's Lodging of the Tower of London. But then, of course, the decision arrived at by the three estates of the realm in mid to late June 1483 officially deprived her of royal status and recognised Eleanor Talbot as Edward IV's legal royal consort. Eventually it also made Richard III king. Even so, subsequently Elizabeth Widville obviously still trusted Richard III (as he had then become) in respect of her daughters, because she accepted his plea that she should pass them into his care. Moreover, as we have seen, she also reportedly recommended her eldest son, Thomas Grey, to return to England and trust the new king. It is therefore difficult to imagine how Elizabeth Widville would have felt when she heard the news of Richard III's defeat and death at the battle of Bosworth.

Possibly she may have been aware of the fact that the new monarch, Henry VII, reputedly already had a plan to marry her own eldest daughter, Elizabeth of York. Indeed, by some historians the incredible suggestion has been advanced that Edward IV – working with the future Henry VII's mother, his distant cousin, Margaret Beaufort – might himself have negotiated such a possible marriage for his eldest daughter some years earlier.[3] That assertion is ludicrous for two reasons. First, in reality the proposed source for the claim in question – a source which is not precisely contemporary, but which dates from August 1486 – merely has Margaret's third husband, Thomas, Lord Stanley, Earl of Derby, testifying:

> that long before communing was had between the said lord Henry and lady Elizabeth about contracting marriage, the said sworn [witness] heard Richard, earl of Salisbury, and the lady Margaret, wife of this sworn [witness], mother of the said king that now is, and divers other noble and illustrious persons saying that the said king Henry and lady Elizabeth were related in the fourth and fourth degrees of kindred, and reciting the degrees aforesaid, and affirming that they were true degrees lineally drawn from the said duke of Lancaster. This sworn [witness] also says that he knows that the said Edward IV, father of the said lady Elizabeth, and the lady Margaret, mother of the aforesaid king Henry, reputed and held themselves to be kinsmen.[4]

This is merely evidence in respect of kinship – which for Henry VII and Elizabeth of York meant that a papal dispensation was required for marriage. It certainly does not comprise evidence that King Edward IV ever considered the possibility of such a marriage for his eldest daughter. Presumably therefore Elizabeth Widville would never have heard her own royal partner contemplating such an abominable, low-quality marriage for Elizabeth of York.

Secondly, the clear fact is firmly established that for seven years, between 1475 and 1482, an entirely different marriage plan had been in place for the daughter in question. 'As part of the treaty of Picquigny ..., it was agreed that Elizabeth [of York] should marry the dauphin Charles, with a jointure of £60,000 to be provided by Louis XI.'[5]

Elizabeth of York had thus been firmly committed to a diplomatic royal marriage by the treaty concluded between her father and the king of France. In other words, between 1475 and 1482 she had been assumed to be already firmly committed in terms of wedlock. In fact she was understood to be on her way to becoming the future Queen of France – a prospect for her eldest daughter, which, given her own maternal-line family background, would undoubtedly have delighted Elizabeth Widville.

So seriously was that commitment taken at the English royal court, that in 1482, when Louis XI was suddenly discovered to be planning a *different* diplomatic marriage for his son and heir, Edward IV suddenly 'found himself deluded in his hopes for a marriage between his daughter and the Dauphin; a marriage which he and his wife, the queen, had desired above everything else in this world.'[6] In fact, the enormous shock produced by that news is reported by one contemporary source to have been what caused Edward IV to fall ill, and to have led subsequently to the king's death.[7]

Of course, it is conceivable that Elizabeth Widville may possibly have heard later (after the death of Edward IV) that at Rennes Cathedral, on Christmas Day 1483, the 'Earl of Richmond' had reportedly voiced a pledge to marry her eldest daughter. However, once again it is important to note that the only source in respect of that information is the account written later by Polydore Vergil.

> Here [at Rennes], after many mutual congratulations, after they had spent several days planning their strategy, they assembled in church on Christmas Day, confirmed everything else on their oath, and Henry vowed that as soon as he had gained the kingdom he would marry King Edward's daughter Elizabeth.[8]

Even if Vergil's later assertion is true in that respect, there is certainly no evidence to suggest that Elizabeth Widville would herself have favoured that proposal. Logically she would have greatly preferred Richard III's subsequent project to marry her eldest daughter to a Portuguese prince.

Nevertheless, earlier published sources have curiously told incredible stories suggesting that Elizabeth Widville herself plotted her eldest daughter's marriage to the 'Earl of Richmond' by working on that plan with that man's mother. For example, one amazing published source claims:

> It was an enormous asset to this conspiracy to be able to attract the support of Edward IV's widow, Queen Elizabeth Wydeville. Rumours of her sons' deaths were bound to inflame the dowager-queen and alienate her from Richard III. This gave Margaret Beaufort and Elizabeth Wydeville a common cause. Contact between them was established by Margaret's physician, the Welshman Lewis Caerleon. ... When Dr. Lewis visited Queen Elizabeth Wydeville in sanctuary at Westminster (whence she had retired as Richard of Gloucester approached London from the north at the beginning of May 1483) it was relatively easy for him to carry messages to and from Margaret Beaufort on the subject of a marriage between Henry Tudor and either Elizabeth of York or, if Elizabeth should die, her younger sister Cecily. Elizabeth Wydeville was much in favour of Margaret's proposal – it had, of course, been in the air for years already – and sent an encouraging message to the London inn of Margaret's fourth husband, Thomas, Lord Stanley. Elizabeth Wydeville promised to urge her own and Edward IV's friends and servants to give it their support too, aware that it implied an attempt to replace Richard on the throne. As for Margaret, she used her agent Reginald Bray, to attract others into the conspiracy, especially young servants of Edward IV from Southern England like Sir Giles Daubeney, Richard Guildford Thomas Rameney and John Cheyne, each of whom swore in oath to adhere to the ladies' plan.[9]

The claims made assert

a) that rumours of her sons' deaths alienated Elizabeth Widville from Richard III. But we have already seen clear evidence that such was not the case.
b) that Lewis Caerleon made contact between Elizabeth Widville and Margaret Beaufort – but not a single piece of evidence is cited to support that claim. (See below.)

c) that plans were made to marry the 'Earl of Richmond' to either Elizabeth of York or her sister, Cecily – but again, no evidence is cited.

d) that such a planned marriage for 'the Earl of Richmond' had been 'in the air for years already'. But we have already seen clear evidence that such was not the case.

Although the published account of Griffiths and Thomas cites not a single source in respect of the claim which it makes, once again the source for this particular story is Polydore Vergil. Vergil, who refers to a physician called Lewis (but who does not employ the name Caerleon) states that:

> the foundation of a new conspiracy had been laid at London by Queen Elizabeth, wife to King Henry, and Henry's mother Margaret, in this way. Because of her ill health Margaret employed a Welsh physician named Lewis. Since he was a grave man not without his uses, she was often accustomed to speak freely with him and sigh in his presence. After she had learned of the killing of Edward's sons, that prudent woman began to have high hopes for her son's fortunes, thinking it would be an action good for the commonwealth, should it come to pass, that the blood of Henry VI and Edward were to be mixed in kinship and these two long-standing and highly ruinous factions ended by one jointure of both families. And so, not letting pass such a great opportunity, in the course of her conversation she informed Lewis that the time had now come when Edward's eldest daughter Elizabeth could be married to her son Henry, and King Richard, regarded by all men as an enemy to his nation, could easily be cast down from all honor and deprived of his crown, and so she asked him that he secretly deal with the queen about this great enterprise. For the queen also employed him [see below], because he was a physician most skilled at the art. Without delay Lewis met with the queen, who was still keeping herself in the asylum, and told her of this thing as if it were his own invention and he was not acting under orders. The queen liked the idea so much that she commanded Lewis to go to Margaret, who was staying at her husband's London mansion. On her behalf he

should promise that she would do what she could so all the friends of her husband Edward would side with Margaret's son Henry, if only he would swear to marry her daughter Elizabeth after gaining the throne, or, should she die before he came to power, to marry her younger daughter Cecily [see below]. Lewis immediately performed this service and easily settled the business between these women, since, being a physician, he could act as a go-between and member of that new conspiracy against Richard without arousing any suspicion.[10]

Vergil's account claims that Dr Lewis was serving as Elizabeth Widville's physician at this time. Earlier, however, she had employed a different physician (see above, Chapter 10). Also, given that her son, the former King Edward V, may well have died naturally in the summer of 1483 (as three of his brothers and sisters had done earlier),[11] it is interesting to note that Elizabeth Widville is apparently alleged to have also contemplated the possible young death of her eldest daughter. However, it seems very strange that here Vergil is claiming that Elizabeth Widville worked against Richard III, while elsewhere he acknowledged that she entrusted her daughters to him (and condemns her for doing so), and claims that she persuaded her son Dorset to desert the 'Earl of Richmond' and trust Richard III.

Certainly, once he had ousted Richard III, and seized the English throne, Henry VII (the former 'Earl of Richmond') rapidly sent to Sheriff Hutton for Elizabeth junior (together with her younger sisters and her royal cousins). A few months later, on 18 January 1485/6, he married her. Their wedding was celebrated at Westminster Abbey, though no evidence survives regarding the nature of that ceremony, or who attended it.

However, in respect of another of Elizabeth Widville's daughters, Henry had her existing marriage annulled. That was the marriage which had been arranged by Richard III for Elizabeth Widville's second surviving daughter, Cecily. After the annulment of that union Henry then arranged a new marriage for Cecily, to one of his own relatives – his maternal uncle, Viscount Welles.

But of course, before either of those marriage proposals, in November 1485 at his first parliament, Henry VII repealed the act of the 1484 parliament of Richard III, known as *Titlus regius*.

Where afore this tyme, Richard, late Duke of Gloucester, and after in dede and not of right King of England, called Richard the III^d, caused a false and seditious Bille of false and malicious ymaginaciones, ayenst all good and true disposicion to be put unto hyme, the beginning of which bill is thus:

'*Please it your noble Grace to understand the consideracions, Elleccion and*

Peticion underwritten' &c.

Which Bill, after that, with all the continue of the same, by auctoritee of Parliament, holden the first yeere of the usurped Reigne of the said late King Richard the III^d, was ratified, enrolled, approved and authorised; as in the same more plainly appereth. The King [Henry VII], atte the special instance, desire and prayer of the Lordes Spirituell and Temporell and Commons in this present Parlement assembled, will it be ordeined, stablished and enacted, by the advys of the said Lordes Spirituell and Temporell and the Comunes in this present Parlement assembled, and by auctoritee of the same, that the said Bille, Acte and Ratificacion, and all the circumstances and dependants of the same Bill and Act, for the fals and seditious ymaginacions and untrouths thereof, be void, adnulled, repelled, irrite, and of noe force ne effecte. And that it be ordeined by the said auctorite that the said Bill be cancelled, destrued, and that the said Acte, Record and enrollinge shall be taken and avoided out of the Roll and Records of the said Parliament of the said late King, and brente, and utterly destroyed. And over this, be it ordeined by the same auctoritee, that every persoune having anie Coppie or Remembraunces of the said Bill or Acte, bring unto the Chaunceller of England for the tyme being, the same Coppies and Remembraunces, or utterlie destrue theym, afore the Fest of Easter next comen, upon Peine of ymprisonment, and making fyne and ransome to the Kinge atte his will. So that all thinges said and remembered in the said Bill and Acte thereof maie be for ever out of remembraunce and allso forgott.[12]

This is probably the only occasion on which an act of parliament was repealed both unquoted and unsummarised. The provision for the destruction of all copies is also probably unique.

Naturally, in terms of Elizabeth of York's situation, Henry VII's repeal of the earlier act was good in one way. After all, it restored her to the status of a legitimate English princess by restoring her mother's claim to have been the wife and queen consort of Edward IV. Indeed, the restitution of Elizabeth of York (who was then his own planned consort) to legitimate royal status was the whole reason why the repeal was set in motion by Henry VII at his first parliament. He wished to present Elizabeth of York to the nation as Edward IV's heiress.

Nevertheless, in reality that restitution of Elizabeth of York's royal status was actually never *universally* accepted. For example, almost half a century later, on 16 December 1533, Eustace Chapuys, who was then serving as the Imperial ambassador in England, wrote to the Holy Roman Emperor Charles V.

> You cannot imagine the grief of all the people at this abominable government [of King Henry VIII]. They are so transported with indignation at what passes, that they complain that your Majesty takes no steps in it, and I am told by many respectable people that they would be glad to see a fleet come hither in your name ... [for] they say you have a better title than the present King, who only claims by his mother, who was declared by sentence of the bishop of Bath [Robert Stillington] a bastard, because Edward [IV] had espoused another wife before the mother of Elizabeth of York. [13]

And about a year later, on 3 November 1534, Chapuys wrote another letter on the same subject to Charles V, in which he repeated that:

> Richard III declared by definitive sentence of the bishop of Bath that the daughters of king Edward, of whom the [present] king's mother was the eldest, were bastards, by reason of a precontract [earlier marriage contract] made by Edward with another lady before he married their mother. [14]

Ironically, however, the subsequent behaviour of Henry VII actually makes it somewhat questionable to what extent *he himself* truly accepted the royal status of his mother-in-law. It is not clear where Elizabeth Widville had been living during the reign of Richard III. Initially, of course, in June 1483, she had been in sanctuary at Westminster Abbey, with her daughters and other relatives. Then, as we have seen, she accepted Richard III's request and sent her daughters out to him in about March 1483/4. It is not clear whether she herself left the sanctuary at the same time. But given the fact that Richard III then granted her 'the summe of DCC [700] marc of lawfulle money of England',[15] it appears likely that she may very well have done so. Assuming that she did leave Westminster Abbey in about March 1483/4, no surviving evidence exists to indicate where she would then have resided. Might she possibly have stayed with relatives?

It is also equally unclear where she resided in 1485–1486, in the months immediately after Henry VII had seized the throne. But then on 5 March 1485/6 the new sovereign granted her not only a number of small annuities (totalling a sum in the region of £800), but also the tenure for life of various properties.[16] So at that point she would have acquired access to various possible residences of her own.

The actual properties which she was given on that occasion were the manors of Waltham (probably both Great Waltham and Little Waltham, which lie just to the north of Chelmsford), Great Baddow (just to the south of Chelmsford), Mashbury (just to the north west of Chelmsford), (Great) Dunmow (to the north of Chelmsford), (Great) Leighs (to the north of Chelmsford) and Farnham (just to the north of Bishops Stortford). All the manors in question were in the county of Essex. Indeed, most of them were in the vicinity of the county town. In modern terms it therefore seems possible that at this rather late stage in her life Elizabeth Widville may have been categorised by her son-in-law as an 'Essex Girl' – 'a female viewed as promiscuous and unintelligent'![17] Indeed, that may have been the disparaging vision of her which had always been in the mind of Henry VII.

About six months later, on 20 September 1486, Elizabeth Widville found that she had become the grandmother of England's new Prince of Wales (Prince Arthur). Subsequently she was also asked to become the godmother of that new heir to the throne, when the little boy was baptised. Even so, there is no evidence of the existence of a close personal relationship between Henry VII and his mother-in-law. Indeed, it seems possible that, in terms of her personal knowledge of certain key aspects of the existing situation, Elizabeth Widville may subsequently have worried her son-in-law considerably in relation to one serious event he found himself forced to confront. The event in question was the rival claim to the English throne which was put forward in 1486–1487 on behalf of the boy who was crowned at Dublin Cathedral as 'King Edward VI'.

The boy in question is generally referred to by historians as 'Lambert Simnel'. However, automatic use of that appellation seems rather ridiculous. The surviving official records of Henry VII's government only actually formally apply that name to the boy on one single occasion – in November 1487, in the act of attainder against his deceased supporter, the Earl of Lincoln.[18] But a little earlier in 1487 one of Henry VII's heralds officially reported a different identity for the pretender. That account stated that the boy's true name was 'John [Blank]'.[19] In other words there is no real proof to back the widespread assumption that his real name was 'Lambert Simnel'.

Detailed examination of the full evidence currently available in respect of 'King Edward VI' can be found in an earlier publication by the present writer,[20] and will not all be repeated here. But it is absolutely clear that the boy in question was said in the Low Countries and in Ireland to be Edward, Earl of Warwick, the son and heir of George, Duke of Clarence. He may indeed have been the real son and heir of the Duke of Clarence – taken or sent by his father to Ireland in 1476/7 (presumably together

The Yorkist pretender, 'King Edward VI', redrawn from his official seal.

A contemporary record of his name, redrawn from York City Archives.

with documentary evidence confirming his identity), and then brought up there by the Earl of Kildare. Certainly he was recognised as that genuine Yorkist prince by key close relatives: Margaret of York, dowager Duchess of Burgundy (Warwick's aunt), and John de la Pole, Earl of Lincoln (Warwick's senior surviving first cousin) – both of whom may have been shown by the Earl of Kildare supporting documentary evidence which had been left with him ten years earlier, in 1476/7, by the Duke of Clarence.

As for the possibly-substitute boy bearing the title 'Earl of Warwick' in England, who, following the execution of his alleged 'father', the Duke of Clarence, had initially been brought up in that country by Elizabeth Widville's son, the Marquess of Dorset, and who in 1486 was living under the guardianship of Henry VII's mother, there is no possible way in which Edward IV or his family – or Henry VII and his mother – or the citizens of London to whom Henry VII publicly displayed him – would have been able to identify him for certain as the true son of the late Duke of Clarence by physical recognition. After all, if King Edward IV had ever actually seen the original (genuine) little boy in question prior to the execution of his father (Edward's brother, George), the only potential occasion would have been at the baptism of that little baby – when Edward IV became one of his two godfathers – and when the child himself had only been a few days old. As for Henry VII and the citizens of London, none of them had ever seen for certain the genuine son of the Duke of Clarence.

It is therefore intriguingly possible that the Yorkist pretender, 'King Edward VI', may have been considered in 1486–1487 to be the genuine son of the Duke of Clarence by Elizabeth Widville. Also she may well have felt close to that boy's key supporters, Margaret of York, dowager Duchess of Burgundy, and John de la Pole, Earl of Lincoln. After all, about twenty years earlier, at a banquet following her churching after the birth of her first royal child, Elizabeth of York, Elizabeth Widville had been attended by the 'king's sister' (as she then was) – Margaret (later Duchess of Burgundy).[21] It has also been suggested that, for her part, Margaret of York may have considered Elizabeth Widville a good role model.[22] The Widville family had been the power behind the throne which, in the 1460s had encouraged Edward IV to go for his youngest sister's Burgundian marriage, and which had actively participated in that splendid event. As for the Earl of Lincoln, as we have seen he was married to one of Elizabeth Widville's young nieces – though that marriage was never actually consummated because of the young age of the bride.

Moreover, as we know, Elizabeth Widville had later played a key role in the execution of the boy's claimed father. As a result of her activities in that respect she must therefore have been very well aware of two key issues which had been cited in the attainder which had been enacted against George ten years earlier, in 1476/7.

> The same Duke purposyng to accomplisse his said false and untrue entent, and to inquiete and trouble the Kynge, oure said Sovereigne Lorde, his Leige People and this his Royaulme, nowe of late willed and desired the Abbot of Tweybury, Mayster John Tapton, Clerk, and Roger Harewell Esquier, to cause a straunge childe to have be brought into his Castell of Warwyk, and there to have beputte and kept in likelinesse of his Sonne and Heire, and that they shulde have conveyed and sent his said Sonne and Heire into Ireland, or into Flaundres, oute of this Lande, whereby he myght have goten hym assistaunce and favoure agaynst oure said Sovereigne Lorde; and for the execucion of the same, sent oon John Taylour, his Servaunte, to have had delyveraunce of his said Sonne and Heire, for to have conveyed hym; the whiche Mayster John Tapton and Roger Harewell denyed the delyveraunce of the said Childe, and soo by Goddes grace his said false and untrue entent was lette and undoon.[23]

In other words Elizabeth Widville must have been well aware that – even though in 1476/7 it had been believed that his plan had not been fully carried out – George was definitely known to have been plotting to substitute a false child for his son and heir in the Clarence nursery at Warwick Castle. She would also have known that the object behind that plan had been to enable George to ship the real Earl of Warwick out of England to safety, either in Ireland or in Flanders.

Thus, when he appeared on the scene, in 1486, Elizabeth Widville may well have shared the belief of Margaret, Duchess of Burgundy, and Margaret's nephew, the Earl of Lincoln, that the young Yorkist pretender, 'King Edward VI', really was the genuine son and heir of the late Duke of Clarence. Obviously the belief of his supporters was simply that the little boy in question actually had been successfully smuggled out of the country by his own father.

In addition, Elizabeth was also well aware of the significant fact that:

> the said Duke continuyng ín his false purpose, opteyned and gate an exemplificacion undre the Grete Seall of Herry the Sexte, late in dede and not in right Kyng of this Lande, wherin were conteyned alle suche appoyntements as late was made betwene the said Duke and Margaret, callyng herself Quene of this Lande, and other; amonges whiche it was conteyned, that if the said Herry, and Edward, his first begoton Son, died withoute Issue Male of theire Bodye, that the seid Duke and his Heires shulde be Kyng of this Lande; which exemplificacion the said Duke hath kepyd with hymself secrete.[24]

In other words Elizabeth Widville knew that, if 'Edward VI' really was the son and heir of George, Duke of Clarence, then in 1486–1487 that boy – not King Henry VII – would have been the rightful (true and legitimate) *Lancastrian* heir to the English crown.

It is therefore intriguing that, in February 1486/7, when 'Edward VI' was claiming the English throne, and in spite of the fact that she was then his own mother-in-law and his son's godmother, for some reason action appears to have been taken against Elizabeth Widville by Henry VII. The history written some years later by Polydore Vergil reports that:

> after lengthy deliberation, some advisors' opinion inclined to producing the Duke of Clarence's son to be shown to the people, so the false [*sic*] opinion that the boy was in Ireland might be erased from men's minds. Many other decrees were promulgated pertinent to the condition of the realm.

Among other things, Elizabeth, the one-time consort of King Edward, was mulcted of all her possessions because she had entrusted herself and her daughters to King Richard, contrary to what she had promised at the beginning of the conspiracy against Richard, and undertaken for those lords who, turning their backs on all the fortune they had in England, had, chiefly at her behest and for her sake, crossed the sea to Henry in Brittany, and had extracted from him an oath binding him to marry her eldest daughter, and yet she herself had not stood by this agreement, rendering it void and consigning those lords who had followed Henry to perpetual exile. This assuredly was a grave offence, but its outcome had seemed much less in need of legal reprisal, since, thanks to it, King Richard dared pile crime on crime and had neglected religion in seeking marriage with his niece, and for this reason had made God all the more angry at him, so that his downfall ensued. From this we may assuredly learn that the wicked are not impelled by human counsel but by the will of God, just as if they were voluntarily hastening to their deserved ruin. And so in her light-mindedness the queen earned herself great unpopularity, and, after achieving this, she henceforth led a wretched life. Our affairs are always as inconstant as we ourselves are. But fortune could not diminish one of her accomplishments. During Edward's reign, at an excellent place in Cambridge she founded a college for young students of the best disciplines and arts and gave it an endowment for their living. This is called Queen's College, and it is assuredly worthy of that name, because at all times it abounds in right learned men, educated by their assiduous study.[25]

It is certainly true that Vergil's account contains some highly questionable material, such as the groundless, and officially denied claim that Richard III had planned to marry his bastard niece, Elizabeth of York, himself. After all, authentic contemporary evidence clearly shows that, in reality, while such a story was put out by his enemies, actually Richard was planning to marry a Portuguese infanta – and to arrange a wedding for Elizabeth of York, not with himself, but with a minor member of the Portuguese royal family.[26] Obviously, however, that was a plan which greatly annoyed the so-called 'Earl of Richmond' (the future King Henry VII). After all *he* had apparently been hoping to marry Elizabeth of York *himself.* Therefore 'Henry VII dared not allow her to marry anyone else.' After all, potentially 'her claim to the English throne was too strong for Henry VII to risk allowing her to be married to anyone else.'[27] In other words, it was supporters of the 'Earl of Richmond' who spread gossip in respect of a mythical planned marriage of Elizabeth to the king, her uncle. Their motivation was a desperate attempt on their part to impede and undermine King Richard III's ongoing negotiations with the Portuguese royal court.

It is also highly intriguing to find ourselves informed by Vergil that the defeat and death of Richard III at the battle of Bosworth, in August 1485, comprised a divine punishment, carried out against Richard by an angry God. So why did Vergil think that God was angry with Richard? Was it because he believed that the king had murdered the so-called 'Princes in the Tower'? Certainly elsewhere in his account Vergil does accuse Richard of having:

> decided to kill his nephews, for as long as they were safe he could by no means be free of danger. Therefore he wrote a letter to Robert Brackenbury, the Governor of the Tower of London, commanding him to find some honorable way of quickly killing his nephews.[28]

Curiously, however, no such claim is mentioned by Vergil in the present context. Instead, and ridiculously, we find ourselves assured that it was Richard's alleged project to marry his own niece – a claim which was actually a lie – which 'had made God all the more angry at him, so that his downfall ensued'. In other words, according to Vergil it seems that Richard III's most serious misdemeanour had been a plan to marry his own niece.

Of course, some people have claimed that there was no quarrel between Elizabeth Widville and her son-in-law, Henry VII. Instead they have argued that her own rather poor health, coupled with her religious devotion, simply inspired Elizabeth to give up her lands in favour of her daughter and namesake, the young queen, while she herself abandoned court and retired to a monastery. Yet the relevant evidence which was examined earlier left big questions in the air in respect of Elizabeth's religiosity.

In any case, in spite of the fact that it contains some obvious nonsense, Vergil's account clearly states that her lands were confiscated from her by Henry VII as a punishment – not that she herself chose to give them up. At all events, when her son-in-law had been wearing the English crown for barely eighteen months, she definitely seems to have found herself more or less segregated from her children and effectively confined in a more or less penniless state at Bermondsey Abbey.

Chapter 19

Religious Life?

In the case of several other prominent fifteenth-century women there appears to have been true religious devotion which led them to take on the role of an oblate (lay person linked to an order of monks) or a tertiary (lay person linked to an order of friars). For example, Cecily Neville, dowager Duchess of York, and the mother of Edward IV, George, Duke of Clarence, and Richard III, became a Benedictine oblate. Cecily then took her religious life very seriously.[1] Nevertheless she never became permanently resident in a religious house. She remained a laywoman, residing in her own homes.

Edward IV's first partner, Eleanor Talbot, acted in a similar way, linking herself to the Carmelite order.[2] As for her sister, Elizabeth Talbot, dowager Duchess of Norfolk, she also attached herself to a religious order as a laywoman. However, in her case, unlike Eleanor Talbot and Cecily Neville, she actually became resident – together with other associated laywomen – at the religious house of the Poor Clares in London.[3] Significantly, perhaps, unlike Cecily Neville and Eleanor Talbot, whose links were with male religious communities, Elizabeth Talbot's link was with nuns.

Obviously in the case of Elizabeth Widville, like Elizabeth Talbot she became an actual resident at the religious house she chose – or which was chosen for her. But that apparent resemblance between the two women in question is actually superficial and misleading. For whereas Elizabeth Talbot linked herself to a female religious community of Franciscan nuns (Poor Clares), Elizabeth Widville's religious community was male. In the fifteenth century the religious community at Bermondsey Abbey comprised Benedictine monks. Thus the logical line for Elizabeth Widville to have followed in the case of a true religious commitment would have been the route taken by Cecily Neville. What *she* did was simply visit a Benedictine Abbey and take there the vow of a Benedictine oblate, and then return home and follow daily the Benedictine hours of prayer.

However, in the case of Elizabeth Widville, there is no evidence showing that she took the vows of an oblate, and no evidence showing that she performed the Benedictine hours of prayer. Thus there seems to have been no strong personal religious commitment of that kind on her part. Instead, in her case, it was apparently thanks to the action taken by her son-in-law, Henry VII, that she eventually found herself more or less excluded from the secular world and resident at Bermondsey Abbey.

In February 1486/7 she was deprived of all the property she had been granted by her son-in-law. About eight weeks later, on 1 May 1487, Henry VII recorded his action in that respect as follow:

> To the treasourer and chamberlains of our Eschequier that nowe be and that for the tyme hereafter shalbe, greting.
>
> Wher as of late by thadvise of the lords and other nobles of our counsaill for diuers consideracions vs and theym moeuyng have seased into our hands all honors, castelles, manoirs, lordships, knights fees, aduousons, and alle othr lands and tenements, with their apportenaunces and all maner fefermes and annuitees by vs late assigned vnto Queene Elizabeth, late wif to the full noble prince of famous memorye Edward the Fourth, and all and every of the saide honoures, castells, manoirs, lordships, knights fees, aduousons, and all other lands, tenements with their appertenaunces, fefermes, and annuities haue assigned vnto our derrest wif the quene.[4]

Meanwhile, on 12 February 1486/7, Elizabeth Widville became resident at Bermondsey Abbey, where she received free accommodation.[5]

In November 1489 she appears to have briefly left the Abbey for a time to join her daughter, the queen. Elizabeth of York was then awaiting her second confinement, at Westminster, which ultimately resulted in the birth of her daughter, Margaret (later Queen of Scots).[6] It had been 'upon All Halow Even' (the eve of the feast of All Saints – Saturday 31 October

1489) that 'the Quene tooke her Chamber at Westmynster' to prepare for her forthcoming childbirth:

> From thens forthe no Maner of Officier came within the Chamber, but Ladies and Gentilwomen, after the olde Coustume. Within a littell Season after, thier came a great Ambassade oute of Fraunce, among the whiche ther was a Kynsman of the Quenes called Francois Monsieur de Luxenburg [*c*.1445–*c*.1511], the Prior of Saint Mattelyns, and Sir William de Zaintes, Bailly of Senlis, and Monjoie, King of Armes of Frenshemen, which desired to se the Quene, and so they dide, in her awne Chambre. Ther was with her hir Moder Quene Elisabeth, and my Lady the Kinges Moder.[7]

The precise purpose of the French embassy is not on record, but obviously it was good for François of Luxembourg to have a chance of seeing his cousins the two royal consorts. Maybe therefore it was at his request that Elizabeth Widville briefly left Bermondsey Abbey and rejoined her daughter at Westminster on this occassion. Since François was the son of Thibaut, Count of Brienne (died 1477) – one of the brothers of Jacquette de St Pol – François himself was one of Elizabeth Widville's first cousins (see above, Family Tree 4).

Incidentally, in the summer of 1486, a few months before she became resident at Bermondsey Abbey, a possible third marriage for Elizabeth Widville – with King James III of Scotland – had apparently been contemplated as a possibility by Henry VII.[8] None of the other fifteenth-century royal and aristocratic widows who devoted themselves sincerely to lay religious life as oblates and tertiaries ever appear to have considered the possibility of making themselves available for potential remarriage, because for them their focus on religious life had become serious. However, in the case of Elizabeth Widville no evidence in support of the notion that she was then in the process of becoming completely devoted to religious life seems to exist, so perhaps in her case she too had been willing at that point to seriously consider a Scottish third marriage.

Chapter 20

Death and burial

On Tuesday 10 April 1492, Elizabeth wrote and signed her will at Bermondsey Abbey. Since she had nothing of consequence to bequeath to her children, she simply left her blessings together with instructions for her 'smale stufe and goodes' to be used to settle any debts 'as farre as they will extende'.

The writing of wills at that period normally began by identifying the dying person and commending their soul to God. For example the long will written for Edward IV in 1475 begins by naming the king:

> In the name of the moost holy and blessed Trinitie, the
> Fader, the Sonne and the holy Goost, by and undre whoom

Bermondsey Abbey.

187

alle Kings and Princes reigne. We Edward, by the grace of God, King of England and of Fraunce and Lord of Irland, … at oure Towne of Sandwich make this oure last Wille and testament in the manere and fourme herafter enswing.[1]

Next the king commends his soul to God, to the Virgin Mary, and to relevant named saints, and then names his burial place.

Furst we bequeth [our soul] to allmighty God and to his glorious Moder oure Lady Saint Marie, Saint George, Saint Edward and all the holy Companie of heven, and oure body to bee buried in the Church of the Collage of Saint George within oure Castell of Wyndesore by us begonne of newe to bee buylded.[2]

As for Elizabeth Widville, the text of her will is quite short. It begins as follows:

In Dei nomine, Amen. The xth daie of Aprill, the yere of our Lord Gode MCCCCLXXXXII.

I Elisabeth, by the grace of God Quene of England, late wif to the most victoroiuse Prince of blessed memorie, Edward the Fourth, being of hole mynde, seying the worlde so traunsitorie, and no creature certayne whanne they shall departe frome hence, havyng Almyghty Gode fressh in mynde, in whome is all mercy and grace, bequeath my sowle into his handes, beseechyng him, of the same mercy, to accept it graciously, and oure blessed Lady Quene of comforte, and all the holy company of hevyn, to be good meanes for me.[3]

Obviously she begins, as Edward had done, by naming herself. And she also commits her soul to God, to the Virgin Mary, and to saints. However, in her case the wording sounds slightly less standard. Interestingly she describes the world as transitory, and says that 'no creature [is] certayne whanne they shall departe frome hence.' And although she then bequeaths her soul into the hands of God and hopes for comfort from the Virgin Mary, unlike Edward IV she does not name any specific saints relevant in her case. St George, St Elizabeth and St Paul are among the most obvious saints who would have been relevant patron saints for her who might have been named.

The will then continues as follows:

> Item, I bequeith my body to be buried with the bodie of my Lord at Windessore, according to the will of my saide Lorde and myne, without pompes entreing or costlie expensis donne thereabought.
>
> Item, where I have no wordely goodes to do the Quene's Grace, my derest doughter, a pleaser with, nether to reward any of my children, according to my hart and mynde, I besech Almyghty Gode to blisse here Grace, with all her noble issue, and with as good hart and mynde as is to me possible, I geve her Grace my blessing, and all the forsaide my children.
>
> Item, I will that suche smale stufe and goodes that I have be disposed truly in the contentacion of my dettes and for the helth of my sowle, as farre as they will extende.
>
> Item, yf any of my bloode wille any of my saide stufe or goodes to me perteyning, I will that they have the prefermente before any other.
>
> And of this my present testament I make and ordeyne myne Executores, that is to sey, John Ingilby, Priour of the Chartourhouse of Shene, William Sutton and Thomas Brente, Doctors. And I besech my said derest doughter, the Queue's grace, and my sone Thomas, Marques Dorsett, to putte there good willes and help for the performans of this my testamente. In witnesse wherof, to this my present testament I have sett my seale, these witnesses, John Abbot of the monastry of Sainte Saviour of Bermondesley, and Benedictus Cun, Doctor of Fysyk. Yeven the day and yere abovesaid.[4]

It is interesting that, while she wishes to be interred in Edward's royal tomb at Windsor, she specifies that the burial shall not be pompous or costly.

It is also interesting that – unlike Cecily Neville – Elizabeth Widville does not mention King Henry VII in her will in any way. Cecily Neville must have hated him. However, in order to secure respectful passage for all her other wishes she left the king a couple of gold cups. The items in question were not specified in any way (unlike most of the other things Cecily was leaving), so it does not sound as if they themselves were of any significance in her opinion – except, of course in terms of their value as items which were made of gold. But as Elizabeth Widville really had no specific bequest wishes which she would have been anxious to ensure, she simply does not bother to mention the hateful reigning monarch at all.

Presumably when she chose to write her will Elizabeth was feeling ill. In fact she died just two months later, on Friday 8 June 1492, at the approximate age of 55. Interestingly her age at death was more or less identical to that of her mother, Jacquette, Duchess of Bedford. However, the precise cause of her death – and also that of her mother – is unknown. Four days later, in a very simple wooden coffin (see below), her remains were interred at St George's Chapel, Windsor, adjacent to those of King Edward IV.

On the viij day of June thyer off our lord m^{l}iiij^{c}iiij^{xx} et xij at Barsey in Swthwerke discessed the right noble pryncese Qwen Elizabeth, some tyme wiff of Kyng Edward the iiijth and modir to Qwene Elizabeth, wiff to Kyng Henry the vijth, whiche was the Friday before Whitsonday as that yere ffell.

And the said qwen desired in her dethe bedde that assoone as she shuld be decessed, she shuld in all goodly hast without any worldly pompe [be] by water conveied to Wyndesore and ther to be beried in the same vaut that her howsband the kyng was beryed in. On Whitsonday [10 June 1492] she was accordyng to her desire by water conveied to Wyndesore and ther prevely thorow the litill parke conveied into the castell, with out ryngyng of any belles or receyvyng of the dean or chanons in their habites or accompanyed as whos sayes, but with the prior of the Charterhous of Shen, Docter Brent, her chapelain, and oon of her executores, Edmond Hault, Maistres Grace, a bastard dowghter of kyng Edwarde, and upon an other gentlewomen.[5]

So two days after her death at Bermondsey Abbey, Elizabeth's body was conveyed westwards up the Thames to Windsor. But no bells at St George's Chapel were tolled for her when she arrived. It was her own chaplain –

accompanied by one of her executors, a bastard daughter of Edward IV, and another unnamed gentlewoman – who travelled with the body.

> And as it told to me, oon prest of the college and a clerke receyved her in the castell And so prevely about xj of the clocke in the nyght. She was beried with oute any solempne Direge [*Dirige* = matins for the dead] or the morne any solempne masse doon for her owbehytt [*obiit* = dying].[6]

Normally the arrival of a body at a church at 11 pm would have been received with a service of matins/morning prayer for the dead (*Dirige*), later followed by a mass. But in the case of Elizabeth Widville, although a priest of the chapel received the remains, nothing religious was done for her.

> On the morne [Monday 11 June] theder came the lord Awdeley, bysshop of Rochester to doo the service, and the substaunce of the officers of armes of this realme, but that day ther was nothyng doon solemply for her savyng a low herse, suche as they use for the comyn peple, with liii wooden candilstikkes abowte hit and a clothe of blacke cloth of gold over hit, with iiij candilstikkes of silver and gilt everyche havyng a taper of noo gret weight, and ij scochyns of her armes crowned pynned on that Clothe.[7]

Usually a very majestic hearse, with a canopy, and surrounded by many candles, was used for significant dead bodies. But Elizabeth's coffin was probably just placed on low tressels and covered with a black cloth to which her coats of arms were pinned. Her low hearse was simply surrounded by four candlesticks.

> On the Tewsday [12 June] theder came by watre iiij of kynges Edwardes doughters and heirs, [*sic* – only three are named and subsequently mentioned] that is to say the Lady Anne, the Lady Katherine, the Lady Bregett accompeygned with the Lady Marquys of Dorsset, the Duc of Buckyngham doughter of nyce of the fore said qwene. Alsoo the doughter of the Marquis of Dorsset, the Lady Herbert, alsoo nyce to the said qwene, the Ladye Egermont, Dame Katheryne Gray, Dame

[blank] Gilford, whiche after duryng the derige [*Dirige* –
passage missing?] and oon the morne, that is to say the Wensday
[13 June] at the masse of Requyem, and the three doughters at
the hed their gentilwomen behynde the thre ladyes.[8]

Elizabeth's coffin remained standing on its low hearse before the altar of
St George's Chapel, and some (apparently in reality only three) of her
royal daughters, together with other relatives, arrived on the evening of
Tuesday 12 June for the celebration of matins of the dead, followed the
following morning by a requiem mass (but see below).

Alsoo that same Tewsday theder came the lords that folowyn:
the Lord Thomas, Marquys of Dorsett, soon to the foresaid
qwene, the Lord Edmond of Suffolke, thErll of Essex, the
Vicount Welles, Sir Charles of Somerset, Sir Roger Coton,
Maister Chaterton. And that nyght began the direge [*Dirige*],
the foresaid bisshop of Rochestre and vicars of the college
were rectors of the qwer, and noo chanons; the Bisshop of
Rochestre red the last lesson at the direges of the chanons the
other two, but the Dean of that college red noon, thowgh he
were present at that service.[9]

Male relatives also attended the matins on the night of Tuesday 12 June,
and the requiem mass the next morning.

Nor att direge [*Dirige*] nor at non at they was [*sic*] ther never
a new torche, but old torches, nor poure man in blacke gowne
nor hoods [deleted] whod, but upon a dozeyn dyvers olde
men holdyng old torches and torches endes.[10]

Apparently Elizabeth Widville was only given second-hand torches.

And on the morne oon of the chanons, called Maistre Vaughan,
sange Our Lady masse, at the whiche the Lord Marquys offred
a piece of gold. At that masse offred no man savyng hym selff
and in likewise at the masse of the Trenytie, whiche was songen
by the dean, and [he] kneled at the hers hed [hearse head] by
cause the ladyes came not to the masse of requiem.[11]

It is here reported that 'the ladies' did not attend the requiem mass. But possibly that term does not include Elizabeth Widville's own three daughters, who do seem to have attended (see above and below).

> And the lordes before reherced sat above in the qwer into thoffryng tyme, when that the foresaid lordes and alsoo the officiers of armes ther beyng present went before my Lady Anne, whiche offred the masse penny in stede of the qwene, wherfore she had the carpet and the cusshyn leid; and the Vicount Welles toke her offryng, which was a very penny in ded of silver, and Dame Katherine Gray bere the said Lady Agnes trayne. In tyme she was turned to her place ageyn then everyche of the kynges dowgthers bere ownes traynes and offred a pece of gold. After the ladies had offred in like wise the Lord Marquys offred a pece of gold, than the other foresaid lordes offred their pleasirs; than offred the dean and the qwere and the poure knyghtes; then Garter Kyng of Armes, with hym all his company. Then offred all other esquyers present and yemen and the servauntes that wold offer, but ther was non offryng to the corps during the masse. Ther was geven certayne money in almes after masse the Lord Marquys rewarded [blank] their costes xl s. I pray to God to have mersy on her sowle. At this same season the qwen her doughter toke her chamber, wherfore I cannot tell what dolent abbeyt [deleted] hewue it she goth in, but I suppose she went in blew in likewise as Qwen Margaret, the wif of Kyng Henry the vj, went in when her mother the Qwene of Cecille deyed.[12]

It appears that the way in which the burial of Elizabeth Widville was carried out was in every way of the cheapest possible kind. When King Edward IV's tomb at St George's Chapel, Windsor, was opened in 1789, that revealed 'the decayed parts of a stout wooden coffin, a skull, and some bones, [which] were found over the king's coffin. The king's [own] coffin was of lead.'[13]

> The wood of the coffin which contained the remains of the queen, upon a strict examination of its texture, appears to be pine, and not cedar, as some have imagined: which is further

193

The bones of Edward IV as found in 1789.

confirmed by observing that cedar is the produce of America, which country had not been yet discovered at that time when this coffin was made.[14]

If Elizabeth was buried in pine that would have been very cheap wood and obviously she was not enclosed in lead. After the exploration of the royal tomb it is reported that 'many relics were removed. John Douglas, Dean of Windsor and Bishop of Carlisle, presented the Society [of Antiquaries] with some of the finds. These included ... wood from the adjacent Queen's coffin.'[15] Therefore in theory it might still have been possible to confirm now the report written in 1796 which claims that Elizabeth Widville was merely buried in highly perishable pine wood. However, when I enquired whether the Society of Antiquaries – which definitely has the lock of Edward IV's hair – also still has a sample of wood from Elizabeth's coffin, I received the following reply.

I have successfully located the lock of hair of Edward IV (LDSAL 122) but as yet have not found any mention of the wood remaining in our collection. The items, including the missing vial, were first catalogued by Albert Way FSA in 1847, but much of our collections management came as a result of the organisation of Beatrice de Cardi FSA, who in the late 1970s – early 1980s used Way's catalogue to ascribe numbers to each item. When she found objects of multiple parts she subdivided the numbers a, b, c etc. However, for the description of the group from the chapel she only listed one number – LDSAL 122. Which suggests she only had the one find – in this case the lock of hair.

So I suspect the wood fragments might have become separated and/or misplaced in the period between 1847 and 1970, most likely with the vial. Unfortunately this is fairly common with the Society's collections, as they were not really thought of as 'museum collections' until fairly recently so were not closely managed.[16]

It therefore appears that it is not currently possible to verify the wood of Elizabeth's coffin.

Chapter 21

Descendants

In the initial stages of my search for the mtDNA of Elizabeth Widville and her children, about ten years ago I traced some close and rather intriguing descendants of Elizabeth herself. They included Henry Stuart, Lord Darnley, the second – and murdered – husband of Mary, Queen of Scots, and the ancestor of all subsequent Kings of England. They also included Lady Jane Grey, 'the nine-days queen', who was later executed.

I myself did not trace a living all-female-line descendant. That was done for me (and with a little help from me in respect of Latin source material) by Glen Moran.

This eventually revealed Elizabeth Roberts, a living opera singer, as a descendant of Elizabeth Widville's younger sister, Margaret, Countess of Arundel. Her kind donation of samples for testing then revealed the mtDNA haplogroup of Elizabeth Widville and all her siblings.

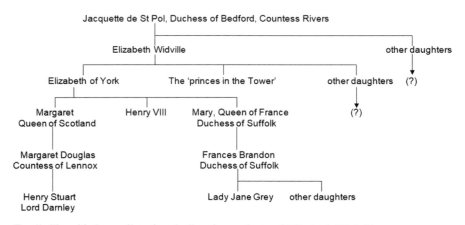

Family Tree 13: Immediate female-line descendants of Elizabeth Widville.

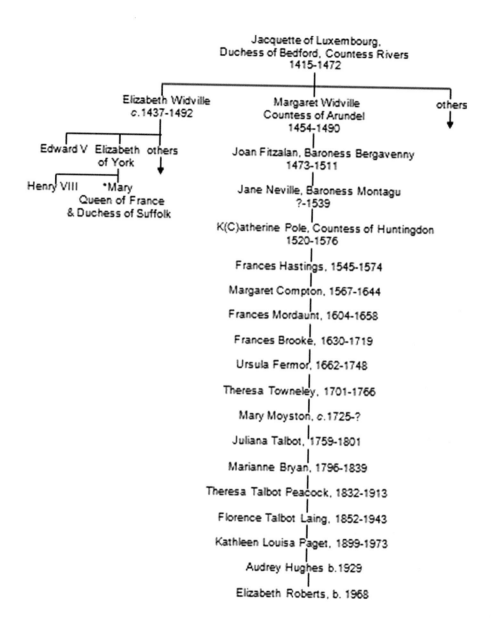

Jacquette of Luxembourg,
Duchess of Bedford, Countess Rivers
1415-1472

Elizabeth Widville
c.1437-1492

Margaret Widville
Countess of Arundel
1454-1490

others

Edward V Elizabeth others
of York

Joan Fitzalan, Baroness Bergavenny
1473-1511

Henry VIII   *Mary
Queen of France
& Duchess of Suffolk

Jane Neville, Baroness Montagu
?-1539

K(C)atherine Pole, Countess of Huntingdon
1520-1576

Frances Hastings, 1545-1574

Margaret Compton, 1567-1644

Frances Mordaunt, 1604-1658

Frances Brooke, 1630-1719

Ursula Fermor, 1662-1748

Theresa Towneley, 1701-1766

Mary Moyston, c.1725-?

Juliana Talbot, 1759-1801

Marianne Bryan, 1796-1839

Theresa Talbot Peacock, 1832-1913

Florence Talbot Laing, 1852-1943

Kathleen Louisa Paget, 1899-1973

Audrey Hughes b.1929

Elizabeth Roberts, b. 1968

* Source of the hair samples.

Family Tree 14: The line of descent from Elizabeth's sister, Margaret Widville, to Elizabeth Roberts.

```
   1 GATCACAGGT CTATCACCCT   ATTAACCACT CACGGGAGCT CTCCATGCAT TTGGTATTTT
  61 CGTCTGGGGG GTGTGCACGC   GATAGCATTG CGAGACGCTG GAGCCGGAGC ACCCTATGTC
 121 GCAGTATCTG TCTTTGATTC   CTGCCTCATC CTATTATTTA TCGCACCTAC GTTCAATATT
 181 ACAGGCGAAC ATACTTACTA   AAGTGTGTTA ATTAATTAAT GCTTGTAGGA CATAATAATA
 241 ACAATTGAAT GTCTGCACAG   CCGCTTTCCA CACAGACATC ATAACAAAAA ATTTCCACCA
 301 AACCCCCCCT CCCCCGCTTC   TGGCCACAGC ACTTAAACAC ATCTCTGCCA AACCCCAAAA
```

```
16021 CTGTTCTTTC ATGGGGAAGC   AGATTTGGGT ACCACCCAAG TATTGACTCA CCCATCAACA
16081 ACCGCTATGT ATTTCGTACA   TTACTGCCAG CCACCATGAA TATTGTACGG TACCATAAAT
16141 ACTTGACCAC CTGTAGTACA   TAAAAACTCA ATCCACATCA AAACCCCCTC CTCATGCTTA
16201 CAAGCAAGTA CAGCAATCAA   CCCTCAACTA TCACACATCA ACTGCAACTC CAAAGTCACC
16261 CCTCACCCAT TAGGATACCA   ACAAACCTAC CCACCCTTAA CAGTACATAG TACATAAAGC
16321 CATTTACCGT ACATAGCACA   TTACAGTCAA ATCCCTTCTC GTCCCCATGG ATGACCCCCC
```

A = ADENINE; C = CYTOSINE; G = GUANINE; T = THYMINE

This belongs to a subgroup of haplogroup U ('Ursula') - particularly U5a2b.
Differences from the revised Cambridge Reference Sequence are shown highlighted.

The mtDNA of Elizabeth Widville, revealed by Elizabeth Roberts' samples.

The mtDNA haplogroup in question is the one which is known as U ('Ursula'). Specifically it seems from the sample produced in 2017 by Elizabeth Roberts, the living descendant of Margaret Widville, Countess of Arundel, that Elizabeth Widville – and all her children – belonged to the mtDNA subgroup U5a2b.

Conclusion

It is not possible – and probably never will be – to produce an absolutely solid and completely accurate and authenticated account of the whole of the life story of Elizabeth Widville. For example, her place and date of birth are not recorded in any contemporary fifteenth-century source, though curiously, as we have seen, a very definite – but probably erroneous – birth place has been put forward for her, and it has been asserted by a number of previous writers. Moreover, it is also worth remembering that even if contemporary fifteenth-century sources did exist in her case, they still might not be accurate – as in the case of the dates of birth and death which are often alleged for her royal partner, King Edward IV.

There are also aspects of her character and her conduct which remain debatable. Those include, for example, her religious attitude. Was she ever willing to explore the black arts? Did she finally devote herself to a religious life, in spite of the fact that during her life there is very little evidence to show that she regularly went on pilgrimages? The picture presented in respect of such questions in the present study remains, in the end, a hypothesis. However, in that and all other respects the present author follows what has hopefully become his normal approach in respect of history. In other words he seeks for authentic contemporary evidence in respect of everything, and is wary of accepting subsequent, non-contemporary source material – even when that has generally been accepted by other historians.

For example, in respect of Elizabeth's religion, one of the pieces of authentic contemporary evidence which has been explored in this present account is the interesting wording which she herself employed in her will. It is interesting to note that, unlike other contemporaries, she names none of the specific saints whom she might have been expected to regard as her patrons. It is also interesting that she expresses the fact that she has God fresh in her mind.

Other contemporary evidence has been explored by comparing what precisely Elizabeth Widville did towards the end of her life – in respect of residing in an abbey – with the actions taken by other contemporary women of similar status who definitely did commit themselves as laywomen to religious lives. In that context it seems rather worrying that other published accounts of the life of Elizabeth tend simply to have assumed that, because she lived at an abbey which was held by a male order, she must have been truly committed to a religious life. In reality, other contemporary evidence appears to show that if she had wished to live in the house of a relgious community because she herself shared their religious commitment, the normal procedure would have been for her to choose a female religious house, rather than the male religious house where she actually resided. Once again, what I have said in that respect is presented, not as an absolutely certain conclusion, but as a hypothesis. However, evidence has been presented to support the proposal in question.

In a similar way I have explored the possibility that Elizabeth Widville may have had people put to death in order to strengthen her own position. Her involvement in the execution of the Duke of Clarence seems absolutely certain, and it was reported by contemporary chroniclers. Her involvement in the execution of the Earl of Desmond also seems highly probable in my view. Although the main surviving source was written more than half a century later, it was written by Desmond's heir, who addressed it to Elizabeth Widville's heir (Henry VIII) in order to verify why a certain concession had been granted to the Fitzgerald family by Edward IV. So why would he have chosen to invent denigration of Elizabeth unnecessarily in that context? Moreover, as we have seen, the hypothesis that Elizabeth was the person behind the execution of Desmond is also supported (albeit less specifically, since the document in question does not actually name her) by an earlier letter written by King Richard III.

As for the hypotheses that Elizabeth Widville may have been the person responsible for the murders of the wife and younger son of George, Duke of Clarence, no absolutely solid evidence exists in its support. But it has been suggested before, and the action in question would have been consistent, given the context – i.e. the obvious enmity which existed between Elizabeth and George at that time. As for the further hypotheses that Elizabeth may also have been behind the early and unexpected deaths of Eleanor Talbot and her brother-in-law, John Mowbray, Duke of Norfolk, of course they are not backed by any solid surviving contemporary evidence. However, both of those curious deaths were undoubtedly beneficial to Elizabeth Widville in various ways.

As for the accounts of Elizabeth which have previously been published, they are rather worrying in some respects. For example, MacGibbon asserts in his version of her story that she was kept in restraint by Richard III – but not by Henry VII. That is a very odd assertion. Although she dwelt for a time in the sanctuary at Westminster in 1483, there is no contemporary evidence in support of the notion that she was in any way kept in restraint by Richard III – who did his best to persuade her to leave the sanctuary. Indeed, as we have seen, all the surviving contemporary evidence supports the view that, in the end, she completely trusted that king. Subsequently, however, once again based on genuine contemporary evidence, she definitely does appear to have been restrained by Henry VII.

Of course, MacGibbon also claims that the Yorkist pretender to the throne in 1486–1487 was an impostor whose real name was Lambert Simnel. But as I have shown elsewhere, there is actually very little contemporary evidence for that alleged name. Also, as I have shown in this present study, given her own involvement in the earlier fate of the Duke of Clarence, Elizabeth Widville must have been very well aware of two key pieces of evidence which may potentially have made the 1486–1487 Yorkist pretender a very strong claimant in her view, leading her into trouble with her son-in-law, Henry VII.

Baldwin's account also contains worrying inaccuracies. For example, ignoring the authentic contemporary evidence in that respect, Baldwin asserts that in 1484/5 Richard III planned to marry his bastard niece, Elizabeth of York. That assertion ignores the surviving contemporary Portuguese evidence, which proves conclusively that Richard III was actually planning to marry both himself and his illegitimate niece to members of the Portuguese royal family. It also ignores the fact that when the allegation in question was put out by enemies in England, Richard III was both distressed by it and publicly denied it.

As for Elizabeth's relationships with Edward IV, and with his very loyal youngest brother, Richard, Duke of Gloucester (later Richard III), they both appear to have been mostly positive. She may sometimes have argued with Edward – as is the human norm. But they seem to have loved one another, and they certainly produced numerous children. Moreover, there is no real evidence to show that Edward was consistently unfaithful to her, as is generally alleged.

And in respect of Gloucester – unlike his middle brother, Clarence – Elizabeth Widville never appears to have feared or distrusted him. The only problem she ever experienced in respect of Richard was in connection with the coup which she attempted in April 1483, and which was aimed at making herself the regent for her son, Edward V. Yet even that seems to have caused no long-term problem between them. Indeed, the subsequent evidence appears to confirm that genuine trust existed between them.

That, of course, raises the intriguing issue of what Elizabeth understood to have been the fate of her royal sons. As in so many aspects of her story, once again, no specific evidence exists in that respect. Yet her conduct in connection with her royal daughters, and her advice to her eldest son, Thomas Grey, clearly shows that she had no worries in respect of Richard III. Therefore she cannot possibly have believed that he had harmed her royal sons.

It may be the case that, through one of her own family connections, she knew that, while the newly-crowned King Richard III had been on his royal tour, in July 1483, her two sons had been extracted from the Tower of London by Kentish supporters of Edward V. She may also have known that, like some of her other children, young Edward had then been in a fragile state of health, and had subsequently died naturally. But probably neither she nor King Richard III ever knew where young Richard of Shrewsbury had been taken.

As for the first question raised earlier in the introduction, Elizabeth Widville was clearly aware throughout approximately the last twenty-eight years of her life that in spite of having been officially crowned as England's queen consort, in actuality her status in that respect was questioned by various people. Indeed, that point caused her considerable concern in respect both of herself and of her children by Edward IV. As we have seen, at two different points – and in different ways – the title of 'queen' was taken away from her and although, in the end, she was recognised as a dowager queen when she died, and was buried in a royal context (though not in a very royal manner), the reality of her claim to that title remains highly questionable. What is more, Henry VII's conduct in respect of her claim to the royal title actually had nothing whatever to do with either Elizabeth Widville herself, or the genuine available evidence. Instead, like everything else he did, it was based purely upon Henry VII's own personal ambitions.

Notes

Introduction – problems in this story

1. D. MacGibbon, *Elizabeth Woodville A Life* (hereinafter *EW*), 1938, republished Stroud 2014.
2. J. Ashdown-Hill, *The Mythology of Richard III*, Stroud 2015, and *The Mythology of the so-called Princes in the Tower*, Stroud 2018.
3. https://en.wikipedia.org/wiki/Elizabeth_Woodville (consulted January 2018).
4. T. Hearne, ed., J. Rous, *Historia Regum Angliae*, Oxford 1745, p. 213.
5. *CPR, 1476–1485*, p. 336.
6. A.R. Myers, ed., G. Buck, *The History of the Life and Reigne of Richard the Third*, London 1646, reprinted Wakefield 1973, p. 113.
7. Rolls of Parliament 9, Edw. IV, as published in J. Strachey, ed., *Rotuli Parliamentorum ut et Petitiones et Placita in Parliamento, 1767–77*, vol 6, London 1777, rolls 1472–1503 (hereinafter *RP*), p. 232.
8. J. Gairdner, *The Paston Letters*, Gloucester 1983, vol. 5, p. 64, citing an MS in Magdalene College, Oxford.
9. J. Stevenson, ed., *Letters and papers Illustrative of the Wars of the English in France during the reign of Henry VI, King of England*, vol. 2, part 2, London 1864, p. 524. Though he does not specify the source, he is actually citing Lambeth Palace Library, MS 506, f. 4r.
10. *RP*, vol. 6, p. 241.
11. H.T. Riley, ed., *Ingulph's Chronicle of the Abbey of Croyland*, London 1908, p. 457.

1. Imperial Ancestry

1. J. Ashdown-Hill, *The Last Days of Richard III*, Stroud 2010, chapters 14 and 15.

2. Descended from a Water-Fay?

1. S. Baring-Gould, *Curious Myths of the Middle Ages*, London 1877, p. 472.
2. Baring-Gould, *Curious Myths*, p. 474.
3. https://en.wikipedia.org/wiki/Melusine (consulted January 2018).
4. Baring-Gould, *Curious Myths*, p. 475.
5. 1275–1313, first Holy Roman Emperor of the house of Luxembourg. Son of Henry VI, Count of Luxembourg, and grandson of Count Henry V (see Family Tree 2).
6. Baring-Gould, *Curious Myths*, pp. 482–3.
7. https://en.wikipedia.org/wiki/Melusine (consulted January 2018).
8. https://en.wikipedia.org/wiki/Melusine (consulted January 2018), citing J. Flori, *Richard Coeur de Lion: le roi-chevalier*, Paris 1999.

3. Anglo-Norman Ancestry?

1. https://opendomesday.org/place/SK8829/wyville/ (consulted January 2018).
2. G. Baker, *History of Northamptonshire*, vol. 2, London 1844, p. 161.
3. T.D. Hardy, ed., *Rotuli Litterarum Clausarum in Turri Londinensis*, vol. 1, 1204–1224, London 1833, pp. 244, 254; C. Roberts, ed., *Excerpta è Rotuli Finium in Turri Londinensi*, 1216–1272, London 1836, p. 306 *et al.*; MacGibbon, *EW*, pp. 15–16.
4. Roberts, ed., *Excerpta è Rotuli Finium*, 1216–1272, p. 306 refers in 1259 to a Hugh de Wyvill and his wife, Juliana. But in terms of the date he seems unlikely to be the Hugh from whom Elizabeth was descended.

4. Born in France?

1. *ODNB*, M. Hicks, 'Woodville [Wydeville], Richard, first Earl Rivers'.
2. *CPR, 1429–1436*, p. 356.
3. *CPR, 1429–1436*, p. 359. It seems his father, the elder Richard Widville was never knighted – ODNB, Hicks, 'Woodville [Wydeville], Richard'.
4. *CPR, 1429–1436*, p. 388.
5. *ODNB*, Hicks, 'Woodville [Wydeville], Richard'.
6. *CPR, 1429–1436*, p. 489.

7. *ODNB*, L. Diaz Pascual, 'Luxembourg, Jaquetta [*sic*] de, duchess of Bedford and Countess Rivers'.

8. *ODNB*, L. Diaz Pascual, 'Luxembourg, Jaquetta [*sic*] de'.

9. *CPR, 1429–1436*, p. 516.

10. Stevenson, ed., *Letters and Papers Illustrative of the Wars of the English in France, vol, 2, part 2*, pp. 433–37, citing Harl. MS 782, f. 52v.

11. Stevenson, ed., *Letters and Papers Illustrative of the Wars of the English in France, vol, 2, part 2*, p. 436.

12. Leicestershire Record Office B. R. II/3/3: R.A. Griffiths, 'Queen Katherine de Valois and a missing statute of the realm', *Law Quarterly Review*, 93 (1977), 257–8. Catherine of France had wished to marry her late husband's cousin, young Edmund Beaufort.

13. *CPR, 1436–1441*, p. 53.

14. MacGibbon, *EW*, p. 15.

15. A. Licence, *Edward IV and Elizabeth Woodville, a True Romance*, Stroud 2016, p. 25.

16. *ODNB*, L. Diaz Pascual, 'Luxembourg, Jaquetta [*sic*] de'.

17. *CPR, 1436–1441*, p. 426.

18. https://en.wikipedia.org/wiki/Isabel (consulted January 2018).

19. See J. Ashdown-Hill, *Cecily Neville*, Barnsley 2018, chapters 3, 4 and 11.

20. P. Erlanger, *Margaret of Anjou, Queen of England*, London 1970, p. 75.

5. Brought up in England

1. *ODNB*, L. Diaz Pascual, 'Luxembourg, Jaquetta [*sic*] de'.

2. *ODNB*, L. Diaz Pascual, 'Luxembourg, Jaquetta [*sic*] de'.

3. Erlanger, *Margaret of Anjou*, pp. 15, 48.

4. *CPR, 1446–1452*, p. 185.

5. Gairdner, *The Paston Letters*, vol. 4, p. 188.

6. *ODNB*, Hicks, 'Woodville [Wydeville], Richard'.

7. *CPR, 1446–1452*, p. 515.

8. *ODNB*, Hicks, 'Woodville [Wydeville], Richard'.

9. J. Stevenson, ed., *Letters and Papers Illustrative of the Wars of the English in France during the Reign of Henry the Sixth*, vol, 1, London 1861, p. 367.

10. Gairdner, *The Paston Letters*, vol. 1, p. 184, citing *Three Fifteenth Century Chronicles*.

11. Gairdner, *The Paston Letters*, vol. 1, pp. 184–5, citing Letter 400.

12. *ODNB*, Hicks, 'Woodville [Wydeville], Richard'.
13. *CPR, 1461–1467*, p. 97.
14. *CPR, 1461–1467*, pp. 81, 83.

6. Married to Sir John Grey

1. https://www.groby.org.uk/history/grey_family.html (consulted January 2018).

7. Relationship with Edward IV

1. J. Ashdown-Hill, 'The Full Itinerary of Edward IV', https://www.amberley-books.com/community-john-ashdown-hill.
2. A. Crawford, ed., *Howard Household Books*, Stroud 1992, vol. 1, p. 229.
3. M. Clive, *This Sun of York*, London 1973, pp. 100–101.
4. E.E. Reynolds, ed. / trans., T. Stapleton, *The Life of Sir Thomas More*, (Douai 1588), London 1966, p. 2, note 3.
5. J. Ashdown-Hill, *The Private Life of Edward IV*, Stroud 2016, also 'The Full Itinerary of Edward IV', https://www.amberley-books.com/community-john-ashdown-hill.
6. Ashdown-Hill, *The Private Life of Edward IV*, p. 60.
7. J. Ashdown-Hill, *The Secret Queen*, Stroud 2009; 2016.
8. M. Jones, ed., P. de Commynes, *Memoirs*, Harmondsworth 1972, pp. 353–54.
9. Jones, ed., Commynes, *Memoirs*, p. 397. This was written with hindsight. In 1460–61 Robert Stillington was not yet a bishop.
10. Jones, ed., Commynes, *Memoirs*, p. 354.
11. P. Coss, *The Lady in Medieval England 1000–1500*, Stroud 1998, p. 87.
12. Elizabeth Talbot was described in 1468 as '*la duchesse de Norfolck, une moult belle dame d'Angleterre*' ('the Duchess of Norfolk a very beautiful English lady'). H. Beaune and J. d'Arbaumont, eds., *Mémoires d'Olivier de la Marche*, 4 vols., vol. 3, Paris 1885, pp. 106–107.
13. Lambeth Palace Library, MS 265, and the Skinners' Company Book of the Fraternity of Our Lady.
14. http://www.quns.cam.ac.uk/Queens/Misc/Elizabeth.html (consulted February 2018). The college has three later copies of the portrait – some of which show different hair colour – a sign perhaps of later influence.
15. British Library, *Royal 15 E VI, f. 2v*.

16. *CSP Milan, 1385–1618*, 18–19, quoted in *ODNB*, Dunn, 'Margaret of Anjou'.

17. J. L. Laynesmith, *The Last Medieval Queens*, Oxford 2004, p. 52.

18. R.S. Sylvester, ed., St Thomas More, *The History of King Richard III*, New Haven & London 1976, pp. 61–2.

19. Sylvester / Thomas More, *The History of King Richard III*, p. 61.

20. Henry's wife did bear a daughter, but the paternity of that child was disputed.

21. J. Ashdown-Hill, *The Mythology of Richard III*, Stroud 2015, pp. 91–2.

22. J. Ashdown-Hill, *The Private Life of Edward IV*, Stroud 2016, chapter 12.

23. Sylvester / Thomas More, *The History of King Richard III*, p. 62.

24. Sylvester / Thomas More, *The History of King Richard III*, p. 62.

25. Sylvester / Thomas More, *The History of King Richard III*, p. 62.

26. Sylvester / Thomas More, *The History of King Richard III*, p. 62.

27. *ODNB*, M. Hicks, 'Elizabeth, *née* Woodville' (consulted March 2012).

28. This date is also cited in Warkworth's Chronicle, Gregory's Chronicle and Hearne's Fragment.

29. H. Ellis, ed., R. Fabyan, *The New Chronicles of England and France*, London 1811 (text of Fabyan's 1516 edition), p. 654.

30. Ashdown-Hill, *The Private Life of Edward IV* / 'The Full Itinerary of Edward IV', https://www.amberley-books.com/community-john-ashdown-hill.

31. *ODNB*, M. Hicks, 'Elizabeth [*née* Elizabeth Woodville]'.

32. I put that forward as a hypothesis in 2009 (in *Eleanor, the Secret Queen*, p. 176) – before I had seen the contemporary evidence in that respect which is cited here.

33. C. Fahy, 'The marriage of Edward IV and Elizabeth Woodville: a new Italian source', *English Historical Review*, vol. 76 (1960), pp. 660–72 (p. 668, lines 16–18), accessed courtesy of JSTOR.

34. Fahy, 'The marriage ... a new Italian source', p. 668, lines 23–30.

35. A lot of further evidence in that respect was presented recently by me. Ashdown-Hill, *The Private Life of Edward IV*.

36. Fahy, 'The marriage ... a new Italian source', p. 663.

37. Fahy, 'The marriage ... a new Italian source', p. 672, lines 223–4.

38. Fahy, 'The marriage ... a new Italian source', p. 672, lines 214–18.

39. *CPR, 1461–1467*, p. 72.

40. *CPR, 1461–1467*, p. 191.

41. *CPR, 1461–1467*, p. 127.

42. *CPR, 1461–1467*, p. 212.

43. *CPR, 1461–1467*, p. 284.

44. *CPR, 1461–1467*, p. 477.

45. For the evidence in that respect see Ashdown-Hill, *The Secret Queen*, chapter 11.

46. H. Ellis, ed., *Three Books of Polydore Vergil's English History comprising the reigns of Henry VI, Edward IV and Richard III*, London 1844, (hereinafter 'Ellis / Vergil'), pp. 116–17.

47. *ODNB*, Hicks 'Elizabeth [*née* Elizabeth Woodville]'.

8. Married to the King?

1. R.S. Sylvester, ed., St Thomas More, *The History of King Richard III and Selections from the English and Latin Poems*, London 1976, p. 65.

2. Ashdown-Hill, *The Private Life of Edward IV*, chapter 10.

3. Sylvester, ed., St Thomas More, *The History of King Richard III*, pp. 67–8.

4. Armstrong / Mancini, pp. 94–5.

5. Ashdown-Hill, *Cecily Neville*, chapter 11.

6. Ellis / Vergil, p. 183.

7. R. Horrox & P. W. Hammond, eds., *British Library Harleian Manuscript 433* (hereinafter *Harleian MS 433*), vol. 2, London / Gloucester 1980, p. 2.

8. The petition consistently refers to both Eleanor Talbot and Elizabeth Widville under their married surnames – Boteler and Grey.

9. i.e. a church porch. At that time church weddings took place *outside* the church.

10. 'Lord Shrewsbury was regarded as a towering figure and a national hero. Thus, when the act of Parliament of 1484 explicitly characterised Eleanor as his daughter, the effect of this was akin to that of a late twentieth-century writer describing someone as a daughter of Sir Winston Churchill. Eleanor's rank – and her plausibility as a potential royal consort – were immediately established beyond any question'. J. Ashdown-Hill, *Eleanor the Secret Queen*, Stroud 2009; 2016, Introduction).

11. Many historians have misunderstood the term 'precontract'. One could never *make* a precontract. One made a *contract* of marriage, and it only became 'pre-' subsequently if one then committed bigamy.

12. This clause shows that Eleanor can never have borne Edward IV a child.

13. *RP*, vol. 6, pp. 240–42.

14. Ashdown-Hill, *Cecily Neville*, p. 111.

15. Laynesmith, *The Last Medieval Queens*, p. 210.

16. *Fratres vero Eduardi, qui duo tunc vivebant, etsi graviter uterque eandem rem tulerunt; alter tamen, qui ab Eduardo secundo genitus erat et dux Clarentinorum, manifestius suum stomachum aperuit; dum in obscurumn Helisabette genus acriter et palam inveheretur; dumque contra morem maiorem [sic] viduam a rege ductam*

predicaret, quem virginem uxorem ducere opportuisset. Alter vero frater, Riccardus qui nunc regnat tunc Closestriorum dux, tum quia ad dissimulandum aptior erat, tum quia minor natu, minus auctoritatis habebat nihil egit aut dixit quo argui posset. Armstrong / Mancini, p. 62.

17. K. Dockray, *Edward IV, a source book*, Stroud 1999, p. 46, citing The Great Chronicle of London, pp. 202–03.

18. Some pedigrees number Thomas as the eighth earl but this is incorrect. The enumeration followed here is that of the *Complete Peerage* (1916 edition) which argues persuasively that when Maurice, the second earl, died childless in 1356, his next brother and heir, Nicholas, was not immediately recognised as earl by the king because his sanity was in question. After an official investigation which concluded that Nicholas was an idiot the next brother in line, Gerald, was formally recognised as the third earl of Desmond on condition that he care for Nicholas. Earlier pedigrees either mistakenly counted the unfortunate Nicholas as the third earl, and Gerald as the fourth (see for example *Complete Peerage*, 1890 edition) or in some cases erroneously interpolated a younger brother, John, as the third earl from 1358 until his death in 1369. It is certain that neither Nicholas nor John ever held the earldom, and that Gerald was being addressed as earl by 1363 at the latest. The title 'earl of Desmond', created by Edward III in 1329, derives from the Irish *Des-Mumha* ('South Munster'), for the earldom was based in the province of Munster.

19. *CPR, 1461–1467*, p. 196.

20. *CPR, 1461–1467*, p. 270.

21. Although curiously the bishop co-operated with Desmond and his brother-in-law, the earl of Kildare, in the foundation of Fraternities of St Nicholas at Dunsany in 1465.

22. S. Hayman and J. Graves, eds., *Unpublished Geraldine Documents*, Dublin 1870–81, p.80. Hayman and Graves go on to quote from the letters in question. R.J. Mitchell, *John Tiptoft*, London 1938, p. 114, also notes that 'the Anglo-Irish were inclined to like him', an observation which the letters confirm, but which Mitchell herself later, inexplicably, utterly contradicts when she claims (p. 119) without citing any evidence that 'the English settlers were alarmed by his [Desmond's] friendship and popularity with the Irish'.

23. *CPR, 1461–1467*, p. 340.

24. Hayman and Graves, p. 80.

25. J.S. Brewer & W. Bullen, eds, *Calendar of the Carew Manuscripts at Lambeth*, vol. 2, 1575–88, London 1868, pp. cv–cvi. This memorandum is usually cited under this reference, as though it were actually one of the Carew Mss at Lambeth,

but in fact it is not, and its date, apparently 1541–42, does not correspond to the date parameters of the volume in which it is printed, and of which it does not constitute part of the main text, but rather figures in an appendix to the introduction by way of forming an explanatory note. No previous writer on this topic seems to have noticed this anomaly. The editor of the *Calendar* gives no source for the memorandum, and in fact it has so far not been possible to locate the original of this important document (said to have been written in the Irish language) despite having searched at the Public Record Office through the Irish State Papers, the documents of the Privy Council and the Letters and Papers Foreign and Domestic of the reign of Henry VIII.

26. A.F. Sutton & L. Visser-Fuchs, 'A Most Benevolent Queen', *The Ricardian*, vol. 10, no. 129, June 1995, pp. 214–45 (pp. 217–8).
27. Dean of St Martin's; archdeacon of Colchester; archdeacon of Taunton; prebend of York; prebend of St David's; prebend of St Stephen's Chapel, Westminster, and rector of Ashbury. He was confirmed in these posts early in the reign of Edward IV: H.C. Maxwell-Lyte, ed., *The Registers of Robert Stillington, Bishop of Bath and Wells 1466–1491 and Richard Fox, Bishop of Bath and Wells 1492–1494*, Somerset Record Society 1937, p. x, citing Patent Roll 1 Edward IV part v, m. 9.
28. A.J. Mowat, 'Robert Stillington', *Ricardian* vol. 4, no. 53 (June 1976), pp. 23–8 (p. 23).
29. Maxwell-Lyte, ed., *The Registers of Robert Stillington*, p. viii.
30. *CPR, 1461–1467*, p. 387.
31. Maxwell-Lyte, ed., *The Registers of Robert Stillington*, p. viii. Pope Paul II (Barbo) had succeeded Pius II (Piccolomini) at the end of August 1464.
32. Maxwell-Lyte, ed., *The Registers of Robert Stillington*, p. viii, citing Patent Roll 4 Edward IV, part 2, m. 2, nos. 37, 38, 51, 52.
33. *Calendar of Papal Registers*, vol. 12, *Papal Letters 1458–1471*, London 1933, p. 519. On Stillington's appointment, see also Mowat, 'Robert Stillington', p. 23, citing *CPR 1461–67*, pp. 149–50, and Emden, *Oxford*, p. 1778.
34. TNA, Close Roll 8 Edward IV, no. 3 *dorso*, 23 February 1468/9.

9. Crowned as Queen

1. This account is from a fifteenth century manuscript, published in G. Smith, *The Coronation of Elizabeth Wydeville*, London 1935, p. 14.
2. Smith, *The Coronation of Elizabeth Wydeville*, pp. 14–15.

3. https://en.wikipedia.org/wiki/Walter_Beauchamp (consulted February 2018).
4. Smith, *The Coronation of Elizabeth Wydeville*, p. 15.
5. Smith, *The Coronation of Elizabeth Wydeville*, pp. 15–16.
6. Smith, *The Coronation of Elizabeth Wydeville*, pp. 16–17.
7. Smith, *The Coronation of Elizabeth Wydeville*, p. 18.
8. Smith, *The Coronation of Elizabeth Wydeville*, pp. 18–19.
9. https://en.wikipedia.org/wiki/John_de_Vere,_13th_Earl_of_Oxford (consulted February 2018).
10. Smith, *The Coronation of Elizabeth Wydeville*, pp. 19–25.

10. Learning the Truth

1. A. R. Myers, 'The household of Queen Elizabeth Woodville, 1466–7', part 1, *Bulletin of the John Rylands Library*, 1967, vol. 50, pp. 207–235 (p. 208).
2. Myers, 'The household of Queen Elizabeth Woodville, 1466–7', part 1, p. 211, note 2, citing *Calendar of Close Rolls, 1468–1476*, p. 5.
3. MacGibbon, *EW*, p. 96, citing *Archeologia* XXVI, pp. 276–8.
4. For the correct use of the 'Lady' title in English contexts see Ashdown-Hill, *The Secret Queen*, appendix 3.
5. C.L. Scofield, *The Life and Reign of Edward the Fourth*, London 1923; 1967, vol. 1, pp. 377–8.
6. Archbishop Thomas Bourchier was appointred Cardinal on 18 September 1467.
7. https://en.wikipedia.org/wiki/John_Fogge (consulted February 2018).
8. A.R. Myers, *Crown, Household and Parliament in Fifteenth Century England*, London 1985, p. 302, citing Early Chancery Proceedings 31/ 121 and Rymer, Foedera (Hague edition, 1740). Vol. 2, p. 166 (see below).
9. The spelling of his names is in a slightly different form in this context because the text of the record was written in Latin.
10. *CCR, 1468–1476*, pp. 30–31, no. 110; http://www.british-history.ac.uk/rymer-foedera/vol11/pp618-639 (consulted February 2018), citing O. xi. 635. H. v. p. ii. 166, states that the certificate was issued for JOHN rather than JOAN, but that seems likely to be incorrect.
11. Dockray, *Edward IV a Source Book*, pp. 46–7, citing Great Chronicle of London, pp. 202–03.
12. Arundel Castle, MS, f. 26r; *HHB*, part 1, pp. 482–83.

13. BL, Add. MS 46349, f. 99v, Arundel Castle MS, f 26r; *HHB*, part 1, pp. 454 (and see note 2), 483.
14. http://www.dictionary.com/browse/lyard (consulted February 2018).
15. Arundel Castle, MS, f. 26r; *HHB*, part 1, p. 482.
16. C.L. Kingsford, *The Stonor Letters and Papers*, vol. 2, London 1919, pp. 127–8, citing *A.C.*, xliv, 64.
17. A. Crawford, *Letters of Medieval Women*, Stroud 2002, p. 45, citing a letter from Jane Stonor.
18. Kingsford, *The Stonor Letters and Papers*, vol. 2, pp. 150–1, citing *A.C.*, xlvi, 151.
19. Scofield, *The Life and Reign of Edward the Fourth*, vol. 2, p. 452, citing the Account Book of Elizabeth's Receiver General.
20. Sutton & Visser-Fuchs, 'A Most Benevolent Queen', p. 229.
21. Brewer & Bullen, eds, *Calendar of the Carew Manuscripts at Lambeth*, vol. 2, 1575–88, p. cvi.
22. Armstrong / Mancini, pp. 62–63.
23. *Rex fecit Henricum, ducem Bukes, maritare sororem reginae Elizabethae.* William Worcester, *Annales*, published in Stevenson, ed., *Letters and Papers Illustrative of the Wars of the English in France during the Reign of Henry the Sixth, vol, 2, part 2*, p. 785.
24. Ashdown-Hill, *Cecily Neville*, chapters 3 & 11.
25. Stevenson, *Letters and Papers Illustrative of the Wars of the English in France, vol, 2, part 2*, p. 783.
26. Riley, ed., *Ingulph's Chronicle of the Abbey of Croyland*, p. 445.
27. Armstrong / Mancini, pp. 62–63.
28. Armstrong / Mancini, pp. 62–63; present writer's emphasis.
29. Riley, ed., *Ingulph's Chronicle of the Abbey of Croyland*, p. 440.
30. A.F. Sutton & L. Visser-Fuchs, 'The Device of Queen Elizabeth Woodville: A Gillyflower or Pink', *The Ricardian*, vol. 11, no 136, March 1997, pp. 17–24.
31. *Ibid*, p. 23.

11. Dealing with the first Problems

1. *ODNB*, Diaz Pascual, 'Jacquetta [*sic*]'.
2. P. Lindsay, *King Richard III*, London 1933, p. 98.
3. Gairdner, *Paston Letters*, vol. 6, pp. 105–6, with date amendement in vol. 1,p. 340.
4. https://en.wikipedia.org/wiki/John_de_Vere,_13th_Earl_of_Oxford (consulted February 2018).

5. Dockray, *Edward IV a Source Book*, p. 47, citing *Great Chronicle of London*, pp. 207–08.

6. Ellis / Fabyan, *Chronicle*, p. 656–7.

7. Brewer & Bullen, eds, *Calendar of the Carew Manuscripts at Lambeth*, vol. 2, 1575–88, pp. cvi–cvii. Explaining why the Earls of Desmond subsequently had a legal right not to be summoned by the king to meetings was the reason why this account was finally penned.

8. J. Ashdown-Hill & A. Carson, 'The Execution of the Earl of Desmond', *The Ricardian*, vol. 15, 2005, pp. 70–93 (http://www.richardiii.net/downloads/Ricardian/2005_vol15_Earl_Desmond_Execution.pdf).

9. '*Circa festum Purificacionis beatae Mariae in Hibernia Comes Wigorniae fecit decollari Comitem Desmund, unde Rex in principio cepit displicenciam*'. T. Hearne, ed., *Liber Niger Scaccarii, nec non Wilhelmi Worcestrii Annales Rerum Anglicarum*, 2 vols., London 1771, vol. 2, p. 513; Stevenson, ed., *Wars of the English in France*, vol. 2, p. 789. This was written in the second half of the fifteenth century, probably within twenty years of Desmond's execution.

10. J. Gairdner, ed., *Letters and Papers illustrative of the Reigns of Richard III and Henry VII*, 2 vols., vol. 1, London 1861, p. 68; *Harleian MS 433*, vol. 3, London / Gloucester 1982, p. 108 (f. 265v).

11. Armstrong / Mancini, p. 63.

12. L.T. Smith, *The Itinerary of John Leland*, parts 6 and 7, London 1907–10, p. 120.

13. C. Weightman, *Margaret of York Duchess of Burgundy 1446–1503*, Gloucester 1989, pp. 47–59.

14. Ashdown-Hill, *The Secret Queen*, p. 188.

12. Losing the first Relatives

1. Riley, ed., *Ingulph's Chronicle of the Abbey of Croyland*, p. 440.

2. Riley, ed., *Ingulph's Chronicle of the Abbey of Croyland*, p. 445.

3. Ashdown-Hill, *Cecily Neville*, pp. 125–6.

4. Later mythology purports to connect 'Robin Hood' with Sherwood Forest and the Midlands. But in reality – like Sir William Conyers – he probably came from further north. The present author's unpublished research suggests that the real 'Robin Hood' had been a manorial lord from Yorkshire.

5. A.R. Myers, ed., *English Historical Documents, 1327–1485*, London 1969, p. 300; Scoffield, *Edward the Fourth*, vol. 1, p. 495.

6. *Le roy en eut les nouvelles dont il fut moult desplaisant, si dist quil estoit trahy, et fist habillier tous ses gens pour aller audevant de son frere le duc de Clarence et son cousin de*

Warewic lesquelz venoient audevant de luy et estoient desja entre Warewic et Coventry ou ilz furent advertis que le roy venoit a lencontre deulz. si nestoit pas a croire que son frère de Clarence ne son cousin de Warewic voulissent penser trahison a lencontre de sa personne; pourquoy le roy se traist en ung village prez et se loga illec atout ses gens non gueres loingz du lieu ou estoit logie le comte de Warewic. Environ heure de myenuit vint devers le roy larchevesque d'Yorc, grandement adcompaignie de gens de guerre, si buscha tout hault au logis du roy, dissant a ceulz qui gardoient son corpz quil luy estoit necessaire de parler au roy, auquel ilz le nuncherent; mais le roy luy fist dire quil reposoit et quil venist au matin de lors il le orroit voullentiers. De laquele responce larchevesque ne fut pas content, si renvoia les messages de rechief dire au roy que force estoit quil parlast a luy, comme ilz le firent, et alors le roy leur commanda quilz le laissassent entrer pour oyr quil diroit, car de luy en riens ne se doubtoit. Quant larchevesque fut entre en la chambre, ou il trouva le roy couchie il luy dist prestement: 'Sire levez vous', de quoy le roy se voult excuser, disant que il navoit ancores comme riens repose; mais larchevesque comme faulz et desloyal quil estoit, luy dist la seconde fois: 'Il vous fault lever et venir devers mon frere de Warewic, car a ce ne povez vous contrester' Et lors le roy doubtant que pis ne luy en advenist se vesty et larchevesque lemmena sans faire grand bruit au lieu ou estoient ledit comte et le duc de Clarence entre Warewic et Coventry. W. & L.C.P Hardy, eds, Jehan de Wavrin, *Recueil des Chroniques et Anchiennes Istoires de la Grant Bretaigne, a present nommé Engleterre*, vol. 5, London 1891, reprinted Cambridge 2012, pp. 584–86.

7. Rolls of Parliament, 9 Edw. IV (see below).
8. *ODNB*, Diaz Pascual, 'Jacquetta [*sic*]'.
9. ERO, D/B5 Cr73, m. 1v (transcript, p. 7).
10. J. Ashdown-Hill, *Royal Marriage Secrets*, Stroud 2013, pp. 63–65.
11. P. M. Kendall, *Warwick the Kingmaker*, London 1957, 1973, p. 256; M. Hicks, *Anne Neville*, Stroud 2007, p. 74.
12. *RP*, vol 6, p. 232.
13. *RP*, vol 6, p. 232.
14. *RP*, vol 6, p. 232.
15. *RP*, vol 6, p. 232.
16. *RP*, vol 6, p. 232.

13. The first Crown Loss

1. Gairdner, *Paston Letters*, vol. 5, p. 85.
2. H. Marshall Pratt, *Westminster Abbey its Architecture, History and Monuments*, vol. 2, New York 1914, pp. 786–7.

3. D. Baldwin, *Elizabeth Woodville*, Stroud 2002, 2010, p. 43. Scofield, *Edward IV*, vol. 1, p. 546, note 2 appears to cite Warrants for Issues, 49 Hen. VI, 30th Oct. as the source for this.

4. 21 April 1471, *CPR, 1467–1477*, p. 258.

5. H. Ellis, ed., *Original Letters Illustrative of English History*, second series, vol. 1, London 1827, pp. 140–2, citing MS DONAT. BRIT. MUS. 4614. art. 108. BAF. EDW. IV. BUND. 1. No 29.

6. L.J.F. Ashdown-Hill, THESIS, subsection 5.8.8; BL, Add. MS 46349, f. 156v; *HHB*, part 1, p. 436.

7. Soc. Ant., MS 76, f. 30v; *HHB*, part 2, pp. 25–26.

8. M.K. Dale, *The Household Book of Dame Alice de Bryene*, Ipswich 1931, pp. 45–57.

9. 'Hail, Mary, full of grace, the Lord is with thee, blessed art thou among women, and blessed is the fruit of thy womb, Jesus. Holy Mary, Mother of God, pray for us sinners now and at the hour of our death'.

10. *Calendar of Papal Registers*, vol. 13, London 1955, pp. 90–1 (f. 208*r*).

11. *Et insuper cum sicut accepimus in diversis mundi partibus observatur quidam modus orandi noviter non sine magna devotione inventus qui psalterium beate Marie Virginis communiter appellatur. …*

12. *principaliter.*

13. *i.e.* the Rosary.

14. *contra iminentia mundi pericula totiens angelicam salutationem Ave Maria quot sunt psalmi in psalterio davidico.*

15. *de sero.*

16. Introduction of saying the *Angelus*. That comprises just three repetitions of the 'Hail Mary' (see above, note 9). Each 'Hail Mary' is led by an opening responsory sentence. At the end one closing prayer is said. Traditionally the *Angelus* is repeated three times a day (morning, noon and evening) while bells are rung.

17. Sutton & Visser-Fuchs, 'A Most Benevolent Queen', pp. 232–5.

18. Sutton & Visser-Fuchs, 'A Most Benevolent Queen', pp. 232–3.

19. *CPR, 1476–1485*, pp. 133–4.

20. Baldwin, *Elizabeth Woodville*, p. 76.

21. Baldwin, *Elizabeth Woodville*, p. 191, note 23.

22. J. Ashdown-Hill, 'Walsingham in 1469: The Pilgrimage of Edward IV and Richard, Duke of Gloucester', *The Ricardian*, vol. 11 (March 1997), pp. 2–16.

23. Ashdown-Hill, *The Private Life of Edward IV*, p. 208.

24. Gairdner, *Paston Letters*, vol. 5, p. 112.

14. Dealing with more Problems

1. *Chronicles of the White Rose of York*, [Hearne's Fragment], pp. 20–21. The fact that the two men were of the Norfolk affinity is attested by a letter of 9 December 1468 from Godfrey Greene to Sir William Plumpton. This reports that 'one Alford and one Poiner, gentlemen to my [lord] of Northfolk ... were beheaded' on Monday 28 November 1468. J. Kirby, ed., *The Plumpton Letters and Papers*, Cambridge 1996, p. 40.

2. Anne Beaufort's husband was William Paston. They were married in about 1467–1468 and their first child was born in January 1469/70 – Gairdner, *Paston Letters*, vol. 1, pp. 291–2.

3. J. Gairdner, ed., *The Historical Collections of a Citizen of London in the Fifteenth Century* [Gregory's Chronicle], London 1876, pp. 236–37.

4. H. Ellis, ed., R. Fabyan, *The New Chronicles of England and France*, London 1811, p. 657; C.L. Kingsford, ed., *Chronicles of London*, Oxford 1905, p. 180.

5. 21 November 1468 was indeed a Monday.

6. Kingsford, ed., *Chronicles of London*, p. 180.

7. *CPR, 1467–1477*, London 1910, p. 122.

8. N. Davis, ed., *Paston Letters and Papers of the Fifteenth Century*, 2 vols., Oxford 1971 and 1976, volume 1, p. 489.

9. J. H. Blunt, *Tewkesbury Abbey and its associations*, London 1875, pp 84–85. Blunt's account is not always accurate. Corrections have been inserted from Bodleian, MS. Top. Glouc. d. 2, Founders' and benefectors' book of Tewkesbury Abbey, fol. 39 r & v.

10. PROME, citing PRO C49/39/5.

11. *ibid*.

12. C. Ross, *Edward IV*, London 1974, 1991, p. 187, note 3.

13. J. Strutt, *The Regal and Ecclesiastical Antiquities of England*, London (1773), 1793, p. 93.

14. *CPR, 1476–1485*, p. 345.

15. Baldwin, *Elizabeth Woodville*, p. 56.

16. J.E. Jackson, 'The Execution of Ankarette Twynyho', p. 52.

17. *Third Report of the Deputy Keeper of the Public Records* (February 28, 1842), p. 214, citing *Baga de Secretis*, Bundle 1, Mss. 58 & 59.

18. *ibid*.

19. Jackson, 'The Execution of Ankarette Twynyho', p. 53.

20. *FFPC*, p. 123.

21. Mancini, pp. 62–63.
22. *erat quaedam prophetia, quod post E. id est, post Edwardum quartum, G regnaret, sub hoc ambiguo Georgius dux Clarentiae, medus amborum fratrum Edwardi et Ricardi regum, dux ob hoc Georgius peremptus est.* T. Hearne, ed., *Joannis Rossi Antiquarii Warwicensis Historia Regum Angliae*, Oxford 1745, p. 215.
23. Ellis/Vergil, p. 167.
24. *Croke ... Select Cases*, p. 122.
25. Madden, 'Political Poems of the Reigns of Henry VI and Edward IV', *Archaeologia*, vol. 29, 1842, pp. 318–347.
26. H. Grimstone & T.Leach, eds., *Reports of Sir George Croke, Knight, of ... Select Cases*, Dublin 1793, p. 121.
27. For full examination of the Beauchamp murder case, see Ashdown-Hill, *The Third Plantagenet*, chapter 12.
28. N. Pronay and J. Cox, eds., *The Crowland Chronicle Continuations: 1459–1486*, London 1986 (hereinafter *Crowland Chronicle Continuations*), p. 145.
29. This may suggest a connection of some kind with the wife of *Richard*, second Lord Beauchamp.
30. *ODNB*, Thomas Burdet.
31. *CPR* 1476–1485, p. 50.
32. The present writer's translation of H. Grimstone & T. Leach, eds., *Reports of Sir George Croke, Knight, of ... Select Cases*, Dublin 1793, pp. 121–22.
33. Burdet's property was inherited by his son, Nicholas, a minor who was placed under the guardianship of Sir Simon Mountfort; *CPR* 1476–1485, p. 102. Subsequently Sir John Grevyle was appointed to head commissions to examine what Burdet had held in the counties of Warwickshire, Worcestershire and Gloucestershire; *CPR* 1476–1485, p. 50.
34. *CPR* 1476–1485, p. 43.
35. Father Provincial (head) of the Franciscan order in England; doctorate obtained at Oxford University; selected earlier (September 1470) by the Earl of Warwick to preach in favour of Henry VI's Readeption at St Paul's Cross.
36. *Crowland Chronicle Continuations*, p. 145, my emphasis.
37. *CPR 1476–85*, p. 75.
38. J. Ashdown-Hill, 'Norfolk Requiem: the Passing of the House of Mowbray', *The Ricardian*, vol. 12 (March 2001), 198–217 (p. 206).
39. *CPR 1476–85*, p. 75.
40. *RP*, vol. 6, pp. 195 citing *Rot. Pat.* 17 E.IV, p. 2, m.19. The original text is in Latin.

15. Losing Edward IV

1. Fahy, 'The marriage ... a new Italian source', p. 668, lines 29–30.
2. Ashdown-Hill, *The Private Life of Edward IV*, chapter 28.
3. https://en.wikipedia.org/wiki/Elizabeth_Lucy (consulted March 2018).
4. *CPR, 1476–85*, p. 371.
5. A.H. Thomas & I.D.Thornley, eds, *The Great Chronicle of London*, London 1938, p. 233. Lord Hastings was the stepfather of Cecily Bonville, Marchioness of Dorset, being her mother's second husband.
6. Ashdown-Hill, *The Private Life of Edward IV*, chapters 16, 19 & 22.
7. Ashdown-Hill *Cecily Neville*, chapter 3.
8. Ashdown-Hill, *The Private Life of Edward IV*, chapters 19 & 28.
9. Ashdown-Hill, *The Private Life of Edward IV*, chapter 20; Accounts Exchequer K.R. E. 101/412, no. 8, m.3, cited in M. St. Clare Byrne, *The Lisle Letters*, London 1981, vol. 1, p. 139.
10. Ashdown-Hill, *The Private Life of Edward IV*, chapter 20.
11. J. Bruce, ed., *Historie of the Arrivall of Edward IV in England and the Final Recouerye of his Kingdomes from Henry VI A.D. M.CCCC.LXXI*, London 1838, p. 17.
12. S. Bentley, ed, *Excerpta Historica*, London 1831, pp. 366–79, citing Rymer, BL, Add. MS 4615 (part of his miscellaneous collections for the *Foedera*).
13. For the full text of this will see Ashdown-Hill, *The Private Life of Edward IV*, chapter 23.
14. *Crowland Chronicle Continuations*, p. 151 (written 1486); Great Chronicle of London (as cited – but not QUOTED in respect of the DATE – in Dockray, *Edward IV, a source book*, p. 146); H. Ellis, ed., R. Fabyan, *The New Chronicles of England and France*, London 1811, p. 667 (Fabyan died circa 1512, however, his Chronicle, as published concludes with the year 1540 – so it appears not to be contemporary.); C.L. Kingsford, ed., *Chronicles of London*, pp. 189, 278 (Vitellius A XVI – not contemporary – the Chronicle continues to the end of the reign of Henry VII); E. Hall, *Chronicle*, London 1809, p. 341 (published 1548; 1550 – so not contemporary).
15. L. Lyell & F.D.Watney, eds, *Acts of Court of the Mercers' Company 1453–1527*, Cambridge 1936, p. 146.
16. E. Carusi, ed., Jacopo Gherardi da Volterra, *Il Diario Romano dal 7 Settembre 1479 al 12 Agosto 1484*, Castello 1904, p. 116 (translation J.A-H).
17. R. Davies, *Extracts from the Municipal Records of the City of York during the Reigns of Edward IV, Edward V and Richard III* (hereinafter Davies, *York Records*), London 1843, pp 142,143, and footnote.

18. Colchester Oath Book, f.107r (modern foliation).

19. L. Toulmin Smith, ed., R. Ricart, *The Maire of Bristowe is Kalendar*, London 1872, p. 46.

20. '*il termina le quatrième jour après Pasques*'. J-A. Buchon, ed., *Chroniques de Jean Molinet*, vol. 2, Paris 1828, p. 376.

21. '*infra dies octo … vita finivit*'. J. Quicherat, ed., T. Basin, *Histoire des règnes de Charles VII et de Louis XI*, vol. 3, Paris 1857, p. 134.

22. Armstrong / Mancini, p. 59.

23. '*quod ad regni administrationem pertinet, se in principibus et regina maximam spem habere*', Armstrong / Mancini, pp. 76–77.

24. *Crowland Chronicle Continuations*, pp. 154–5.

25. *Crowland Chronicle Continuations*, pp. 156–57.

26. *CPR 1476–1485*, pp. 350–51.

27. *CPR, 1476–1485*, p. 354.

28. J. Ashdown-Hill, 'The Go-Between', *The Ricardian*, vol. 15, 2005, pp. 119–21.

29. Kendall, *Richard the Third*, p. 178.

30. Armstrong / Mancini, p. 81.

31. Armstrong / Mancini, pp. 119–20, note 59.

16. Losing more Relatives

1. Mis-cited by A. F. Sutton and L. Visser-Fuchs as a Friday – *The Royal Funerals of the House of York at Windsor*, London 2005, p. 27.

2. Kendall, *Richard the Third*, p. 164.

3. *Crowland Chronicle Continuations*, pp. 154–55.

4. Kendall, *Richard the Third*, p. 72.

5. J. Bruce, ed., *Historie of the Arrivall of Edward IV*, London 1838, p. 3.

6. Kendall, *Richard the Third*, pp. 164, 173; R. Edwards, *The Itinerary of King Richard III 1483–1485*, London 1983, p. 1.

7. *Crowland Chronicle Continuations*, pp. 154–55.

8. Armstrong / Mancini, pp. 76–77.

9. Armstong translated the phrase … *ab eorum manu in libertatem* … as '… set free … from the clutches …'. But the present writer prefers to use 'release … from the hands'.

10. Armstrong / Mancini, pp. 78–9, with the present writer's correction to the English translation as noted above.

11. *Crowland Chronicle Continuations*, pp. 156–57.

12. P.W. Hammond, & A.F. Sutton, *Richard III: The Road to Bosworth*, London 1985, p. 99; *Crowland Chronicle Continuations*, pp. 156–57. The palace was destroyed during the seventeenth-century Civil War.

13. Armstrong / Mancini, p. 120, note 63.

14. *Crowland Chronicle Continuations*, pp. 156–57.

15. *Isto die lectum fuit iuramentum Richardi ducis Gloucestriae protectoris Anglie, Thomae archiepiscopi Cantuariensis, Thomae archiepiscopi Eboracensis, Henrici ducis Buckinghamiae et dominorum nuper factum domino nostro Regi. Item iuramentum quod dicti domini facere voluissent domine Elizabethae regine Anglie modo existenti in sanctuario Sancti Petri Westminster, si eadem domina privilegium eiusdem loci reliquere voluerit.* Armstrong / Mancini, pp. 124–25, n. 74, citing minutes of the City Council of London (London Guildhall, MS., Journal 9, f. 23v).

16. *Crowland Chronicle Continuations*, pp. 158–59.

17. The new name was first attested in 1544, according to https://en.wikipedia.org/wiki/Traitors%27_Gate (consulted April 2018). Historians at the Tower of London advised me that the name only really became current in the seventeenth century. I am grateful to Philippa Langley for encouraging me to investigate the name.

18. Kingsford, ed., *The Stonor Letters and Papers*, vol. 2, p. 160.

19. 'The death of Anthony Earl Rivers is dated 20 June (instead of 25 June) in inquisitions post mortem of 1486 [footnote: *Inq. P. M. Henry VII*, I, No. 33 (2 Nov. 1486)]'. A. Hanham, *Richard III and his Early Historians 1483–1535*, Oxford University Press 1975, p. 29. Curiously however, one modern source has alleged (on no solid basis) that Rivers was executed after the accession of Richard III – *ODNB*, M. Hicks, Anthony Woodville, 2nd Earl Rivers.

20. … *dominus comes de Rivers Antonius Woodvyle morte instante cilicio ad nudam carnem, ut diu ante usus fuerat, indutus est repertus, In tempore tamen incarcerationis apud Pontem-fractum edidit unum Balet in Anglicis, ut mihi monstratum est quod subsequetur sub his verbis:* [English text of poem] *et sic comites praerecitati adiudicati sunt ad mortem tanquam rei & coniuratores mortis Ricardi ducis Gloucestriae, tunc temporis Protectoris regni Angliae. Et sic innocentes propter id quod no excogitaverunt a tortoribus suis pacifice inimicorum crudeli tormentatione humilime se submisserunt.* Hearne / Rous, *Historia Regum Angliae*, pp. 213–14.

17. The second Crown Loss

1. *Crowland Chronicle Continuations*, pp.158–61.

2. Kingsford, ed., *The Stonor Letters and Papers*, vol. 2, p. 160.

3. Year Book, 1 Henry VII, Hilary Term, plea 1, published in W. Fleetwood (alleged ed.), *Les Reports des Cases en les ans des Roys Edward v. Richard iij. Henrie vij & Henrie viij.*, London 1679, p. 24 (Henry VII, Year 1, p. 5 – Hilary Term, plea 1). With thanks to Philippa Langley for bringing this source to my attention.

4. The meaning of the medieval term 'precontract' has been misinterpreted by many historians, who wrongly assumed it to refer merely to a betrothal. But the supplication very clearly states that Edward IV was *married* to Eleanor.

5. PROME, Edward IV, April 1463, October 1472.

6. PROME, Edward IV, April 1463, October 1472.

7. PROME, Edward IV, November 1461, April 1463.

8. Harl. 433, f. 308v; *Harleian MS 433*, vol. 3, p. 190.

9. *Harleian MS 433*, vol. 3, p. 190 (f. 308v).

10. Kendall, *Richard the Third*, p. 287; Ellis / Vergil, p. 210.

11. For references to Cecily's Scrope marriage see: Ellis/Vergil, p. 215, P. Sheppard Routh "'Lady Scroop Daughter of K. Edward": an Enquiry', *The Ricardian* vol. 9, no. 121, June 1993, pp. 410–16 (pp. 412, 416, n. 12) and Laynesmith, *The Last Medieval Queens*, p. 199.

12. 'casamento da filha delRej Duarte de Inglaterra ... com o duque de Beja Dom Manuel... o qual casamento antes fora a elRej apontado por Duarte Brandão sendo uindo por embaixador delRej Richarte jrmão do ditto Rej Duarte a jurar as ligas e commeter casamento com a Iffante Dona Joana'. A. Mestrinho Salgado and Salgado, Álvaro Lopes de Chaves, *Livro de Apontamentos (1438–1489)*, as cited in A.S. Marques, 'Álvaro Lopes de Cheves [sic]: A Portuguese Source', *Ricardian Bulletin*, Autumn 2008, pp. 25–27.

13. Ellis / Vergil, p. 210.

14. For the evidence in that respect see J. Ashdown-Hill, *The Mythology of the Princes in the Tower*, Stroud 2018, chapter 17.

15. Such was the meaning of the verb *entreprendre* in Old French.

16. Ashdown-Hill, *The Mythology of the 'Princes in the Tower'*, p. 120.

17. Ashdown-Hill, *The Mythology of the 'Princes in the Tower'*, p. 151.

18. *Harleian MS 433*, vol. 2, pp. 48–9.

19. Ellis / Vergil, p. 214.

18. The Queen's Mother

1. J. Hughes, *The Religious Life of Richard III*, Stroud 1997, p. 101, citing Mancini, p. 94 in respect of his alleged Clarence mourning.

2. Mancini, p. 94, my translation.

3. M.K. Jones & M.G. Underwood, *The King's Mother*, Cambridge 1992, p. 61; ODNB, S.J. Gunn, 'Henry VII'.
4. http://www.british-history.ac.uk/cal-papal-registers/brit-ie/vol14/pp.14-30 (consulted April 2018).
5. *ODNB*, R. Horrox, 'Elizabeth of York'.
6. Jones, ed., Commynes, *Memoirs*, p. 393.
7. Jones, ed., Commynes, *Memoirs*, p. 396.
8. D.F. Sutton, ed., Polydore Vergil, *Anglica Historia* (1555 version), on-line 2005, 2010, part xxv (Edward V / Richard III), subsection 14 (http://www.philological.bham.ac.uk/polverg/25eng.html).
9. R.A. Griffiths & R.S. Thomas, *The Making of the Tudor Dynasty*, Stroud 1985, pp. 91–3.
10. Sutton, ed., Vergil, *Anglica Historia* (1555 version), on-line 2005, 2010, part xxv (Edward V / Richard III), subsection 11 (http://www.philological.bham.ac.uk/polverg/25eng.html).
11. Ashdown-Hill, *The Mythology of the 'Princes in the Tower'*, chapter 17.
12. *RP*, vol. 6, p. 289.
13. *L&P*, vol. 6, p. 618.
14. *L&P*, vol. 7, p. 519.
15. *Harleian Manuscript 433*, vol. 3, p. 190 (f. 308v).
16. *RP*, vol. 6, pp. 288; *CPR, 1485–1494*, pp. 75–7.
17. https://en.wikipedia.org/wiki/Essex_girl (consulted March 2018).
18. C. Given-Wilson, ed., *The Parliament Rolls of Medieval England* (PROME), Leicester 2005 – 1487 Parliament, Lincoln attainder [November 1487].
19. E. Cavell, ed., *The Heralds' Memoir 1486–1490*, Richard III & Yorkist History Trust 2009, pp. 116–17.
20. J. Ashdown-Hill, *The Dublin King*, Stroud 2015.
21. C. Weightman, *Margaret of York*, Gloucester 1989, p. 28, citing M. Letts, ed., *The Travels of Leo of Rozmital*, pp. 46–49.
22. C. Weightman, *Margaret of York*, Gloucester 1989, p. 28.
23. *RP*, vol. 6, pp. 194, 'from the original in the Tower of London'.
24. *RP*, vol. 6, pp. 194.
25. Sutton, ed., Vergil, *Anglica Historia* (1555 version), on–line 2005, 2010, part xxvi (Henry VII), subsection 6 (http://www.philological.bham.ac.uk/polverg/26eng.html).
26. J. Ashdown-Hill, *The Last Days of Richard III*, Stroud 2010, chapter 2.
27. Laynesmith, *The Last Medieval Queens*, pp. 45, 58.
28. Sutton / Vergil, part xxv (Edward V / Richard III), subsection 8 (http://www.philological.bham.ac.uk/polverg/25eng.html).

19. Religious Life?

1. J. Ashdown-Hill, *Cecily Neville*, Barnsley 2018, chapter 14.
2. Ashdown-Hill, *Eleanor the Secret Queen*, chapter 15.
3. W.E. Hampton, 'The Ladies of the Minories', *The Ricardian*, vol. 4, no. 62, September 1978, pp. 15–22.
4. W. Campbell, ed., *Materials for a History of the Reign of Henry VII from Original Documents preserved at the Public Record Office*, vol. 2, London 1877, p. 148.
5. https://en.wikipedia.org/wiki/Bermondsey_Abbey (consulted March 2018).
6. Licence, *Edward IV & Elizabeth Woodville*, p. 256.
7. J. Leland, *Collectanea*, vol. 4, London 1774, p. 249.
8. Laynesmith, *The Last Medieval Queens*, pp. 199; 216.

20. Death and burial

1. S. Bentley, ed, *Excerpta Historica*, London 1831, pp. 366–79, citing Rymer, BL, Add. MS 4615 (part of his miscellaneous collections for the *Foedera*).
2. *Ibid.*
3. J. Nichols, *A Collection of all the Wills, now known to be extant, of the Kings and Queens of England*, London 1780, pp. 350–51.
4. J. Nichols, *A Collection of all the Wills, now known to be extant, of the Kings and Queens of England*, London 1780, pp. 350–51.
5. BL, MS Arundel 26, ff. 29v–30; A.F. Sutton & L. Visser-Fuchs, *The Royal Funerals of the House of York at Windsor*, London 2005, pp. 72–3.
6. BL, MS Arundel 26, ff. 29v–30; Sutton & Visser-Fuchs, *The Royal Funerals of the House of York at Windsor*, p. 73.
7. BL, MS Arundel 26, ff. 29v–30; Sutton & Visser-Fuchs, *The Royal Funerals of the House of York at Windsor*, p. 73.
8. BL, MS Arundel 26, ff. 29v–30; Sutton & Visser-Fuchs, *The Royal Funerals of the House of York at Windsor*, p. 73.
9. BL, MS Arundel 26, ff. 29v–30; Sutton & Visser-Fuchs, *The Royal Funerals of the House of York at Windsor*, p. 73.
10. BL, MS Arundel 26, ff. 29v–30; Sutton & Visser-Fuchs, *The Royal Funerals of the House of York at Windsor*, p. 73.
11. BL, MS Arundel 26, ff. 29v–30; Sutton & Visser-Fuchs, *The Royal Funerals of the House of York at Windsor*, p. 73.
12. BL, MS Arundel 26, ff. 29v–30; Sutton & Visser-Fuchs, *The Royal Funerals of the House of York at Windsor*, pp. 73–4.

13. Society of Antiquaries of London, *Vetusta Monumenta*, 3, 1796, Windsor Castle report, p. 1.

14. Society of Antiquaries of London, *Vetusta Monumenta*, 3, 1796, Windsor Castle report, p. 3.

15. http://makinghistory.sal.org.uk/page.php?cat=2 (consulted March 2018).

16. Personal communication from Lucy Ellis, Museum Collections Manager, Society of Antiquaries of London.

Bibliography

Documents

Arundel Castle, MS
BL, Add. MS 46349
Essex Record Office, D/B5 Cr73
Soc. Ant., MS 76

Books

Armstrong C A J, ed., Mancini D, *The Usurpation* [*sic*] *of Richard III*, Gloucester 1989
Ashdown-Hill J, *The Secret Queen*, Stroud 2009; 2016
Ashdown-Hill J, *The Last Days of Richard III*, Stroud 2010
Ashdown-Hill J, *Royal Marriage Secrets*, Stroud 2013
Ashdown-Hill J, *The Dublin King*, Stroud 2015
Ashdown-Hill J, *The Mythology of Richard III*, Stroud 2015
Ashdown-Hill J, *The Private Life of Edward IV*, Stroud 2016
Ashdown-Hill J, *Cecily Neville*, Barnsley 2018
Ashdown-Hill J, *The Mythology of the 'Princes in the Tower'*, Stroud 2018

Baker G, *History of Northamptonshire*, vol. 2, London 1844
Baldwin D, *Elizabeth Woodville*, Stroud 2002, 2010
Baring-Gould S, *Curious Myths of the Middle Ages*, London 1877
Beaune H and d'Arbaumont J, eds., *Mémoires d'Olivier de la Marche*, 4 vols., vol. 3, Paris 1885
Bentley S, ed, *Excerpta Historica*, London 1831
Blunt J H, *Tewkesbury Abbey and its associations*, London 1875

Brewer J S & Bullen W, eds, *Calendar of the Carew Manuscripts at Lambeth*, vol. 2, 1575–88, London 1868

Bruce J, ed., *Historie of the Arrivall of Edward IV in England and the Final Recouerye of his Kingdomes from Henry VI A.D. M.CCCC.LXXI*, London 1838

Buck G – see Myers

Calendar of Close Rolls, 1468–1476, London 1953

Calendar of Papal Registers, vol. 12, *Papal Letters 1458–1471*, London 1933

Calendar of Papal Registers, vol. 13, *1471–1484*, London 1955

Calendar of Patent Rolls, 1429–1436, London 1907

Calendar of Patent Rolls, 1436–1441, London 1907

Calendar of Patent Rolls, 1446–1452, London 1909

Calendar of Patent Rolls, 1461–1467, London 1897

Calendar of Patent Rolls, 1467–1477, London 1900

Calendar of Patent Rolls, 1476–1485, London 1901

Calendar of Patent Rolls, 1485–1494, London 1914

Campbell W, ed., *Materials for a History of the Reign of Henry VII from Original Documents preserved at the Public Record Office*, vol. 2, London 1877

Carusi E, ed., Jacopo Gherardi da Volterra, *Il Diario Romano dal 7 Settembre 1479 al 12 Agosto 1484*, Castello 1904

Cavell E, ed., *The Heralds' Memoir 1486–1490*, Richard III & Yorkist History Trust 2009

Clive M, *This Sun of York*, London 1973

Commynes P de- see Jones

Coss P, *The Lady in Medieval England 1000–1500*, Stroud 1998

Crawford A, ed., *Howard Household Books*, Stroud 1992

Crawford A, *Letters of Medieval Women*, Stroud 2002

Croke G, *Select Cases – see* Grimstone

Dale M K, *The Household Book of Dame Alice de Bryene*, Ipswich 1931

Davis N, ed., *Paston Letters and Papers of the Fifteenth Century*, 2 vols., Oxford 1971 and 1976

Dockray K, *Edward IV, a source book*, Stroud 1999

Edwards R, *The Itinerary of King Richard III 1483–1485*, London 1983

Ellis H, ed., R. Fabyan, *The New Chronicles of England and France*, London 1811

Ellis H, ed., *Original Letters Illustrative of English History*, second series, vol. 1, London 1827

Ellis H, ed., *Three Books of Polydore Vergil's English History comprising the reigns of Henry VI, Edward IV and Richard III*, London 1844

Erlanger P, *Margaret of Anjou, Queen of England*, London 1970

Fabyan R – see Ellis
Fleetwood W, alleged editor (but the book in question was produced anonymously 85 years after his death) – see *Les Reports des Cases en les ans des Roys Edward v. Richard iij. Henrie vij & Henrie viij.*

Gairdner J, ed., *Letters and Papers illustrative of the Reigns of Richard III and Henry VII*, 2 vols., vol. 1, London 1861
Gairdner J, ed., *The Historical Collections of a Citizen of London in the Fifteenth Century* [Gregory's Chronicle], London 1876
Gairdner J, ed., *The Paston Letters*, Gloucester 1983
Gherardi da Volterra J – see Carusi
Given-Wilson C, ed., *The Parliament Rolls of Medieval England* (PROME), Leicester 2005
Gregory's Chronicle – see Gairdner
Griffiths R A, & Thomas R S, *The Making of the Tudor Dynasty*, Stroud 1985
Grimstone H & Leach T, eds., *Reports of Sir George Croke, Knight, of ... Select Cases*, Dublin 1793

Hardy T D, ed., *Rotuli Litterarum Clausarum in Turri Londinensis*, vol. 1, 1204–1224, London 1833
Hardy W & L C P, eds, Jehan de Wavrin, *Recueil des Chroniques et Anchiennes Istoires de la Grant Bretaigne, a present nommé Engleterre*, vol. 5, London 1891, reprinted Cambridge 2012
Hayman S and Graves J, eds., *Unpublished Geraldine Documents*, Dublin 1870–81
Hearne T, ed., Rous J, *Historia Regum Angliae*, Oxford 1745
Hearne T, ed., *Liber Niger Scaccarii, nec non Wilhelmi Worcestrii Annales Rerum Anglicarum*, 2 vols., London 1771, vol. 2
Horrox R & Hammond P W, eds., *British Library Harleian Manuscript 433*, vol. 2, London / Gloucester 1980

Jones M, ed., P. de Commynes, *Memoirs*, Harmondsworth 1972
Jones M K & Underwood M G, *The King's Mother*, Cambridge 1992

Kingsford C L, ed., *Chronicles of London*, Oxford 1905
Kingsford C L, *The Stonor Letters and Papers*, vol. 2, London 1919
Kirby J, ed., *The Plumpton Letters and Papers*, Cambridge 1996

Laynesmith J L, *The Last Medieval Queens*, Oxford 2004

Leland J, *Collectanea*, vol. 4, London 1774

Les Reports des Cases en les ans des Roys Edward v. Richard iij. Henrie vij & Henrie viij., London 1679

Licence A, *Edward IV and Elizabeth Woodville, a True Romance*, Stroud 2016

Lindsay P, *King Richard III*, London 1933

MacGibbon D, *Elizabeth Woodville A Life*, 1938, republished Stroud 2014

Mancini – see Armstrong

Marche O de la – see Beaune

Marshall Pratt H, *Westminster Abbey its Architecture, History and Monuments*, vol. 2, New York 1914

Maxwell-Lyte H C, ed., *The Registers of Robert Stillington, Bishop of Bath and Wells 1466–1491 and Richard Fox, Bishop of Bath and Wells 1492–1494*, Somerset Record Society 1937

Mitchell R J, *John Tiptoft*, London 1938

More T – see Sylvester

Myers A R, ed., *English Historical Documents, 1327–1485*, London 1969

Myers A R, ed., G. Buck, *The History of the Life and Reigne of Richard the Third*, London 1646, reprinted Wakefield 1973

Myers A R, *Crown, Household and Parliament in Fifteenth Century England*, London 1985

Nichols J, *A Collection of all the Wills, now known to be extant, of the Kings and Queens of England*, London 1780

Riley H T, ed., *Ingulph's Chronicle of the Abbey of Croyland*, London 1908

Roberts C, ed., *Excerpta è Rotuli Finium in Turri Londinensi*, 1216–1272, London 1836

Rolls of Parliament – see Given-Watson; Strachey

Ross C, *Edward IV*, London 1974, Yale 1991

Rous J – see Hearne

St. Clare Byrne M, *The Lisle Letters*, London 1981, vol. 1

Scofield C L, *The Life and Reign of Edward the Fourth*, London 1923; 1967, vols. 1 & 2

Smith G, ed., *The Coronation of Elizabeth Wydeville, Queen Consort of Edward IV*, London 1935, reprinted Cliftonville 1975

Smith L T, *The Itinerary of John Leland*, parts 6 and 7, London 1907–10

Stevenson J, ed., *Letters and Papers Illustrative of the Wars of the English in France during the Reign of Henry the Sixth*, vol, 1, London 1861

Stevenson J, ed., Letters and papers Illustrative of the Wars of the English in France during the reign of Henry VI, King of England, vol. 2, part 2, London 1864

Strachey J, ed., Rotuli Parliamentorum ut et Petitiones et Placita in Parliamento, 1767–77, vol 6, London 1777

Sutton A F, and Visser-Fuchs L, The Royal Funerals of the House of York at Windsor, London 2005

Sutton D F, ed., Polydore Vergil, Anglica Historia (1555 version), on-line 2005, 2010 (http://www.philological.bham.ac.uk/polverg/25eng.html; http://www.philological.bham.ac.uk/polverg/26eng.html)

Sylvester R S, ed., St Thomas More, The History of King Richard III, New Haven & London 1976

Vergil P – see Ellis; Sutton

Vetusta Monumenta, Society of Antiquaries of London, vol. 3, 1796

Wavrin, J de – see Hardy

Weightman C, Margaret of York Duchess of Burgundy 1446–1503, Gloucester 1989

Papers

Ashdown-Hill J, 'Walsingham in 1469: The Pilgrimage of Edward IV and Richard, Duke of Gloucester', The Ricardian, vol. 11 (March 1997), pp. 2–16

Ashdown-Hill J, 'Norfolk Requiem: the Passing of the House of Mowbray', The Ricardian, vol. 12 (March 2001), 198–217

Ashdown-Hill J & Carson A, 'The Execution of the Earl of Desmond', The Ricardian, vol. 15, 2005, pp. 70–93 (http://www.richardiii.net/downloads/Ricardian/2005_vol15_Earl_Desmond_Execution.pdf).

Ashdown-Hill J, 'The Go-Between', The Ricardian, vol. 15, 2005, pp. 119–21

Fahy C, 'The marriage of Edward IV and Elizabeth Woodville: a new Italian source', English Historical Review, vol. 76 (1960), pp. 660–72

Griffiths R A, 'Queen Katherine de Valois and a missing statute of the realm', Law Quarterly Review, 93 (1977), pp. 257–8

Hampton W E, 'The Ladies of the Minories', The Ricardian, vol. 4, no. 62, September 1978, pp. 15–22

Jackson J E, 'The Execution of Ankarette Twynyho'

Madden, 'Political Poems of the Reigns of Henry VI and Edward IV', *Archaeologia*, vol. 29, 1842, pp. 318–347

Mowat A J, 'Robert Stillington', *Ricardian* vol. 4, no. 53 (June 1976), pp. 23–8

Myers A R, 'The household of Queen Elizabeth Woodville, 1466–7', part 1, *Bulletin of the John Rylands Library*, 1967, vol. 50, pp. 207–235

Sutton A F & Visser-Fuchs L, 'A Most Benevolent Queen', *The Ricardian*, vol. 10, no. 129, June 1995, pp. 214–45

Sutton A F & Visser-Fuchs L, 'The Device of Queen Elizabeth Woodville: A Gillyflower or Pink', *The Ricardian*, vol. 11, no 136, March 1997, pp. 17–24

ODNB, Diaz Pascual L, 'Luxembourg, Jaquetta [*sic*] de, duchess of Bedford and Countess Rivers'

ODNB, Dunn D E S, 'Margaret of Anjou'

ODNB, Gunn S J, 'Henry VII'

ODNB, Hicks M, 'Elizabeth [*née* Elizabeth Woodville]'

ODNB, Hicks M, 'Woodville [Wydeville], Richard, first Earl Rivers'

ODNB, Horrox R, 'Elizabeth of York'

Unpublished

Ashdown-Hill L J F, PhD THESIS

Internet

Ashdown-Hill J, 'The Full Itinerary of Edward IV', https://www.amberley-books.com/community-john-ashdown-hill

https://en.wikipedia.org/wiki/Bermondsey_Abbey (consulted March 2018) https://en.wikipedia.org/wiki/Elizabeth_Lucy (consulted March 2018)

https://en.wikipedia.org/wiki/Elizabeth_Woodville (consulted January 2018) https://en.wikipedia.org/wiki/Essex_girl (consulted March 2018)

https://en.wikipedia.org/wiki/Isabel (consulted January 2018) https://en.wikipedia.org/wiki/John_Fogge (consulted February 2018)

https://en.wikipedia.org/wiki/Melusine (consulted January 2018) https://en.wikipedia.org/wiki/Traitors%27_Gate (consulted April 2018)

https://en.wikipedia.org/wiki/Walter_Beauchamp (consulted February 2018) http://makinghistory.sal.org.uk/page.php?cat=2 (consulted March 2018)

https://opendomesday.org/place/SK8829/wyville/ (consulted January 2018)
http://www.british-history.ac.uk/cal-papal-registers/brit-ie/vol14/pp14–30 (consulted April 2018)

http://www.british-history.ac.uk/rymer-foedera/vol11/pp618-639 (consulted February 2018)

https://www.groby.org.uk/history/grey_family.html (consulted January 2018)
http://www.quns.cam.ac.uk/Queens/Misc/Elizabeth.html (consulted February 2018)

http://www.philological.bham.ac.uk/polverg/26eng.html (consulted February 2018) – see Books – Sutton / Vergil

Index